I0793384

POSTCARD HISTORY SERIES

# *Kalamazoo*

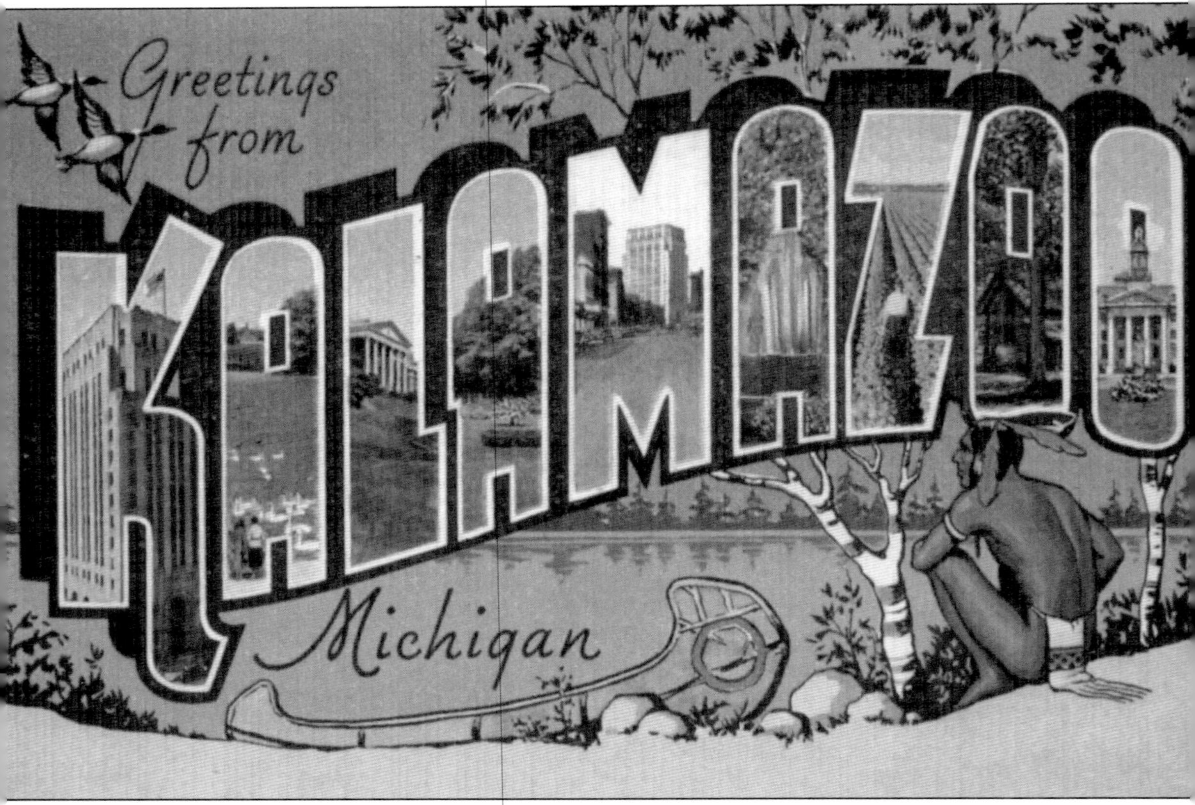


In the 1930s and 1940s, large letter postcards were very popular. These postcards were works of art that featured the name of the town spelled out in oversized letters. Within the letters were images showing local landmarks. The scenes in this mid-1930s example are, from left to right, the American National Bank Building, Kellogg Bird Sanctuary, Western Michigan University, Bronson Park, East Michigan Avenue, Bronson Park's electric fountain, a celery field, the log cabin in Milham Park, and Nazareth College. (Author's collection.)

**On the Front Cover:**
In 1909, Kalamazoo marked its silver anniversary as a city. That October, residents celebrated the milestone in style. Streets, buildings, and even cars were decorated for the several parades held during the celebration. This photograph shows one of the decorated cars, almost completely covered in flowers. (Author's collection.)

**On the Back Cover:**
During the first half of the 20th century, Kalamazoo was known as "the paper city." The concentration of over a dozen paper mills along the Kalamazoo River and Portage Creek provided prosperity, jobs, and pollution. This remarkable interior view shows two workers posing with the rags used to make pulp. (Author's collection.)

POSTCARD HISTORY SERIES

# *Kalamazoo*

*David George Kohrman*

ARCADIA
PUBLISHING

ISBN 978-1-4671-1377-9

Published by Arcadia Publishing
Charleston, South Carolina

Printed in the United States of America

Library of Congress Control Number: 2014951454

For all general information contact Arcadia Publishing at:
Telephone 843-853-2070
Fax 843-853-0044
E-mail sales@arcadiapublishing.com
For customer service and orders:
Toll-Free 1-888-313-2665

Visit us on the Internet at www.arcadiapublishing.com

*To my friends and family,*
*who continue to inspire and nurture my love of history.*

# Contents

# ACKNOWLEDGMENTS

There are several individuals and institutions I would like to thank for their help in making this book possible. I thank Beth Timmerman and the staff of the Kalamazoo Public Library, who not only supplied many of the images found in this book, but care for a collection of historical material that has been invaluable in my research. I also thank Paula Metzner and the staff of the Kalamazoo Valley Museum, who have also assisted in providing images and information used in the book. The faculty of Western Michigan University's Department of History, as well as that of Ball State University's Historic Preservation program, have guided my education. I also thank Sharon Carlson, Sharon Ferraro, Lynn Houghton, and Pamela Hall O'Connor for the inspiration their efforts in local history and preservation have provided me. And, lastly, I thank my parents, for buying me my first postcard those many years ago.

Unless otherwise noted, the images found in this book are from the author's personal collection. The other images are from the Kalamazoo Public Library and the Kalamazoo Valley Museum.

# Introduction

The history and growth of Kalamazoo, Michigan, reflects that of the state, the Midwest, and the nation as a whole. Its first white settler, Titus Bronson, arrived in 1829 and laid out a village, which he named for himself. From this original plat, the core of the current downtown area was born, including the centrally located park that still bears Bronson's name. Soon, other settlers came, and by 1836, the growing village was renamed Kalamazoo. But, the steady stream of new arrivals meant that the pioneer era was fleeting. Within a few decades, Kalamazoo had become a prosperous village boasting fine homes, parks, business blocks, and industries.

It did not take long for that village to transform itself to the point that the residents of the mid-19th century would have a hard time recognizing it. Among other things, the later years of the century saw an explosion in the number of manufacturers as the nation's industrial revolution spread westward. Paper mills, pharmaceuticals, and makers of horse-drawn vehicles were among the varied businesses that helped fuel Kalamazoo's growth. Large department stores opened on its main streets. Impressive new religious structures and public buildings were erected, reflecting the latest architectural trends from the East. This version of Kalamazoo became an oversized village until it was elevated to city status in 1884.

However, it would be the early 20th century that would witness Kalamazoo's biggest growth spurt. More manufacturers came, adding automobiles, corsets, and regalia to the list of Kalamazoo-made products. New institutions, such as the Western State Normal School (Western Michigan University) and Nazareth College, joined the existing Kalamazoo College to make the city a center for learning in the state. Bronson Methodist Hospital, downtown skyscrapers, and entire neighborhoods can trace their beginnings to the early 1900s. Public buildings were quickly outgrown and replaced. Goods and people came to and from the city via railroads, automobiles, and even aircraft. Kalamazoo was transformed into a modern regional center within a generation.

Kalamazoo's early-20th-century transformation coincided with the national popularity of the penny postcard. Although variants of postcards were used in the 19th century, the medium did not really take off until around 1900. By that time, the United States and European governments relaxed postal regulations and enabled publishers to produce photographs stamped with "postcard" on the back. Initially, the back of the card was solely reserved for the address, so the sender had to cram a message into a small space on the picture side of the card. But, in time, those requirements changed, and in 1907, "divided back" postcards allowed room for both address and message, leaving the image on the front to stand out.

For both collectors and historians, postcards are a fascinating example of material culture. On one level, they offer an opportunity to see the Kalamazoo that once was. The majority of the cards provide an image of some aspect of the city's built environment. Buildings, businesses, and streetscapes that have long vanished or been transformed are, in some small way, preserved on paper. Postcards also serve as a gauge of how Kalamazoo's past residents felt about their city. The record left by postcards is far from complete, and many areas of the city were not depicted in postcard form. But, the buildings and scenes that were captured speak of what aspects the residents were most proud of and what they were most interested in sharing with the outside world. The buildings and scenes that were left out, on the other hand, suggest something else.

Over the years, several different styles of postcards came and went. Most were mass produced from photographs. More often than not, postcard publishers had artists on their staff to hand-color the images, making up for the lack of color photography. The quality of these coloring jobs varies, and the accuracy of the color is always suspect. But, when done well, the result could be beautiful. After World War I, postcards were published with white borders around the image. These were generally of a lower quality than their predecessors. Many of the earlier cards had been printed in Germany, and the German postcard industry never recovered from the war. Mass-produced postcard quality further declined in the 1930s with the advent of linen cards. These were so named for the heavy paper on which they were printed. The texture gave the appearance that the card was printed on cloth. These cards are generally more durable than older cards, but, in many cases, the image does not translate as well. Finally, beginning in the 1950s, chrome postcards were produced. These mass-produced color photographs finally eliminated the need for hand-coloring by artists.

Produced concurrently with the different types of mass-printed cards, real-photo postcards are highly prized by collectors. These consist of actual black-and-white photographic prints, produced at a standard postcard size. They were usually made by local publishers, in far fewer numbers than mass-produced cards. Many real-photo postcards are one of a kind, produced by individuals rather than publishers. These postcards offer far sharper images than printed cards. Furthermore, they frequently depict scenes that larger publishers overlooked.

Most of the postcards included in this book are from the author's personal collection. They represent a sampling of over 20 years of collecting. The remaining cards have been pulled from the collections of the Kalamazoo Public Library's Local History Room and the Kalamazoo Valley Museum. Whenever possible, real-photo postcards have been used, due to the sharper images they offer. The majority of the postcards found in the book date to between 1904 and 1944, although a few were published after World War II.

# *One*

# Around Town

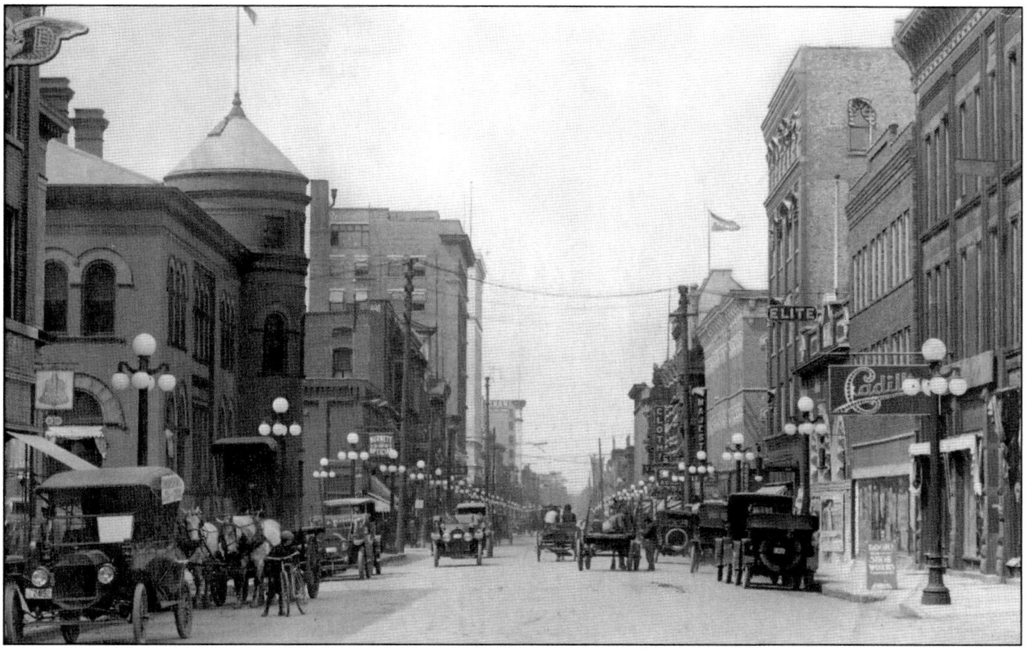


Street scenes, particularly those of downtown areas, were among the most popular subjects for postcards. This 1914 view of South Burdick Street shows a modern city on the move. Steel-frame "skyscrapers" rise above 19th-century blocks. Newly installed electric lights and several automobiles are additional signs of the city's progress. The Cadillac dealership on the right is said to have been the first car dealership in the city.

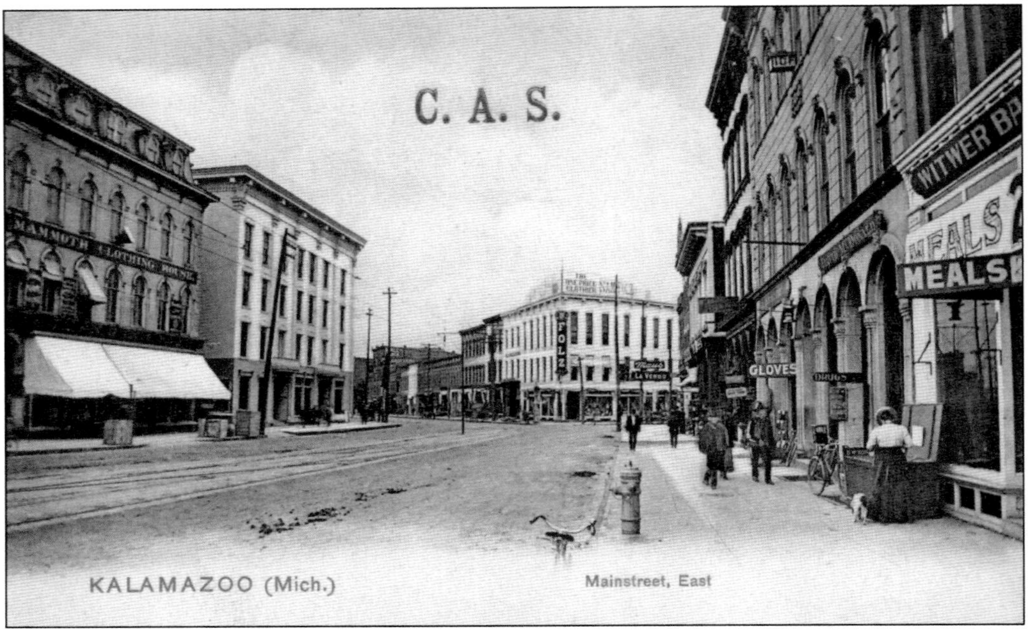


This early postcard of Main Street shows how downtown appeared around 1900. The streets are lined with long rows of Italianate business blocks. This type of building, popular after the Civil War, featured tall, narrow windows, often with arches and window hoods. Stores were located on the ground level, and offices or apartments were housed above. The second building from the left is the Kalamazoo House, one of the city's early hotels. It was razed in 1906.

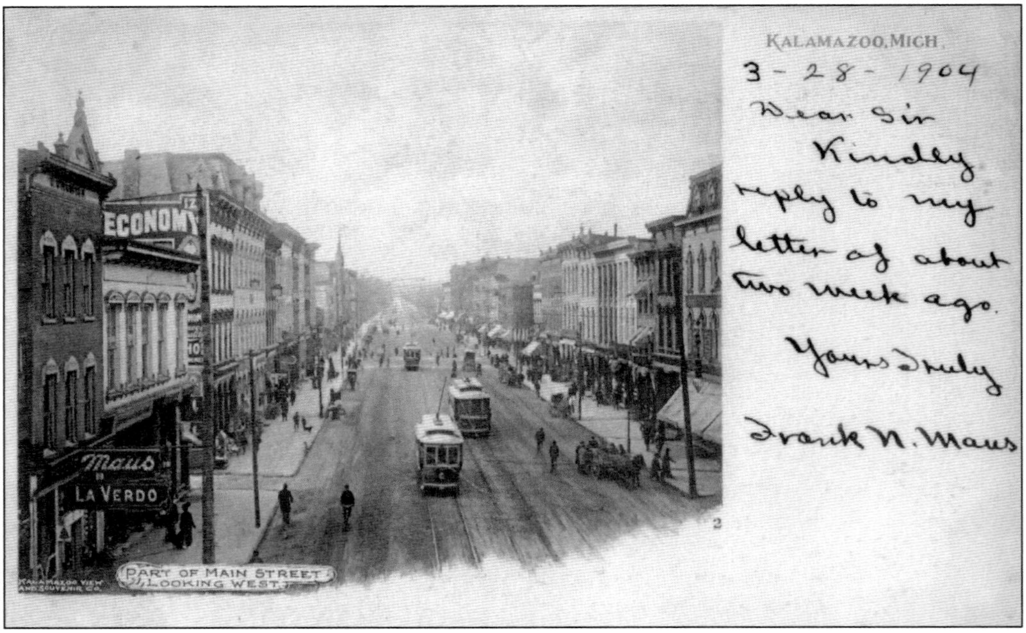


The photographer of this 1904 postcard found a rooftop perch from which to capture this west-facing view of Main Street. Seen here is a prosperous early-20th-century community, with a well-trafficked street. This card provides a good example of the first generation of postcards. Due to postal regulations, the reverse side was reserved only for the address. Therefore, space was made on the front of the card for the message.

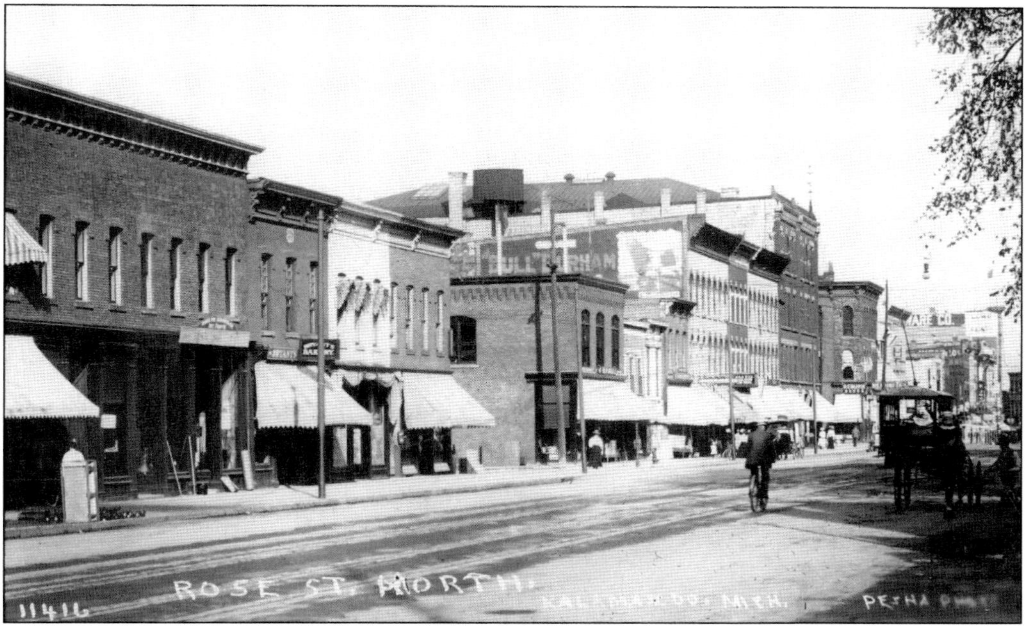


Occasionally, postcard publishers would make a mistake. That is the case with this image, which is incorrectly labeled as depicting Rose Street. In fact, it shows Main Street, looking east from the front of the courthouse. This c. 1910 card provides an excellent view of the rows of 19th-century business blocks that line the street, many of which still stand.

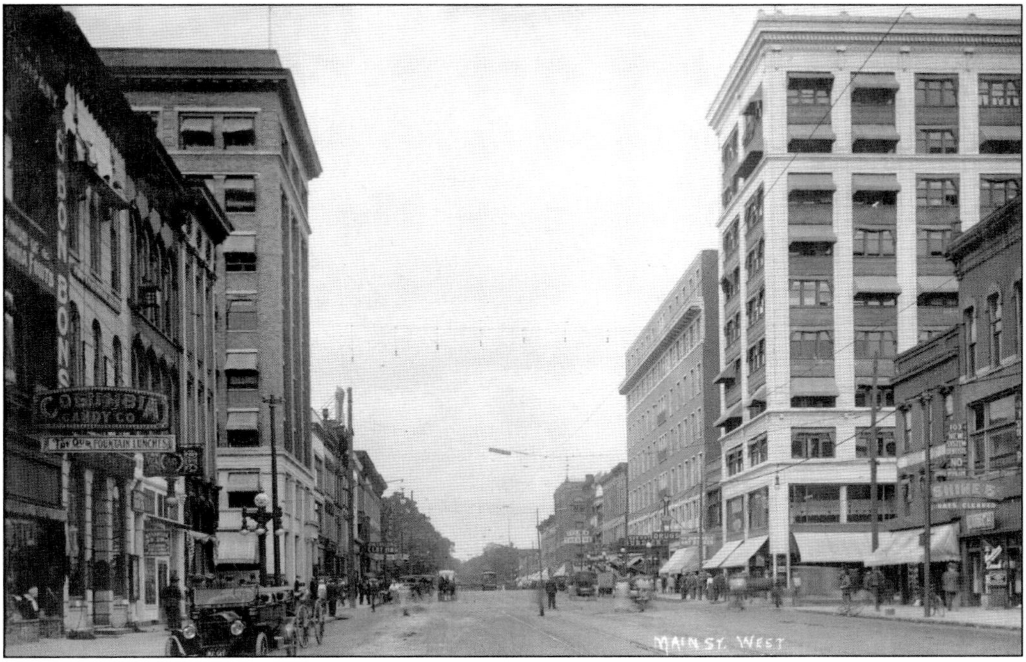


A decade after the earlier images on the preceding pages had been produced, the view had changed significantly, reflecting the growth of Kalamazoo. This c. 1913 photograph is dominated by new steel-framed, high-rise construction. Looking west, Main Street's earlier 19th-century buildings are overshadowed by the new Kalamazoo National Bank Building (left), the Hanselman Building (right), and the new Burdick Hotel (distant right).

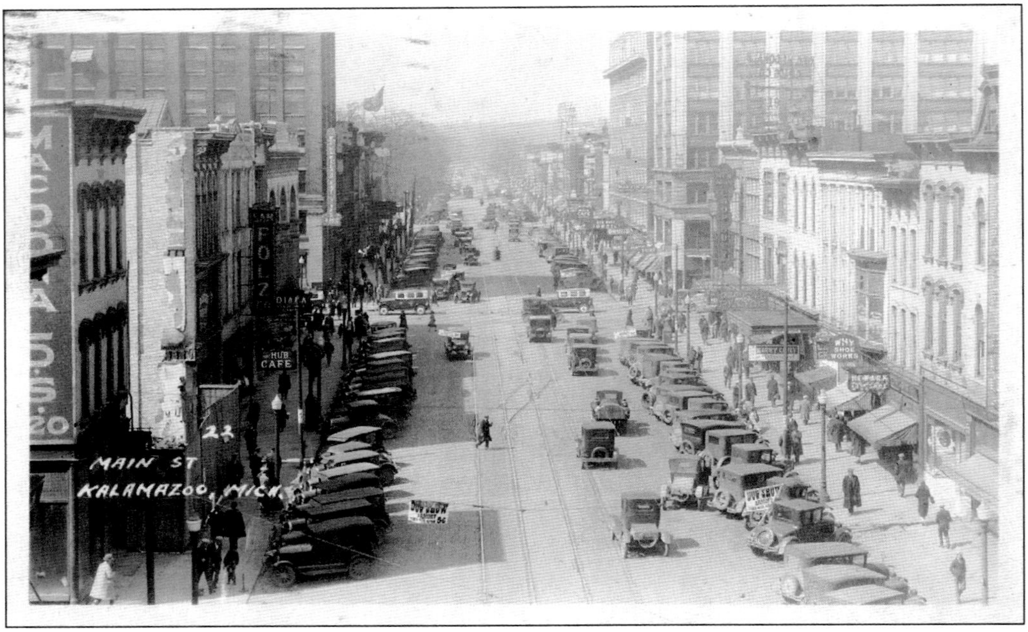


This c. 1928 photograph of Main Street offers a vantage point very similar to the one on page 10. Yet, besides the angle of the camera, the two images have little in common. Not only have the buildings changed, but the traffic has, as well. The arrival of the automobile age is very much in evidence. (From the Collection of the Kalamazoo Valley Museum.)

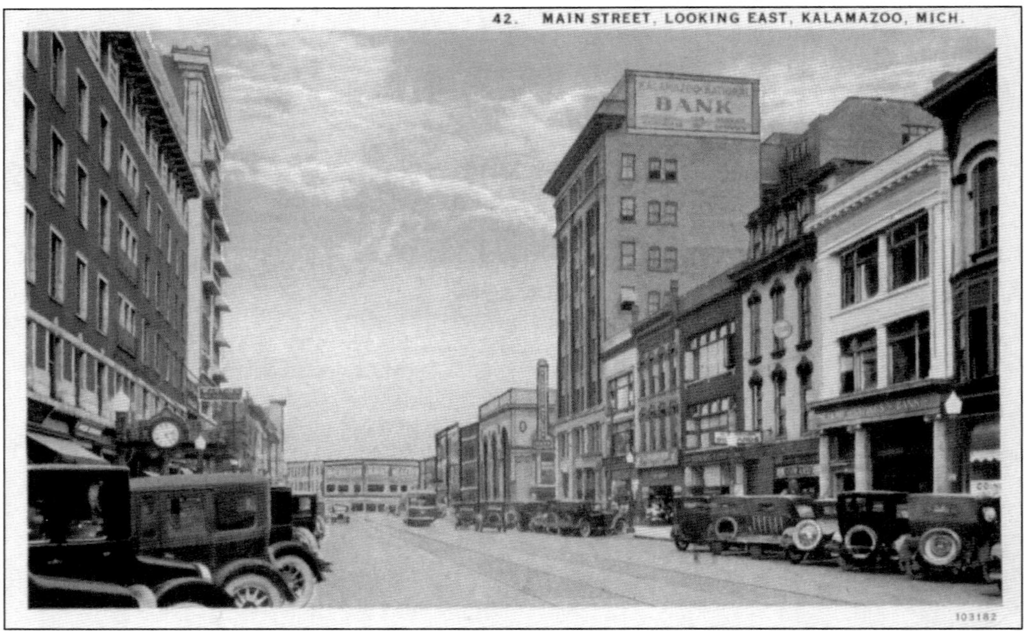


This mid-1920s colored postcard of Main Street suggests the same transformation as in the above photograph. Most of the available parking has been taken. The camera is pointed east, from the intersection with Rose Street. The Burdick Hotel and Hanselman Buildings dominate the left side. The Radisson Plaza Hotel now occupies their place. Across the street, the Kalamazoo National Bank Building towers over a row of older structures. These buildings would steadily fall victim to fires and demolitions, leaving the skyscraper the lone survivor on the block.

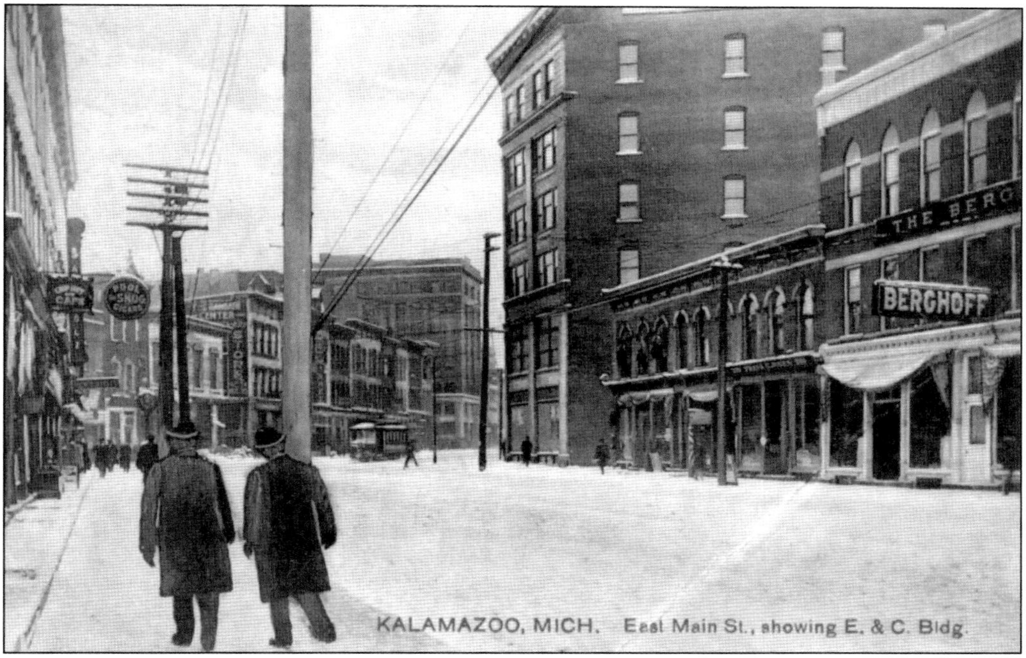


This rare winter view of East Main Street includes the curve where it meets Portage Street. The tall building on the right is the Edward and Chamberlain Hardware Store. The Berghoff Hotel and Café are evidence of the prosperous German American community that thrived here until the outbreak of World War I.

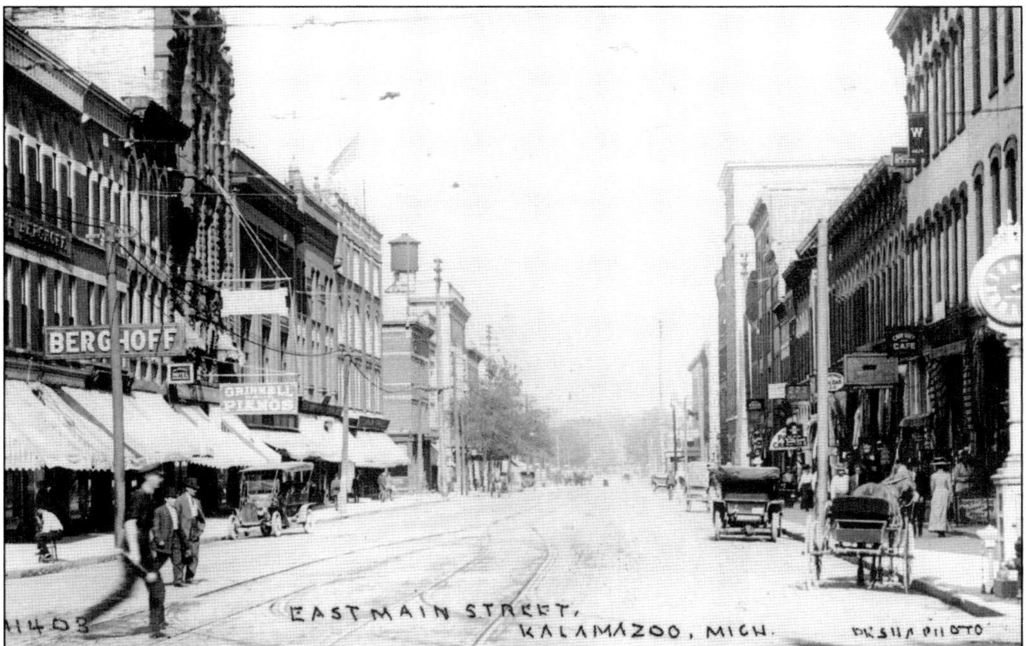


This east-facing photograph of East Main Street was taken from the intersection with Portage Street. The Berghoff is immediately on the left. The buildings seen here housed a number of hotels, restaurants, industries, and saloons.

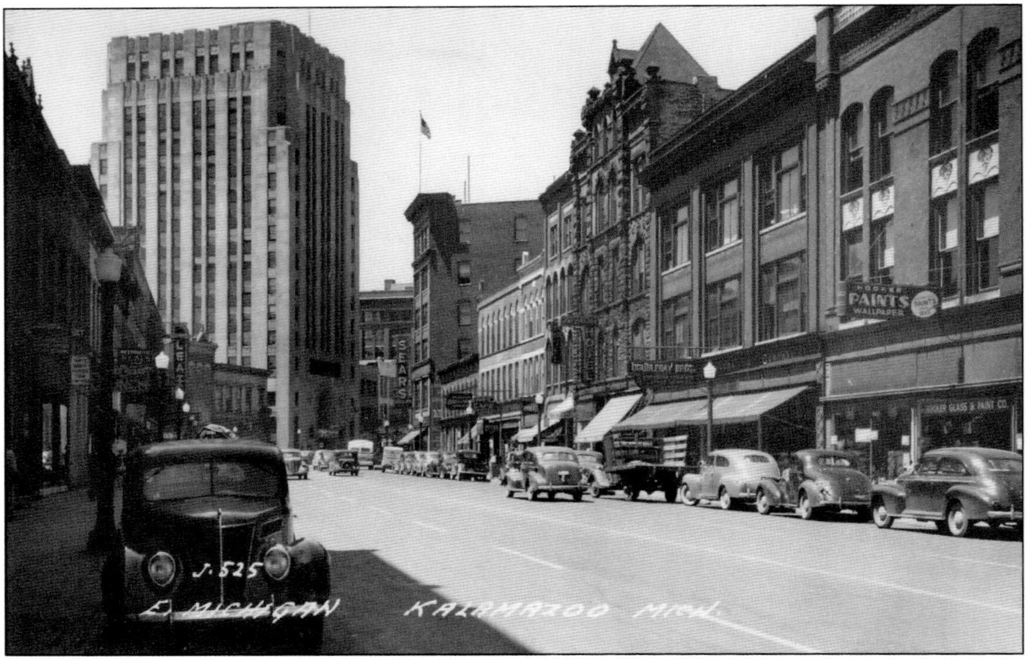


East Main Street, known today as East Michigan Avenue, fell on hard times in the latter half of the 20th century. Fortunately, that downturn ultimately helped preserve many of the buildings seen here. They have been restored as part of the Haymarket Historic District. The street appears much the same today as in this 1944 photograph.

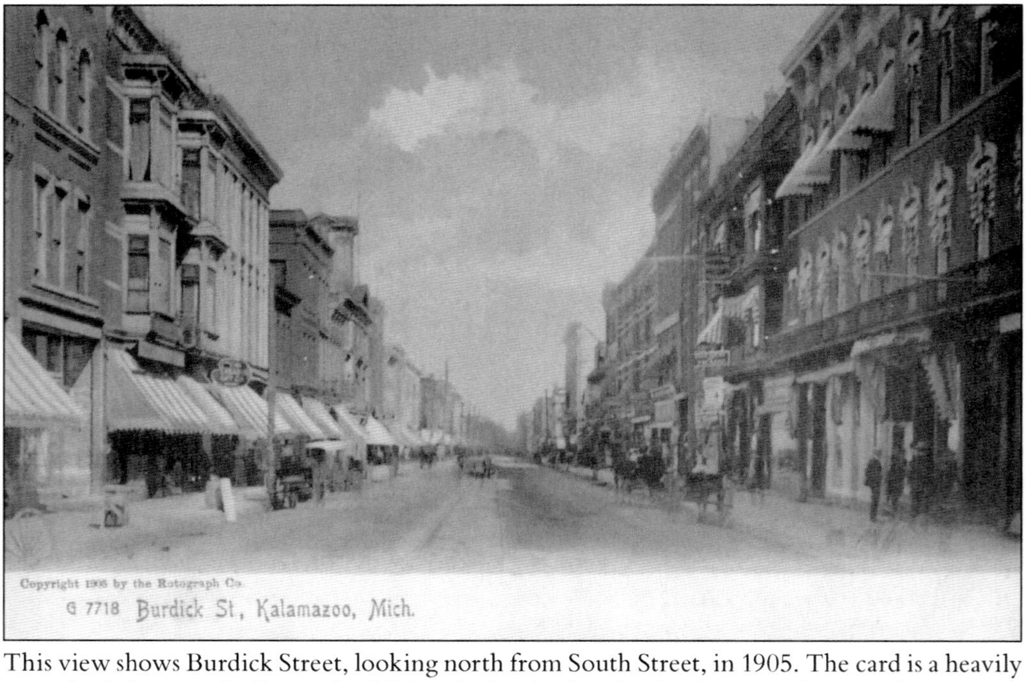


This view shows Burdick Street, looking north from South Street, in 1905. The card is a heavily retouched photograph. Postcard publishers had artists hand-color images to increase their appeal. Since photography at the time resulted in washed-out skies, these artists also added clouds and occasional artistic flourishes.

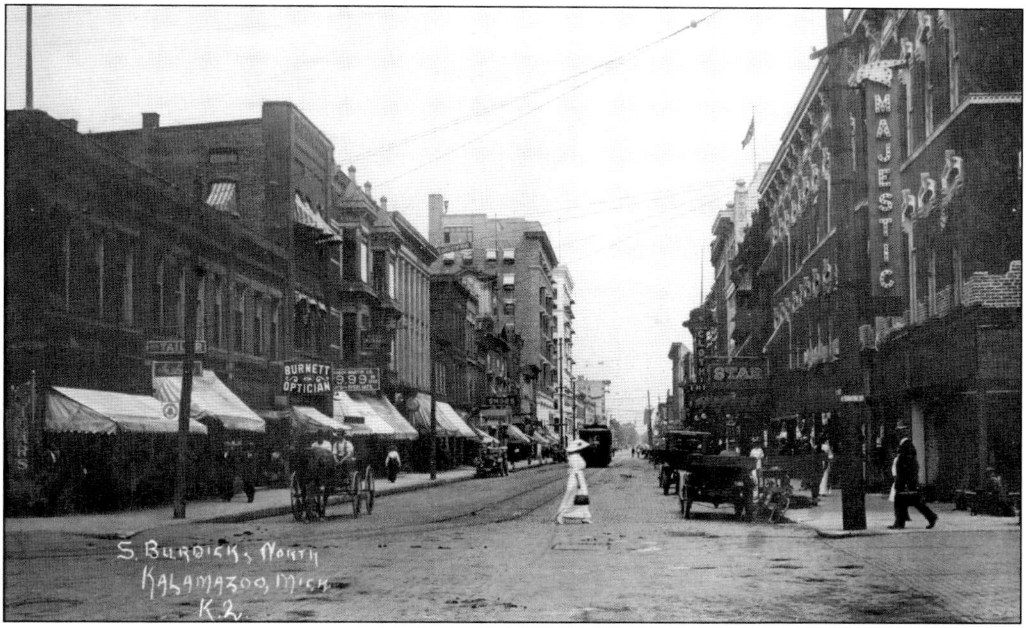


Burdick Street is seen here approximately 10 years after the photograph on the previous page. Several changes are evident, the most startling being the three tall skyscrapers that rise in the distance. Residents looked upon these structures with pride, as they represented the "greater Kalamazoo" and the city's entrance into the modern age. Another development is the electric sign on the right. It directs people to the Majestic Theatre a block down South Street.

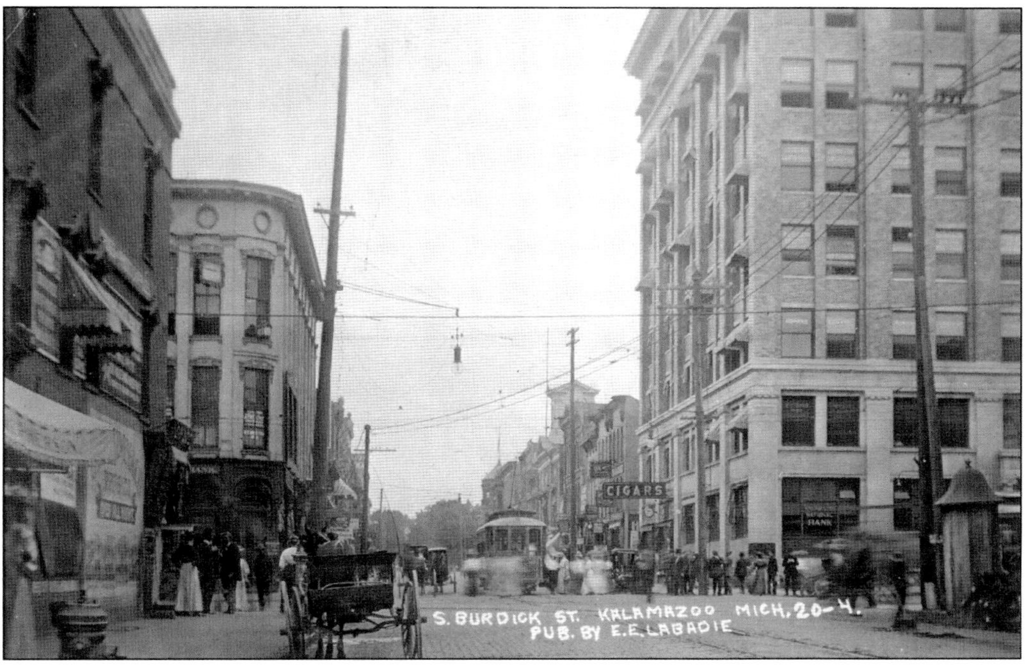


The intersection of Main and Burdick Streets was the busiest in the city for many years, owing to the two streets' status as Kalamazoo's primary commercial thoroughfares. In this c. 1911 photograph, a range of traffic is evident, including buggies and a line of people waiting to board an electric streetcar.

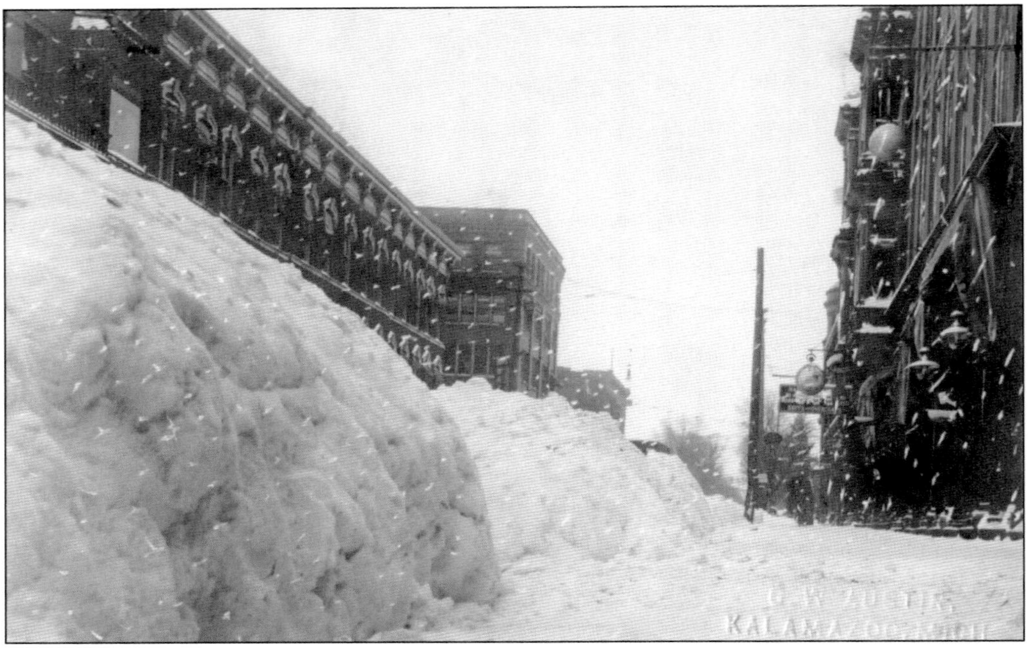

Occasionally, a street scene falls into a category all its own. South Burdick Street is shown here during a particularly bad winter. The photographer, not content with the presence of large piles of snow in the street, took the time in the darkroom to add snowflakes to enhance the effect.

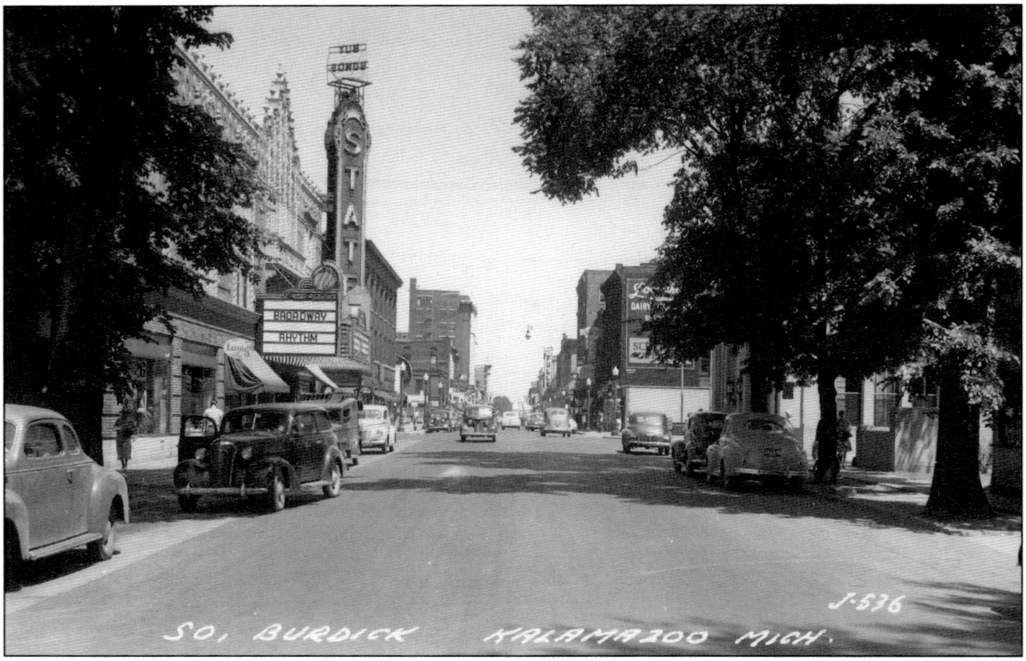


This 1944 view of South Burdick Street, looking north, shows the transition of the south side of downtown, from walls of brick and stone to tree-lined residential streets. The State Theater dominates the view on the left. It continues to do so today, although the original marquees, seen here, are gone. Trees on the right obscure the *Kalamazoo Gazette's* former headquarters.

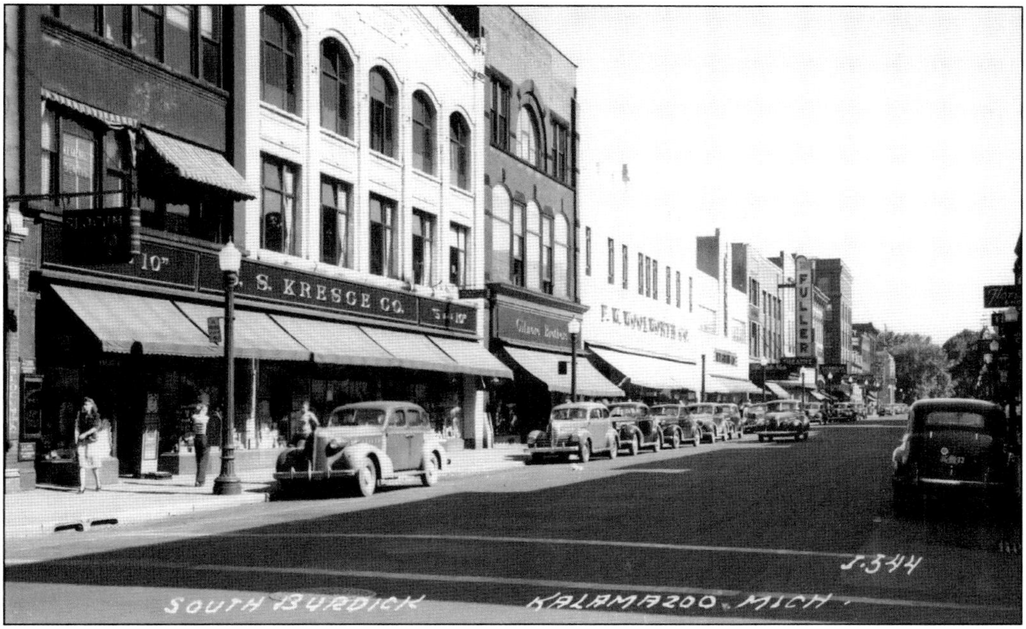


South Burdick Street steadily developed into the heart of Kalamazoo's retail scene, eventually overshadowing Main Street. By 1944, most of the city's department stores could be found here. S.S. Kresge occupies two storefronts on the left. Its neighbor, Gilmore Brothers, would eventually absorb Kresge's space. Farther down the road, the F.W. Woolworth Company and the Fuller Theater are visible.

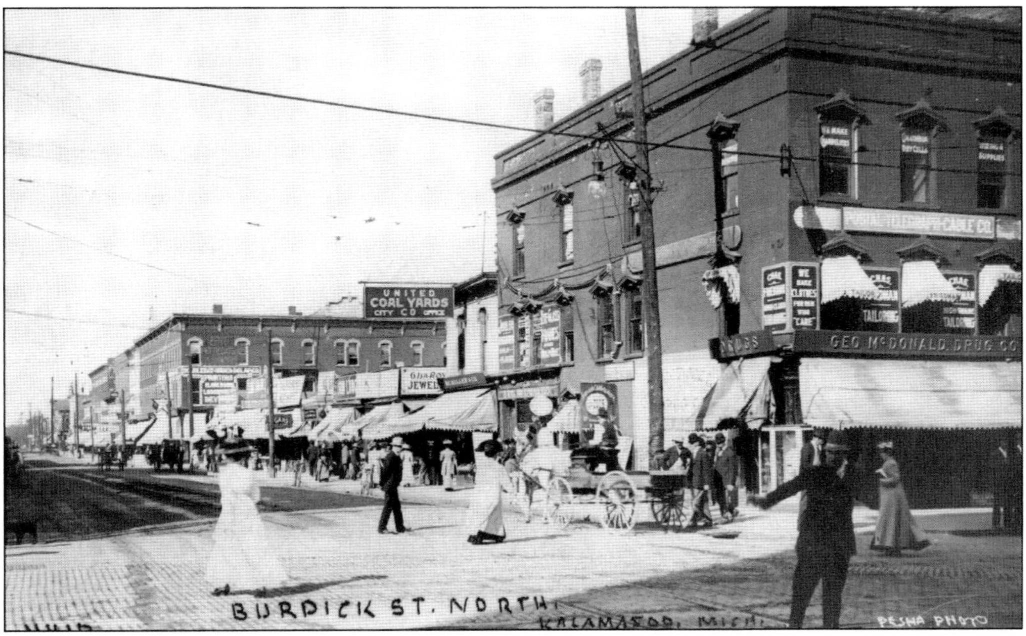


The sidewalks of downtown Kalamazoo are filled with well-dressed pedestrians in this view of North Burdick Street from the intersection with Main Street. The long row of low, wooden buildings seen here was nicknamed "Asbestos Row," due to the block's ability to resist fire, despite the hopes of many residents. The ramshackle collection of buildings was long considered an embarrassment. They were finally razed in 1928 to make way for the Dewing Building.

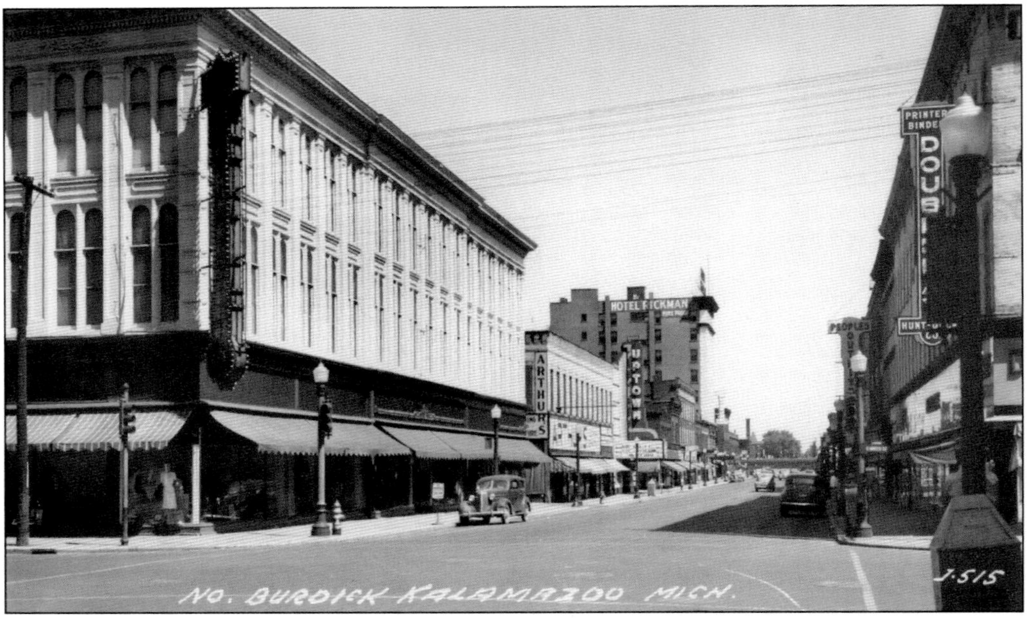


This stretch of North Burdick Street, looking toward the Michigan Central Station from Water Street, has changed dramatically since this 1944 photograph was taken. The street is closed to traffic, the only stretch of Kalamazoo's 1959 pedestrian mall to remain so. Most of the buildings on the left side of the street have given way to green space or new development. On the other hand, most of the structures on the right side of the street survive.

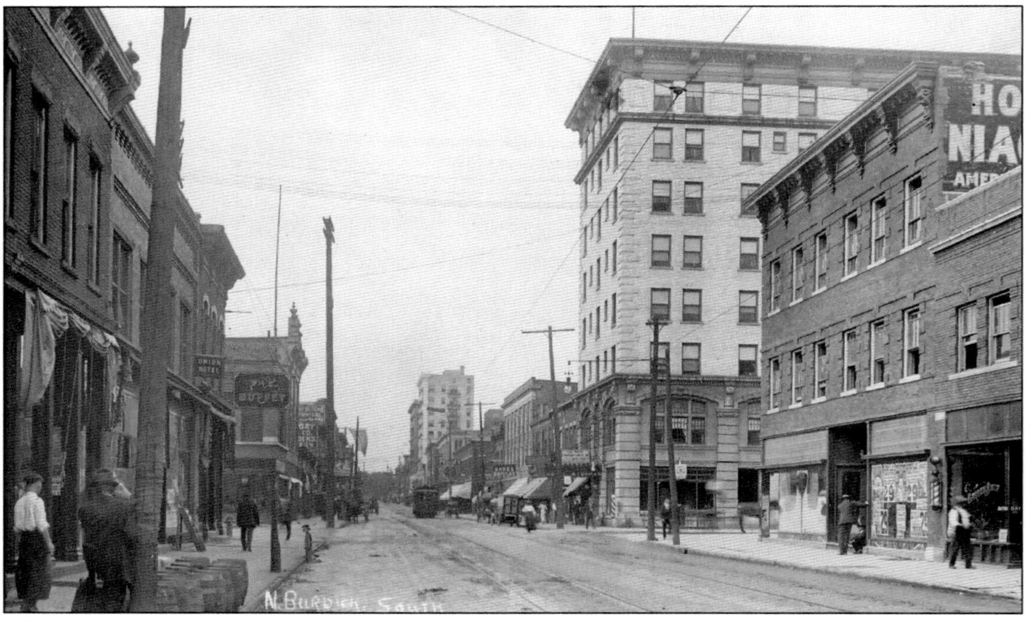

This rare view, postmarked in 1913, shows North Burdick Street looking south from the Michigan Central Station. A number of hotels are visible, including the Hotel Niagara, the Union Hotel, and the towering, eight-story Rickman. These establishments were not unlike the motels found near interstates today. They got most of their business from passengers arriving at the neighboring railroad station. The Rickman still stands, but most of the other structures seen here are long gone.

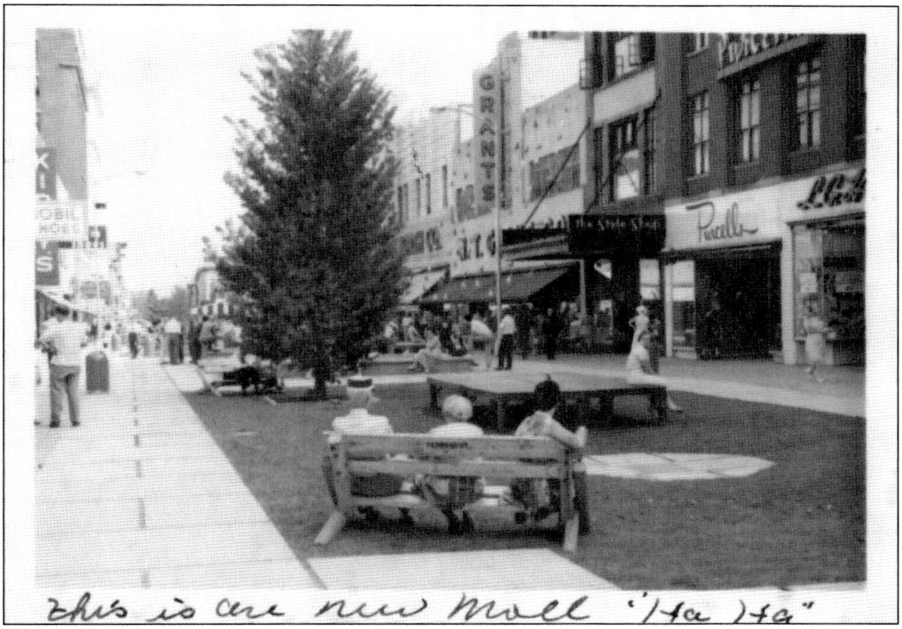


By the 1950s, downtown's status as Kalamazoo's shopping center was being challenged by strip malls being built on the outskirts of the city. In 1958, city officials approved the Kalamazoo 1980 plan, proposed by architect Victor Gruen. It called for a dramatic transformation of the city center, turning the streets into pedestrian zones, building new ring roads that would circle downtown, and razing large areas for parking. However, the Kalamazoo Mall that opened on August 19, 1959, was a vastly scaled-back version of that proposal. Just two blocks of North and South Burdick Streets were closed off, and the pavement was replaced with grass, trees, and pools. In 1960 and 1975, two additional blocks were closed off. It was the first downtown pedestrian mall in the nation, and Kalamazoo became known as the "mall city." These 1959 photo postcards show the original two blocks of the mall.

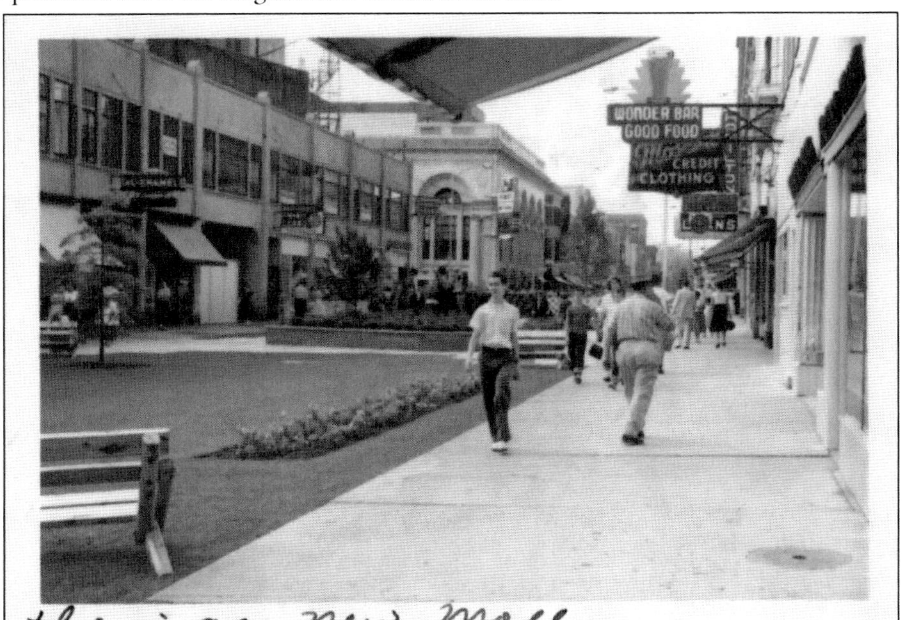

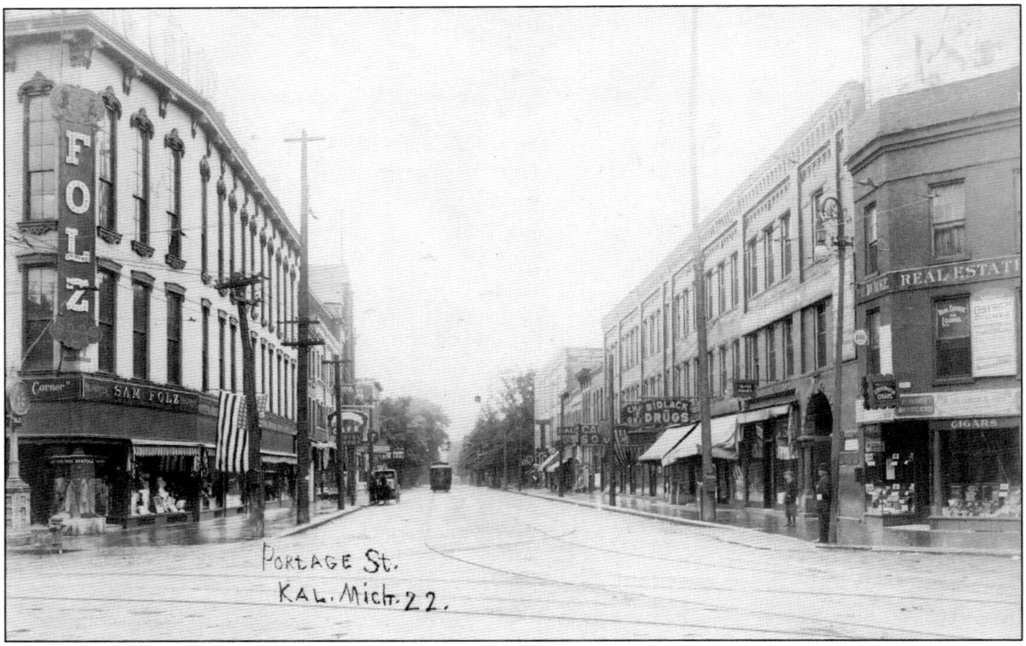


Although somewhat overshadowed by Main and Burdick Streets, Portage Street has been both an important artery and retail strip. This c. 1910 photo postcard shows Portage Street from its terminus with Main Street. The two corner buildings on either side of the street still exist, although they have been heavily altered. Most of the other buildings have been lost to time.

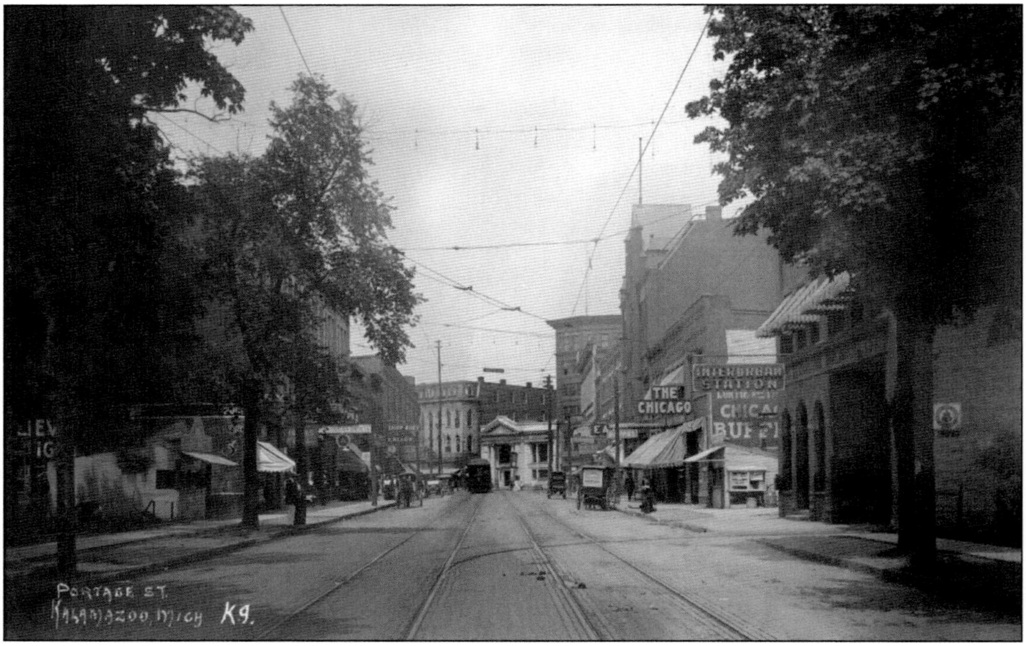


This is a reverse view of the above photograph. Portage Street is seen from Lovell Street. The tallest structure on the right side of the street is the AUV Auditorium, a social hall built in 1898 by Kalamazoo's German community. It and most of the other buildings on that side of Portage Street were destroyed in the 1980 Kalamazoo tornado. (Courtesy of the Kalamazoo Public Library's Local History Room.)

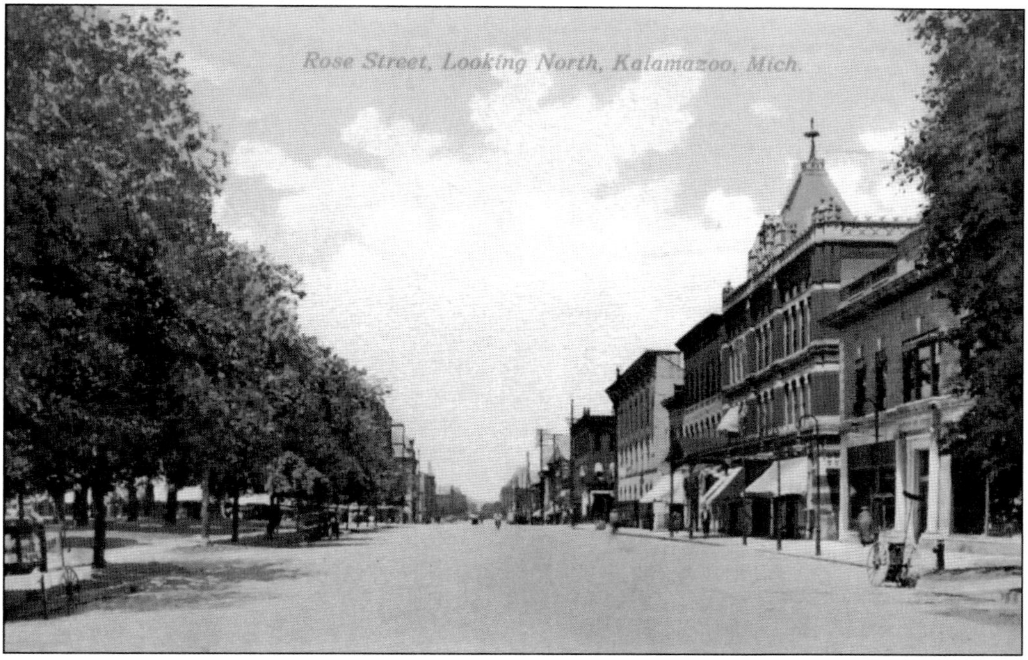


Rose Street was another downtown thoroughfare not frequently captured by the postcard photographer's lens. This north-facing photograph was taken around 1910 from the intersection with South Street. The most prominent building on the right is the Academy of Music, the city's 19th-century opera house. The trees on the left mark the location of Bronson Park.

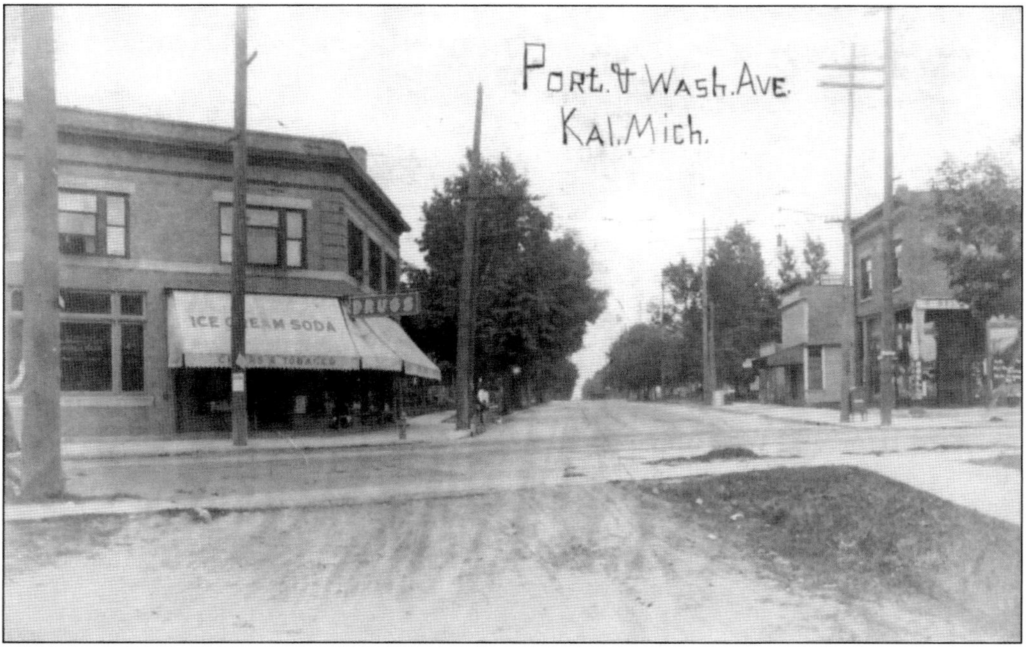


Washington Square was Kalamazoo's first neighborhood business district to develop outside of the downtown area. This view looks down Washington Avenue toward the intersection with Portage Street. The structure on the left housed an A&P for many years. Most of these buildings are now gone, but the area remains an important cornerstone of the Edison neighborhood.

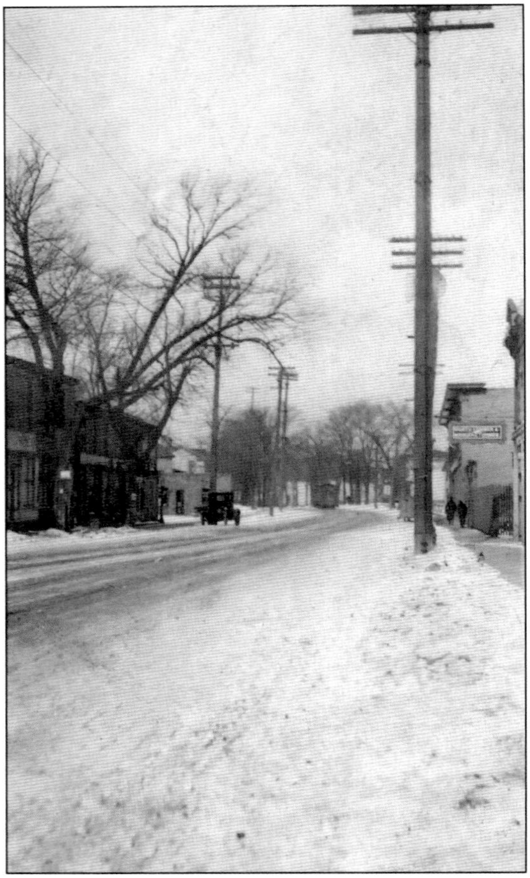

Occasionally, a postcard shows one of downtown's less-glamorous stretches. This winter view of Portage Street looks toward the intersection with Lovell Street. Today, this view would show the massive structures built by the former pharmaceutical manufacturer Upjohn. Those on the left side of the street are now Western Michigan University's new medical school, and those on the right house Zoetis, an animal health company.

One would not know it today, but West Main Street, today known as West Michigan Avenue, was once lined with the most impressive homes in Kalamazoo. The section between Oakland Drive and Park Street was nicknamed "Mansion Row" for all of the 19th-century homes found there. The house on the left was built by Oscar M. Allen, who made his fortune with the Globe Casket Company, a manufacturer of cloth-lined caskets. The gradual westward expansion of the commercial district led to the demise of these mansions. Those seen here fell in 1951 to make way for the new St. Augustine Parish.

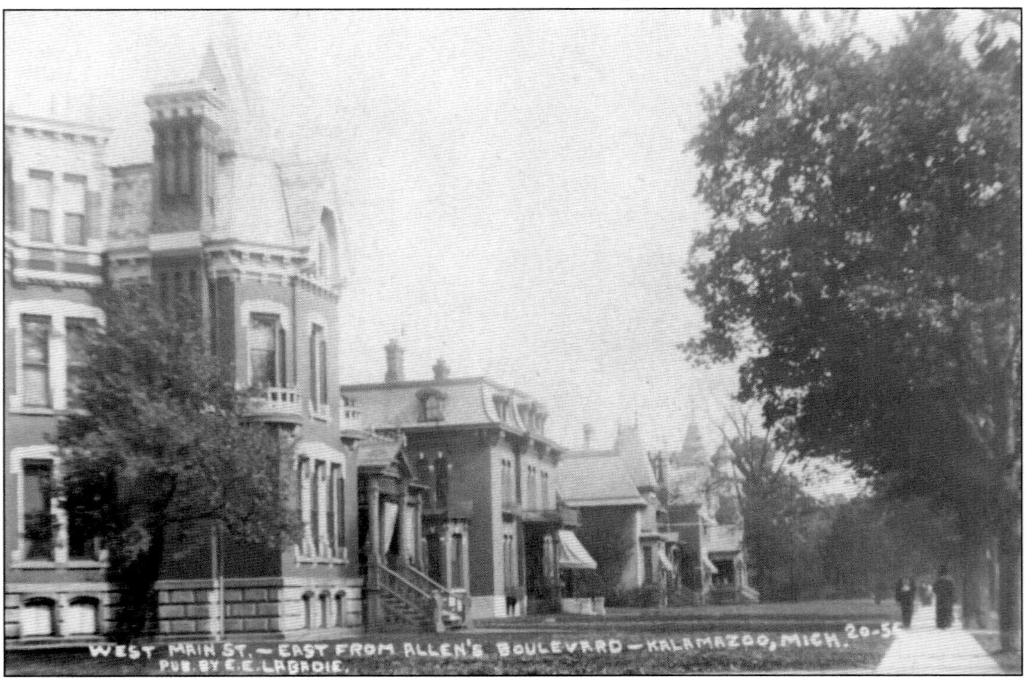

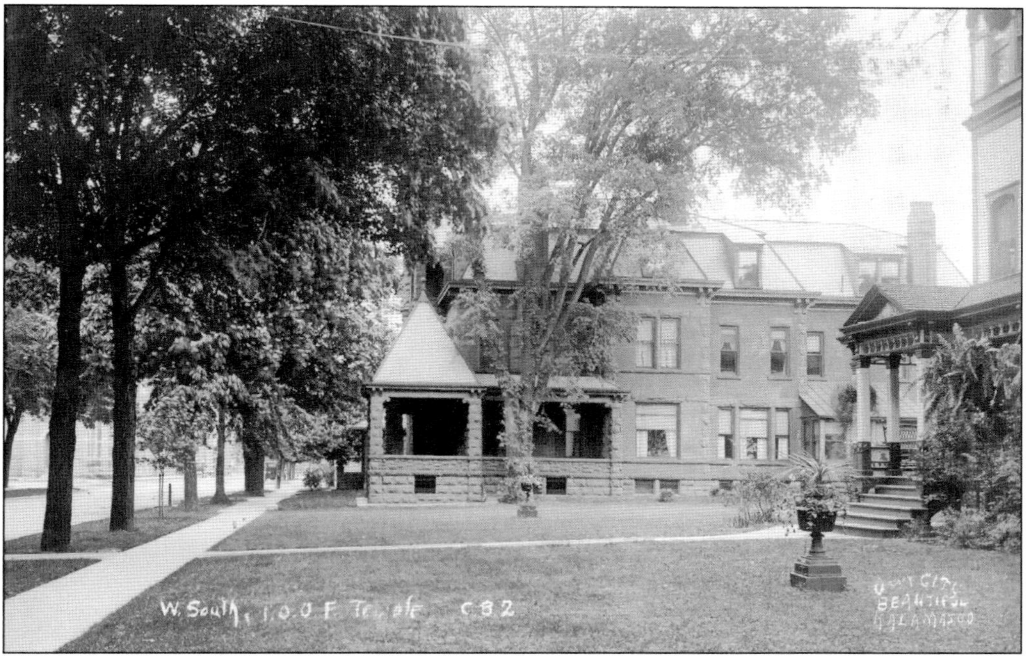


South Street was another location of some of the city's most impressive 19th-century and early-20th-century houses. William S. Lawrence, a local industrialist, built the castle seen here in 1889. At the time of this postcard, the home was occupied by the Independent Order of Odd Fellows. Today, the Park Club occupies it. Visible at right is part of the Perrin-Milham House, which briefly housed city offices in the 1920s before being razed to make room for the current City Hall.

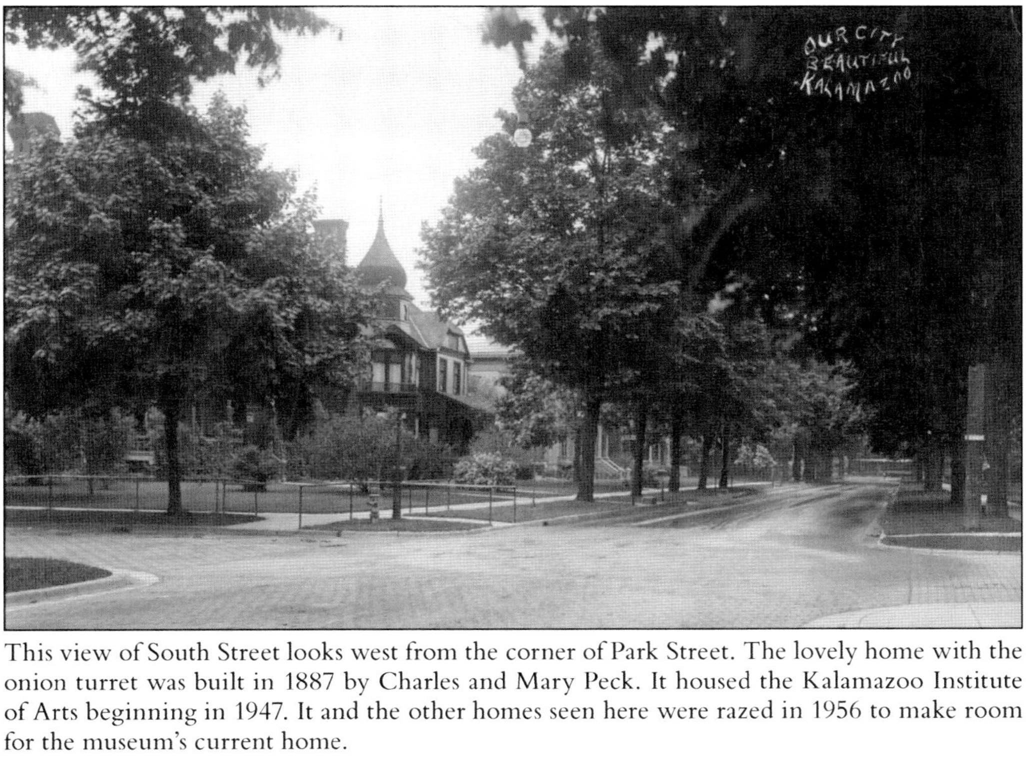


This view of South Street looks west from the corner of Park Street. The lovely home with the onion turret was built in 1887 by Charles and Mary Peck. It housed the Kalamazoo Institute of Arts beginning in 1947. It and the other homes seen here were razed in 1956 to make room for the museum's current home.

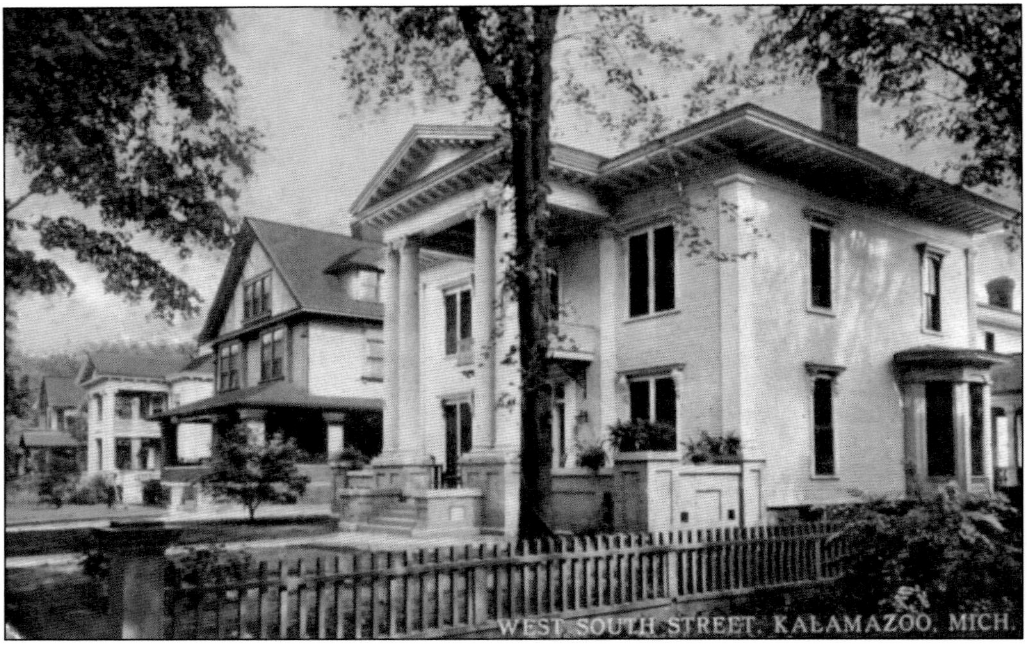


Several blocks of South Street survive today as one of Kalamazoo's most noted historic districts. For example, this view could be replicated today. The homes shown here are, from right to left, the Van Deusen House, the Frank B. Lay House, and the Donald Boudeman House.

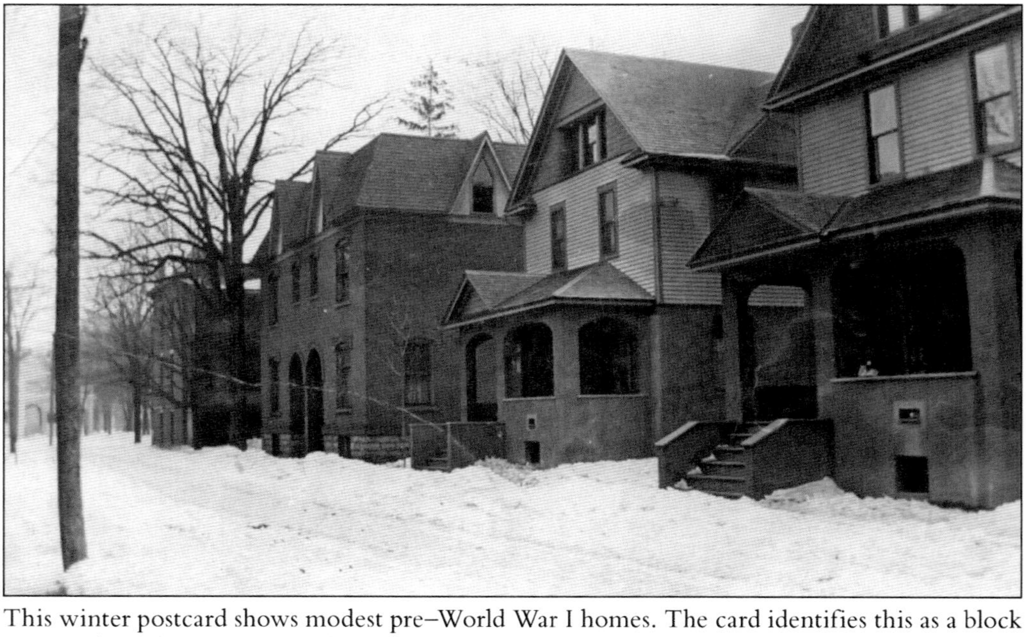

This winter postcard shows modest pre–World War I homes. The card identifies this as a block on North Cedar Street, which no longer exists. The area the street once occupied has been gobbled up by the steady expansion of Bronson Methodist Hospital.

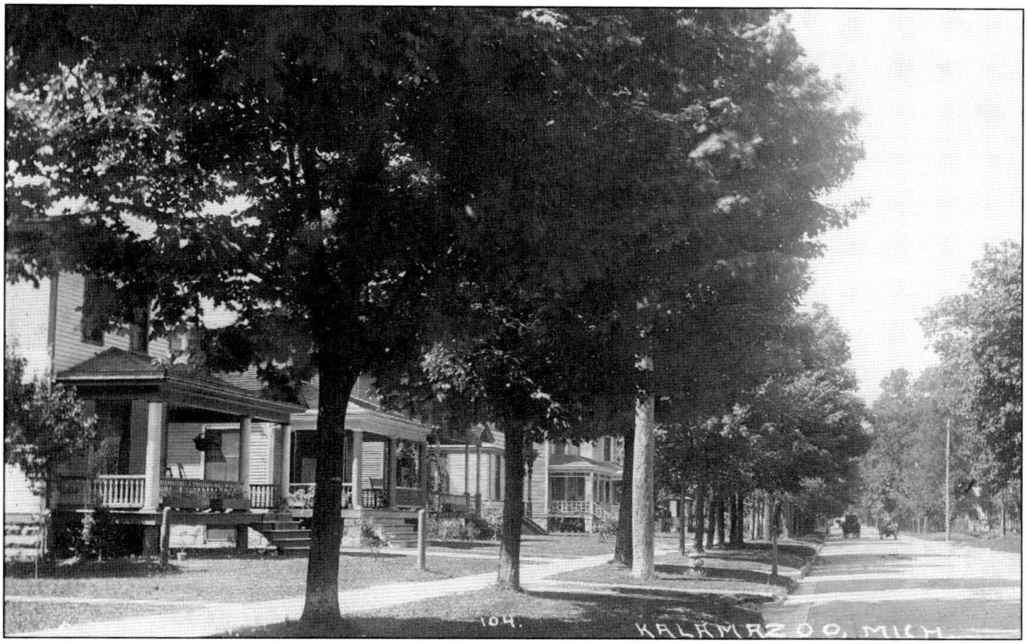


This unidentified residential street is typical of Kalamazoo neighborhoods in the first decades of the 20th century. This is very likely a street in the Vine Neighborhood, just south of downtown. Although more modest than the mansions on West Main and South Streets, these homes are substantial and feature large front porches and verandas.

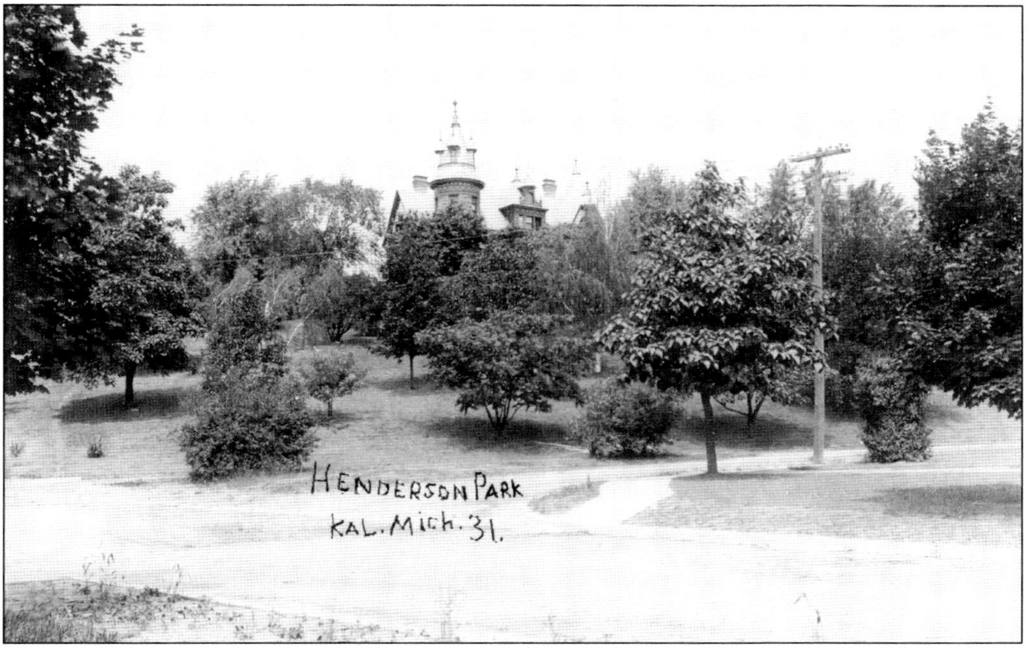


Frank Henderson's "castle," seen here atop a hill overlooking the Henderson Park neighborhood and West Main Street, is one of the most recognizable historic homes in the city. The home was completed in 1895 by the founder of the Henderson-Ames Company, which manufactured uniforms and regalia. Henderson did not enjoy his house for long, dying in 1899. Today, it is a bed-and-breakfast.

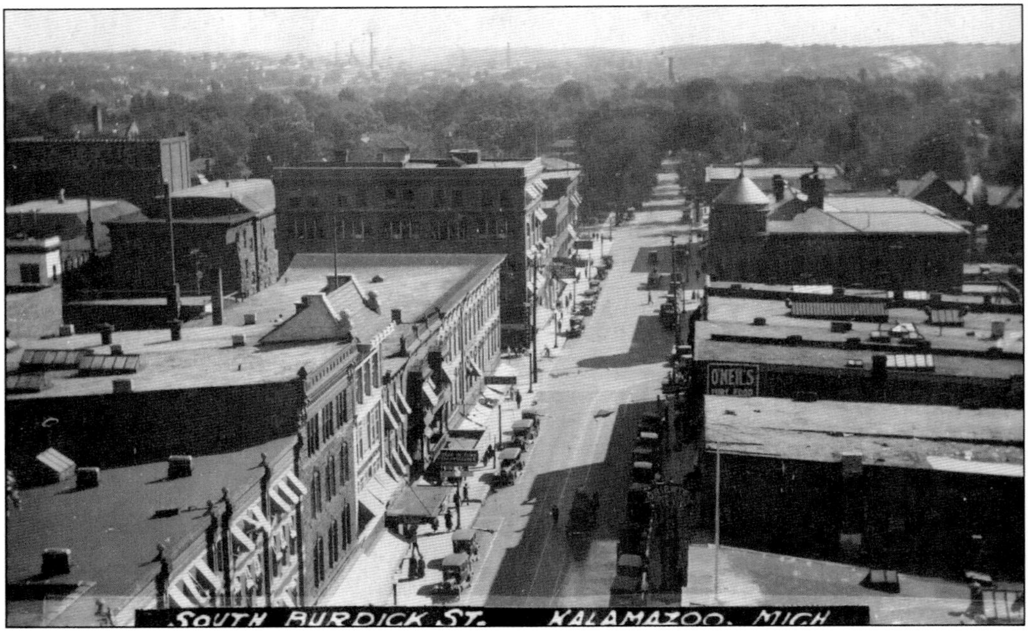


As buildings grew higher, they provided photographers the opportunity to capture the city from a bird's-eye view. This photograph, taken from the roof of the Kalamazoo National Bank Building, looks south down Burdick Street. Note the contrast between the brick, concrete, and stone of the downtown area and the forested neighborhoods beyond. Smokestacks for the Bryant Paper Company are visible on the horizon.

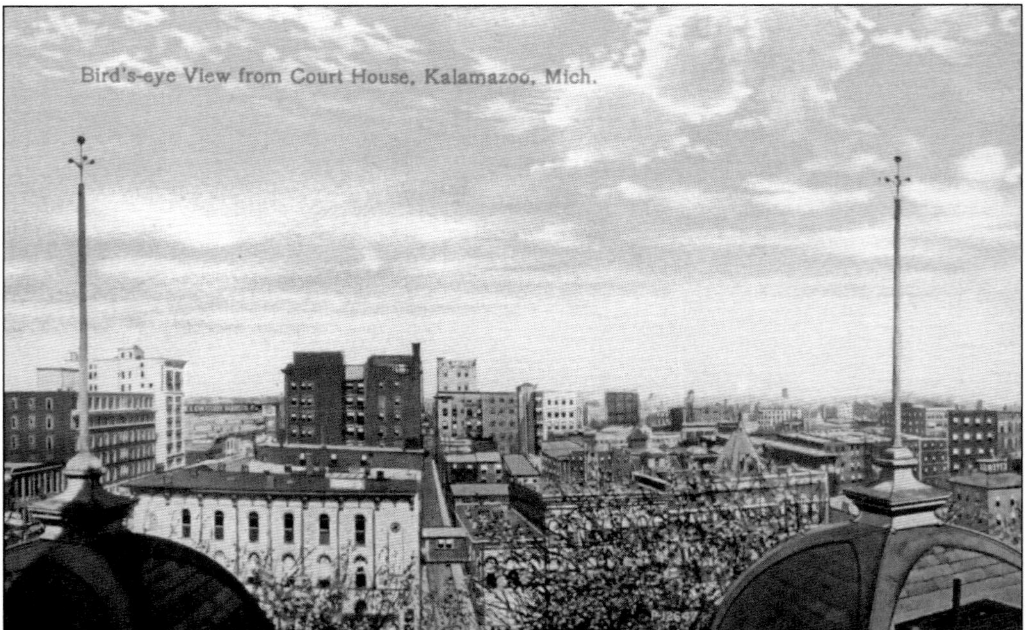


This photograph was taken from the tower of the Kalamazoo County Courthouse. The city's new skyline is framed by the courthouse domes. The tall buildings include the Burdick Hotel, Hanselman Building, Kalamazoo National Bank Building, and Gilmore Brothers Department Store.

## *Two*

# Public Buildings and Infrastructure

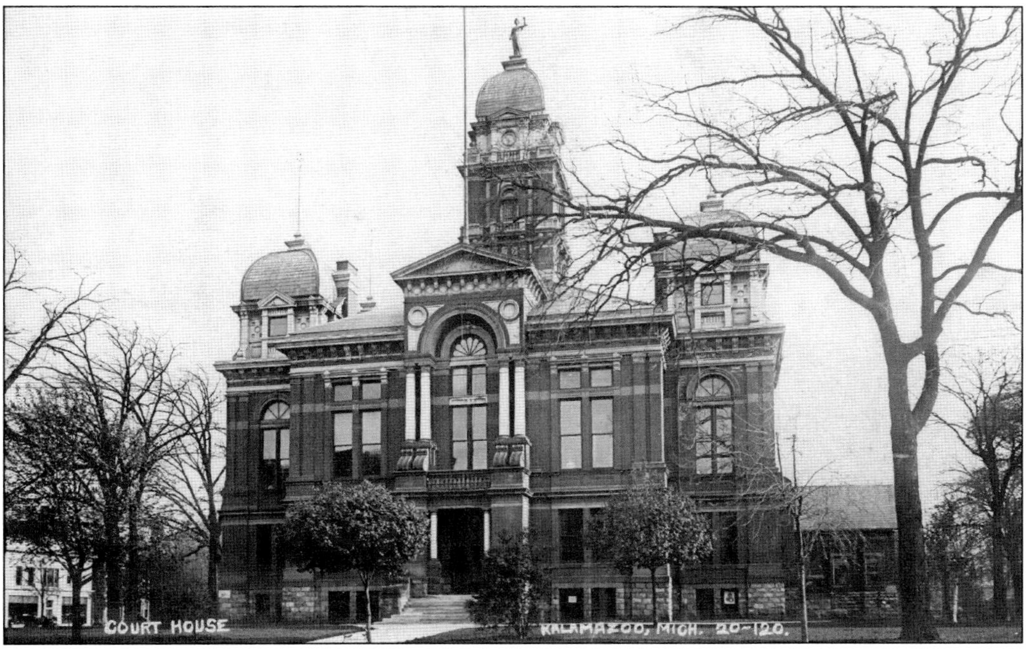


Kalamazoo serves as the county seat for Kalamazoo County. This postcard shows the second courthouse to stand at the corner of Main and Rose Streets, overlooking Bronson Park. The building was opened in 1885 and featured splendid architecture befitting a public building. But, it fell victim to the rapid growth of the city and county. It soon became overcrowded and was torn down in 1935 to make room for a larger structure.

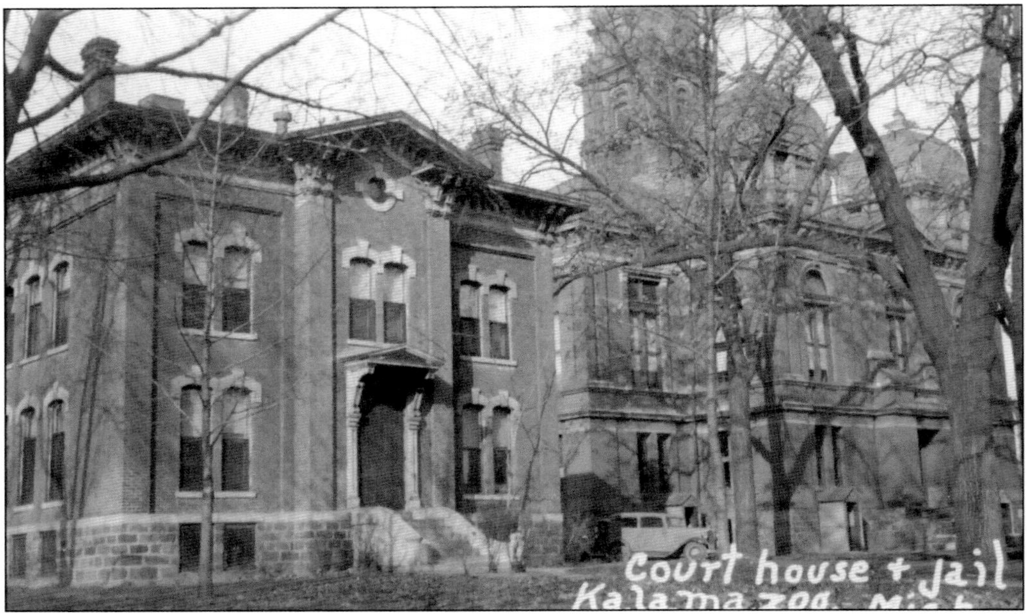


The county jail was located in this structure at the corner of Rose and Academy Streets, just behind the courthouse. Facing Bronson Park, this handsome Italianate brick building was opened in 1866. The courthouse that opened in 1937 had its own jail, and this building was rendered obsolete. It was demolished that year.

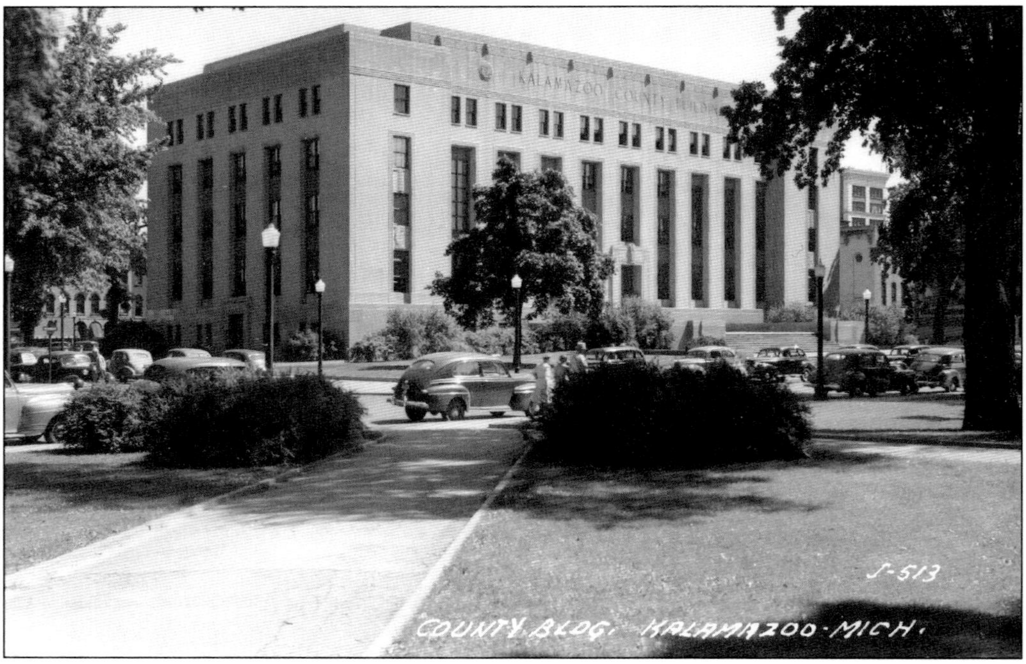


The current courthouse and jail, seen here in 1944, was opened in 1937. It was built with financing from the Public Works Administration, a New Deal program during the Great Depression intended to aid the crippled construction industry and provide needed infrastructure improvements. The building's Art Deco styling matches Kalamazoo's other public buildings of the time.

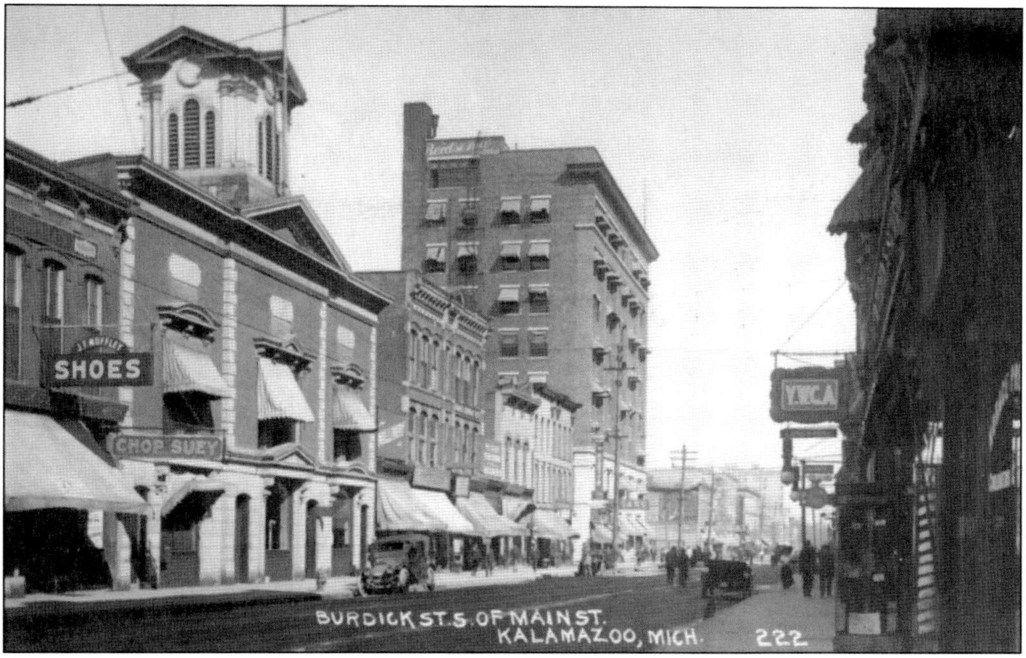


The building at left with the cupola was Corporation Hall. It was built in 1867 to house Kalamazoo's fire and police departments as well as the village offices. The fire department moved out in 1908, and the police followed in 1914. For the next 10 years, the building continued to serve as city hall until the offices were moved to the present site on South Street. The structure was then adapted to retail use and altered beyond recognition. It was razed in 2011.

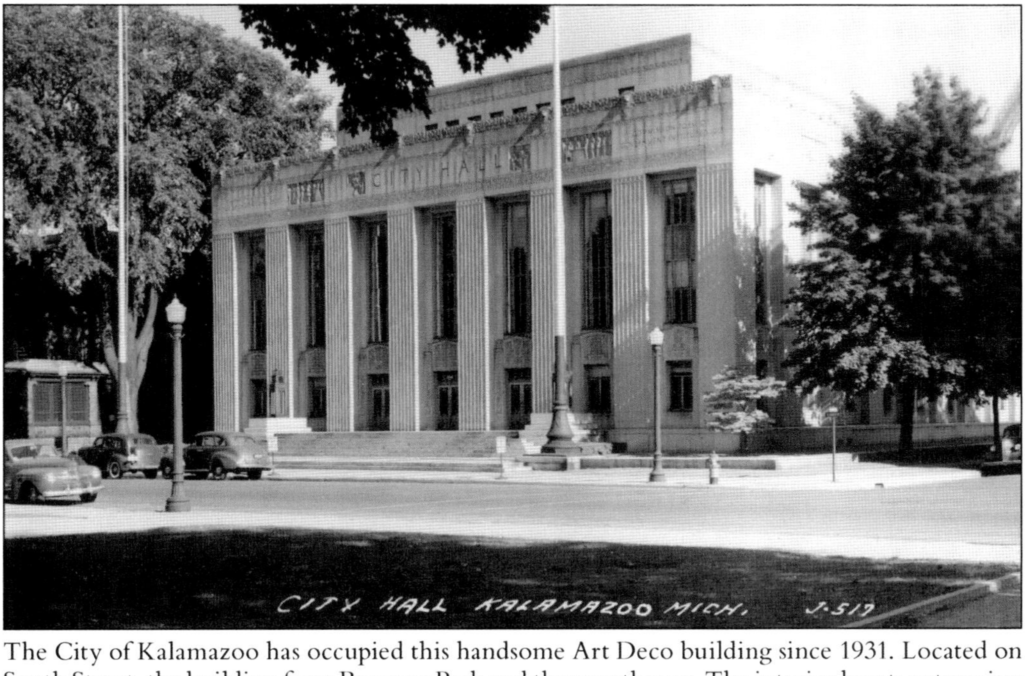


The City of Kalamazoo has occupied this handsome Art Deco building since 1931. Located on South Street, the building faces Bronson Park and the courthouse. The interior boasts a stunning atrium and fine commission chambers. The exterior is covered with relief sculptures depicting scenes of local history. The building appears today much as it does in this 1944 photograph.

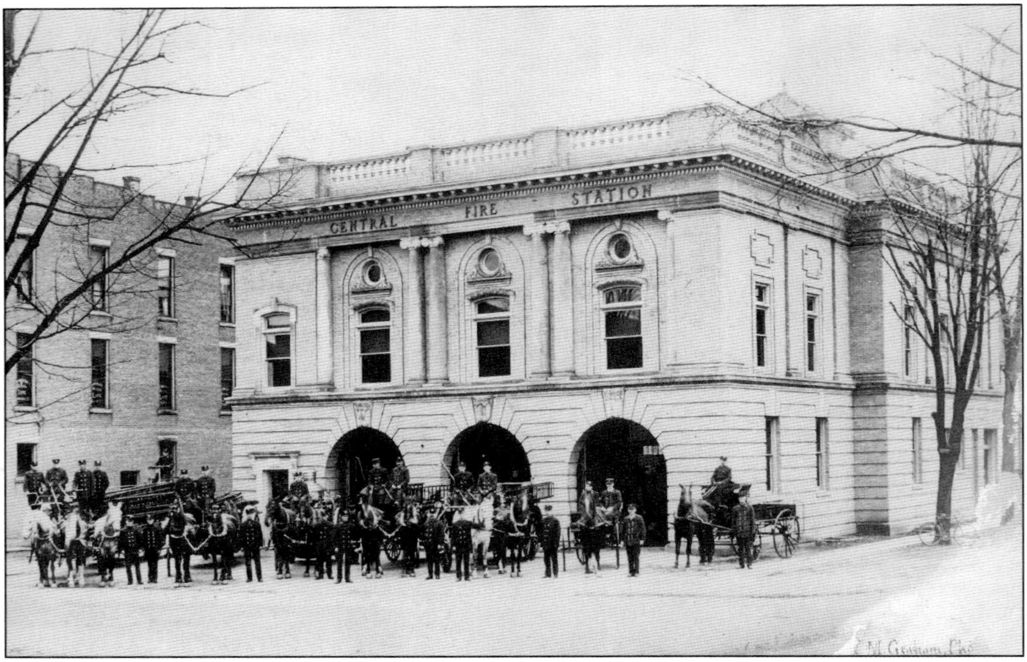


The fire department was proud of its new Central Fire Station. Here, members pose in front of the structure with their horse-drawn equipment. The back of this postcard states that the photograph was taken on the day the building opened in 1908. Although beautiful, the building was razed in 1959 to make room for Jacobson's Department Store, today the site of the Epic Center.

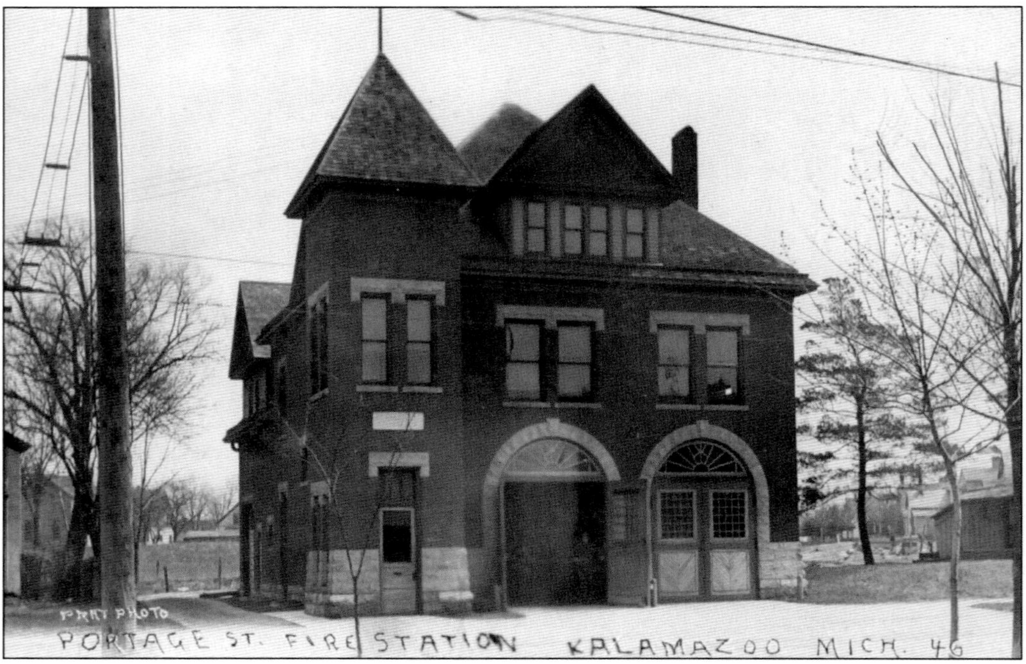


Kalamazoo was too large to be served by one centrally located fire station. Fire House No. 2 was built on Portage Street in 1900. It ceased being a fire station in the 1950s, but it remains a landmark in the Washington Square neighborhood and has since been restored.

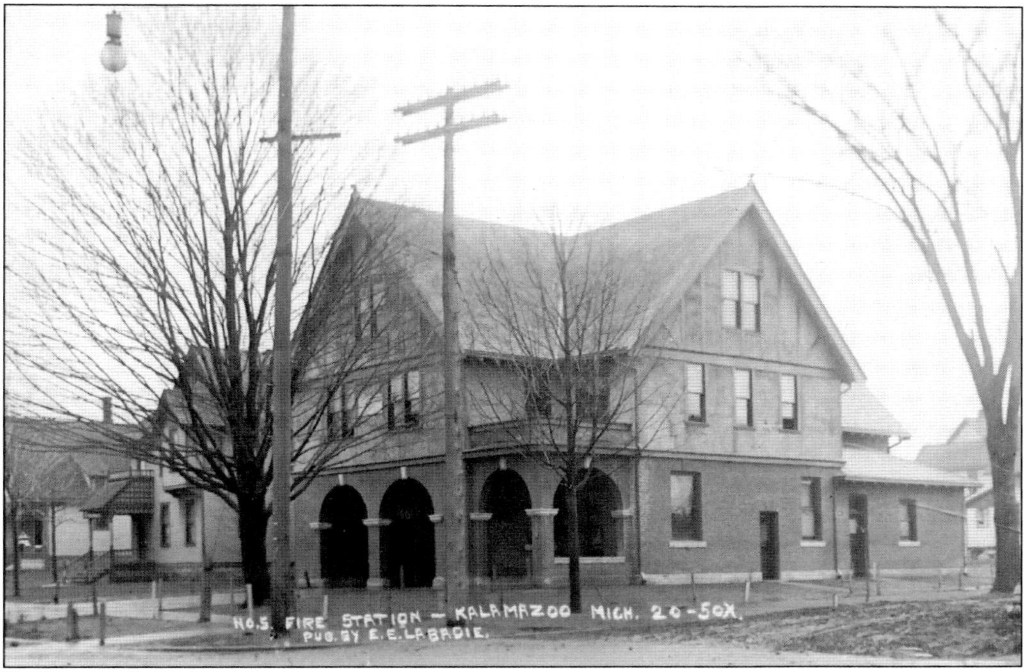


The identical Fire Stations No. 5 and No. 6 were built in 1908 and 1909, respectively, from plans by Forrest Van Volkenburg, architect of the Central Fire Station. Station No. 5 (above) served Kalamazoo's northwest neighborhoods from its location on Douglas Avenue. Station No. 6 (below) was built on South West Street, now known as Westnedge Avenue, and served the south side. Both buildings survive today.

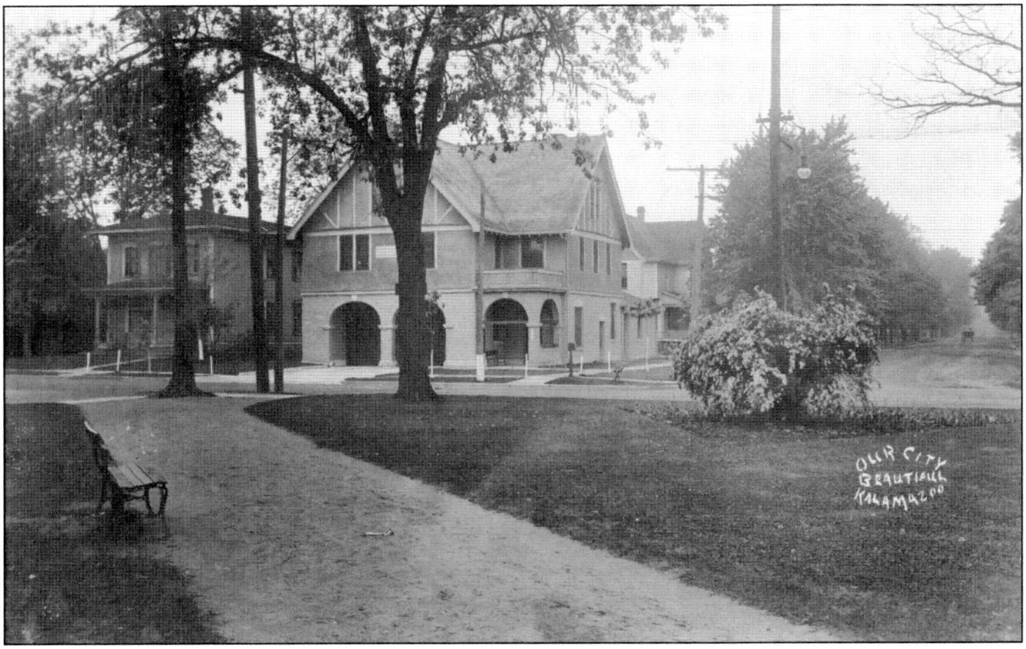

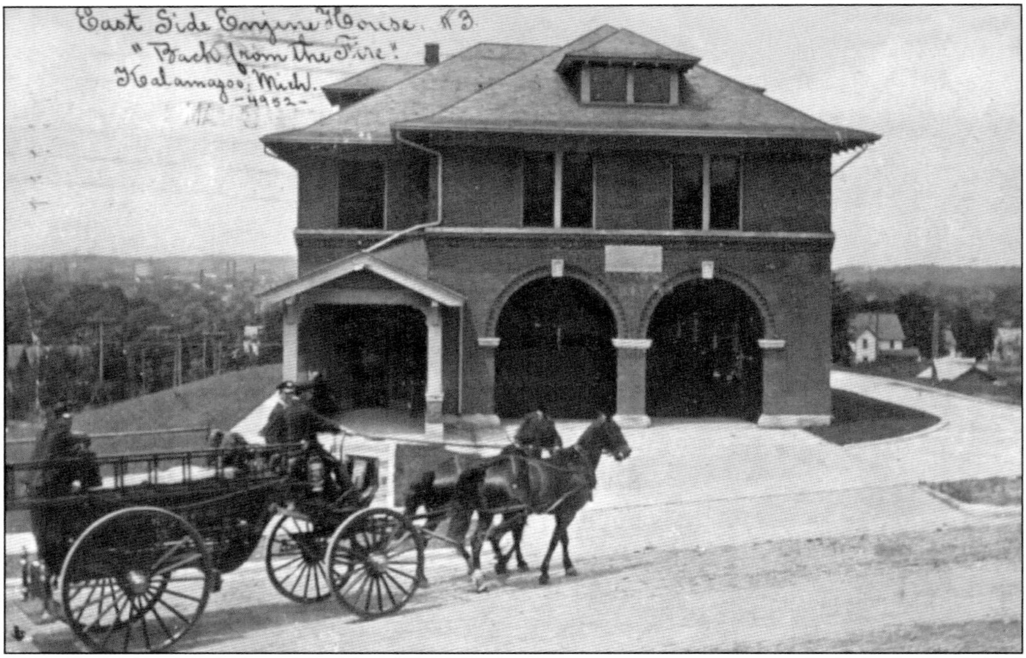


Fire Station No. 3 served the northeast side from its location on Charlotte Street. It was built as a fire station in 1907 and served until 1980. This postcard shows the horse-drawn equipment used when the station was first built. Eventual adoption of motorized firefighting equipment would require widening of the garage entry. The building still stands today.

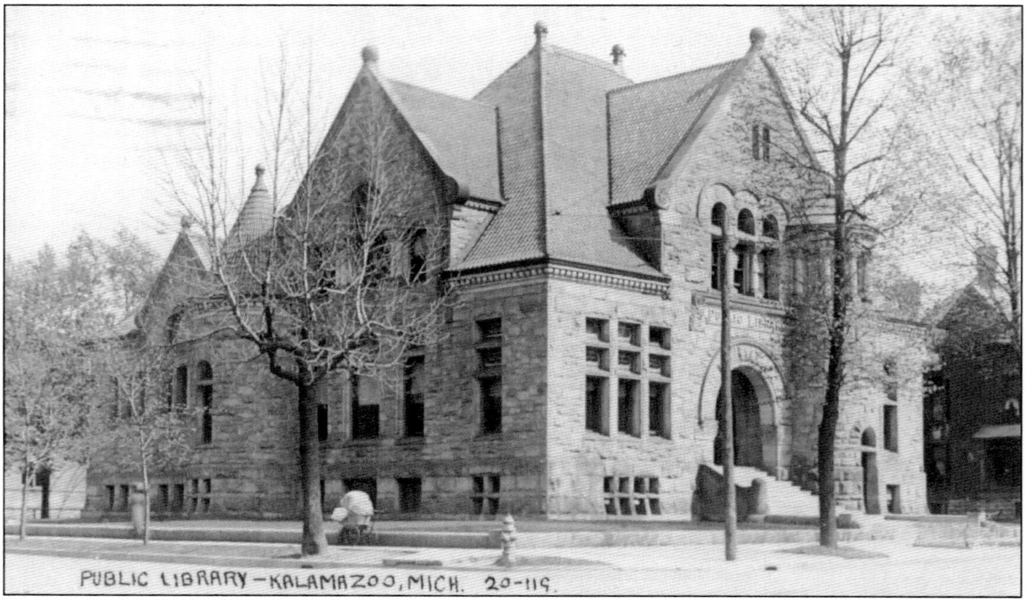


The Kalamazoo Public Library has occupied this corner of South and Rose Streets since this building opened in 1893. But, like many of Kalamazoo's other 19th-century public buildings, it could not meet the demands of a growing city. It was soon overcrowded, but wars and the Great Depression delayed action. It was finally razed in 1958 for a new library. When its successor was renovated in 1998, workers discovered that several stained-glass panels from this building were in storage. They have been reinstalled and can be enjoyed today.

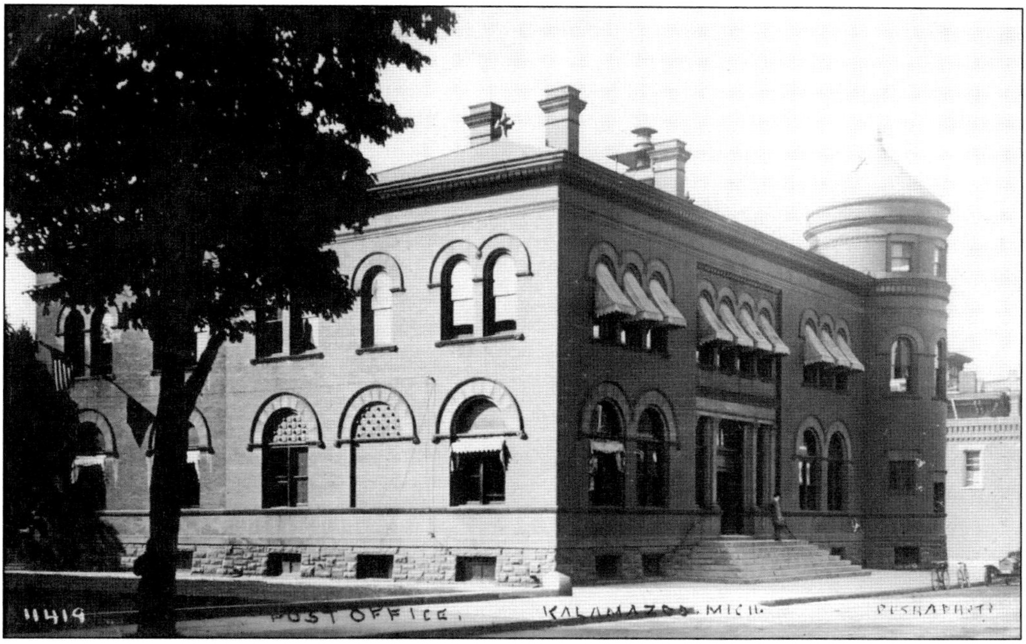


This handsome Romanesque post office stood at Burdick and South Streets. Its rounded corner tower is a landmark in many early postcard views. The building first opened in 1892, but it was quickly outgrown and expanded in 1904. However, that work proved insufficient, and the building continued to suffer from overcrowding until it was replaced in 1939. It was torn down that same year.

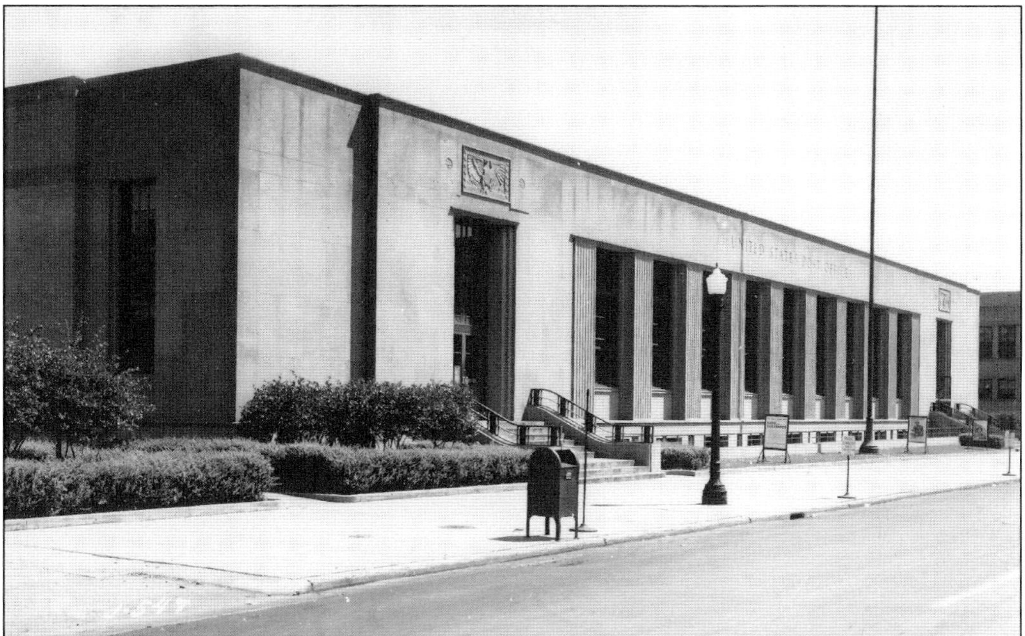


When the post office vacated its Burdick Street home, it moved into this Art Deco structure on West Michigan Avenue. The building's design matches that of both the nearby Kalamazoo County Courthouse and Kalamazoo City Hall. It serves as a federal courthouse today.

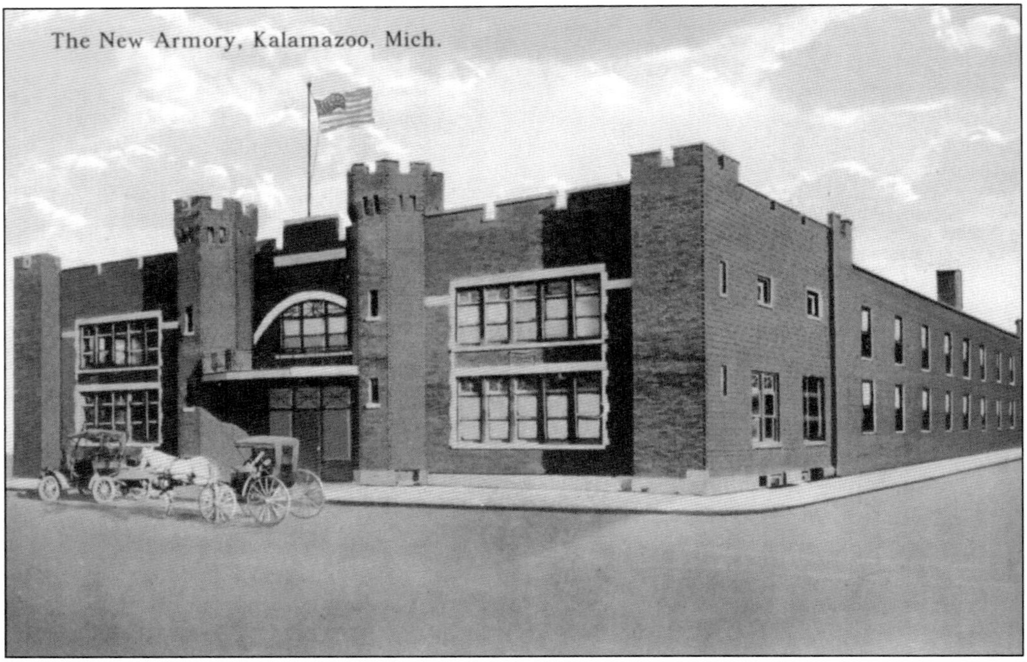


This distinctive brick castle on Water Street was the home of the Michigan State Armory. Its unique architecture reflects the design practice used for armories throughout the country. There was no intention of hiding its military purpose. Kalamazoo's armory opened in 1913 and served until 1978. It was then razed to make room for a parking lot.

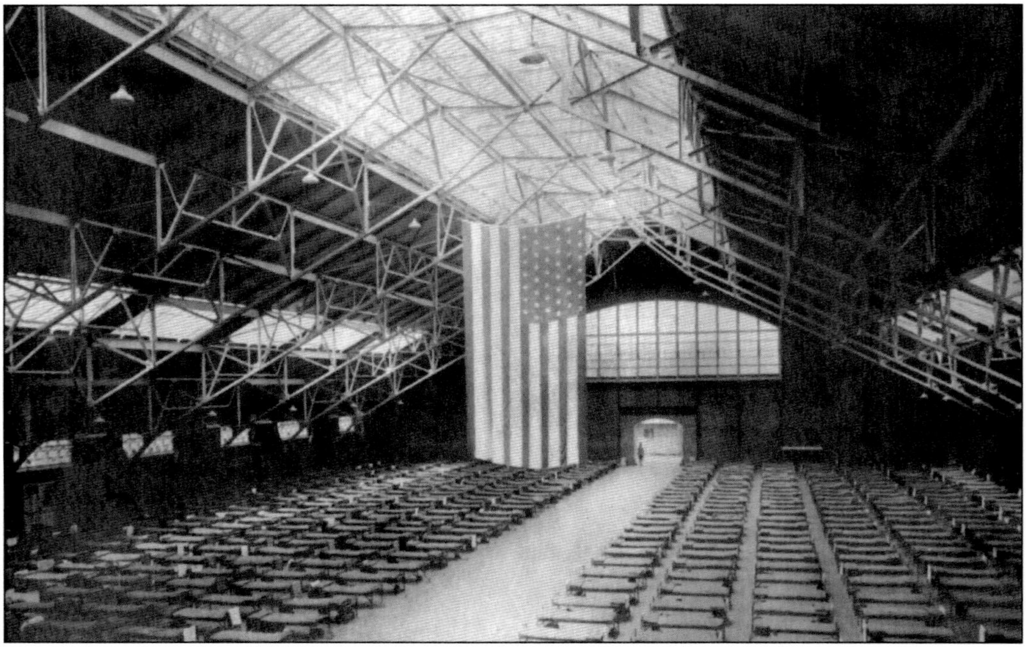

This real-photo postcard shows the vast interior of the Michigan State Armory. If the exterior reflected medieval design, the interior displayed modern industrial architecture, with a steel infrastructure. The hall is seen here filled with countless cots, possibly to serve the needs of troops during World War I.

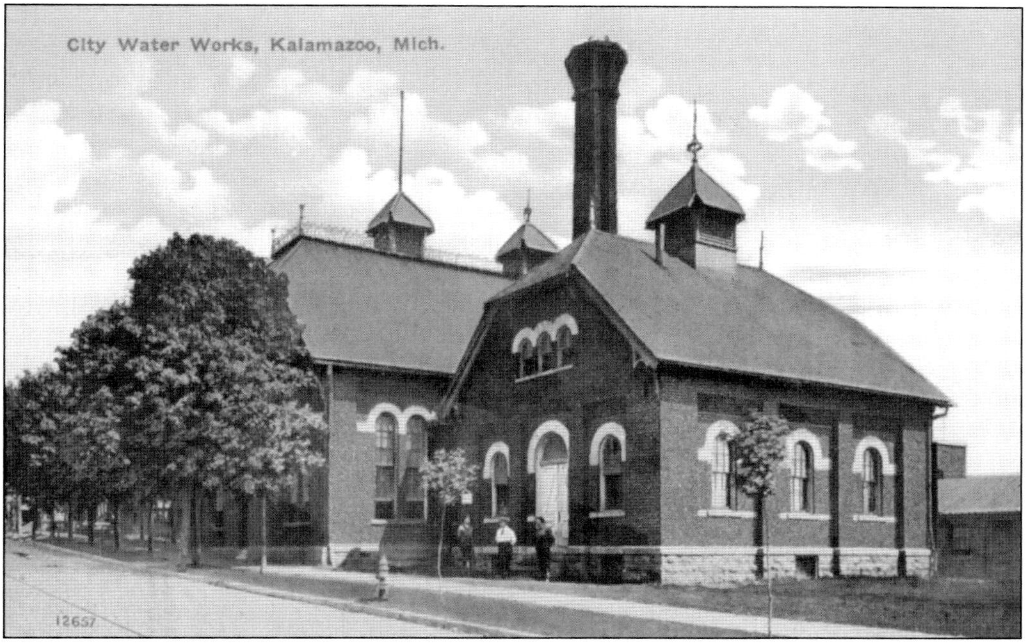


A public water system was the mark of a modern city, and this unusual building housed the city's waterworks beginning in 1884. It was located on the outskirts of the city, on Burdick Street, near the intersection of today's Crosstown Parkway. It was torn down in 1961.

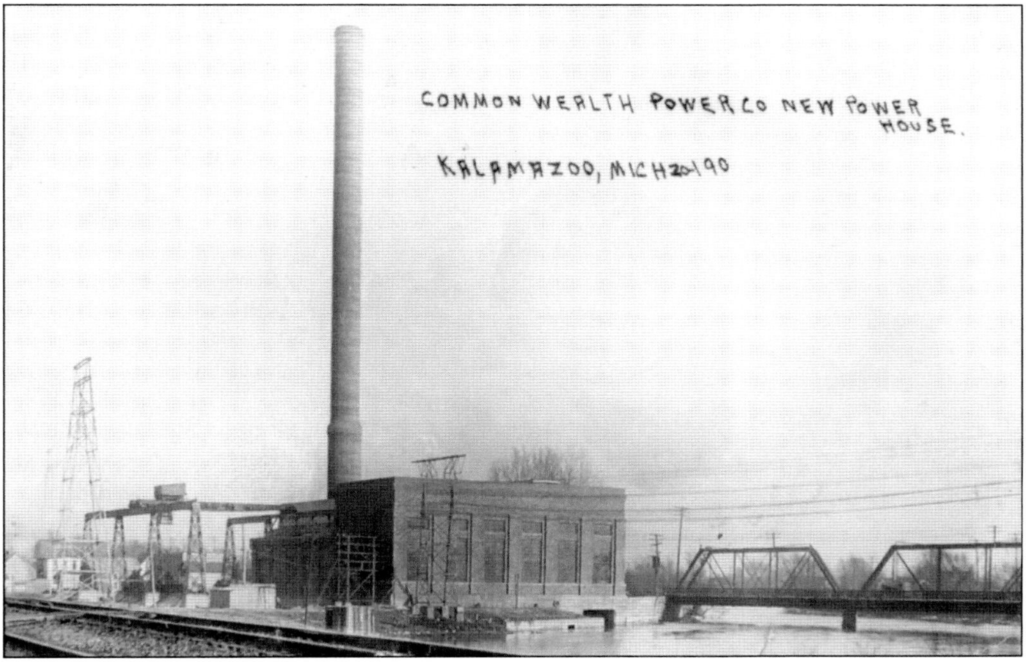


This simple building with a soaring smokestack was located just beyond downtown on East Main Street. It signified Kalamazoo's modernity and prosperity perhaps more than any other structure. The Commonwealth Power Company built it in 1910 to supply electricity to the ever-growing city. The building would be doubled in size in 1927 and continued to serve Kalamazoo's electrical needs until it was demolished in 1976.

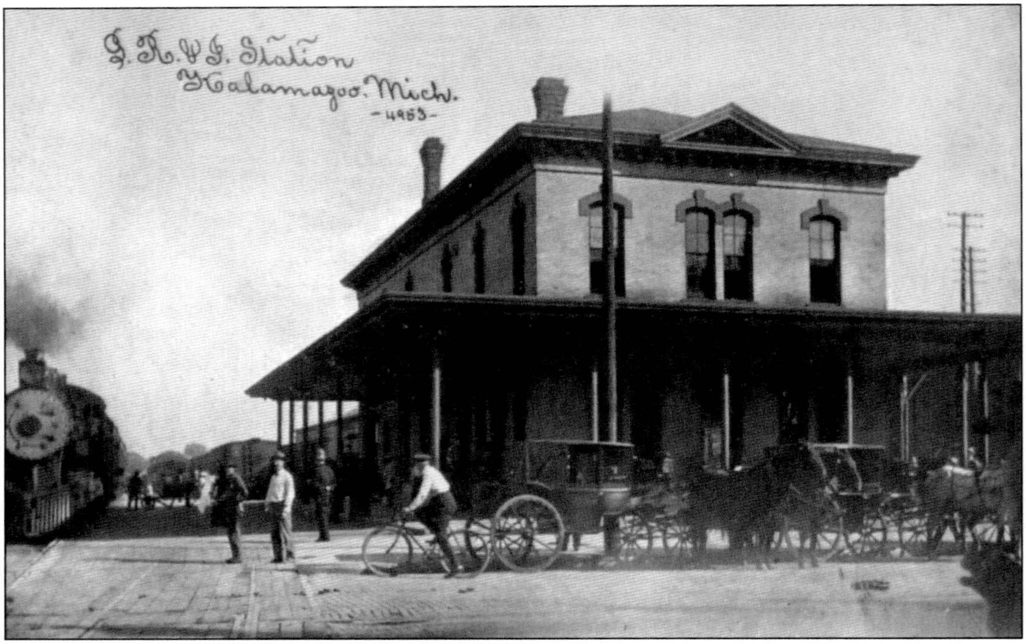


In the late 19th century, the railroad was the primary mode of transportation for both goods and people, and Kalamazoo was well connected. The north-south Grand Rapids & Indiana Railroad's first trains rolled through the town in 1870. The railroad built this handsome Italianate passenger station on East Main Street four years later. It continued as a passenger station until the 1970s. Although the trains have gone, the building still exists as a modern office complex.

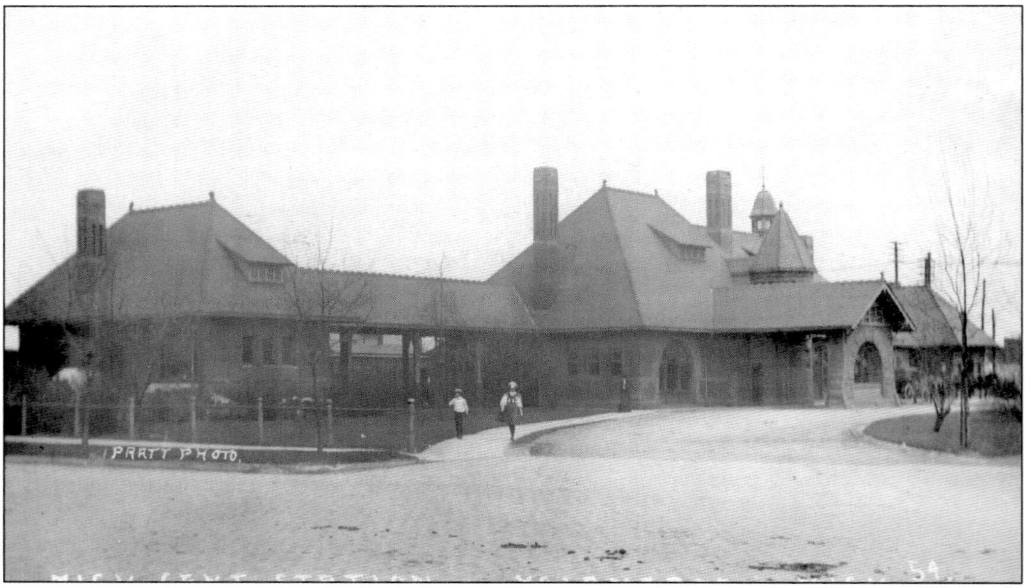


The Michigan Central Railroad, which operated an east-west route, built this Richardson Romanesque station off of North Burdick Street in 1887. The line first came to the city in 1846 and connected Kalamazoo to Detroit and Chicago by 1852. The city's advantageous location halfway between those two cities helped fuel its growth. The Michigan Central Station still serves as Kalamazoo's transit center, with Amtrak and bus service. (Courtesy of the Kalamazoo Public Library's Local History Room.)

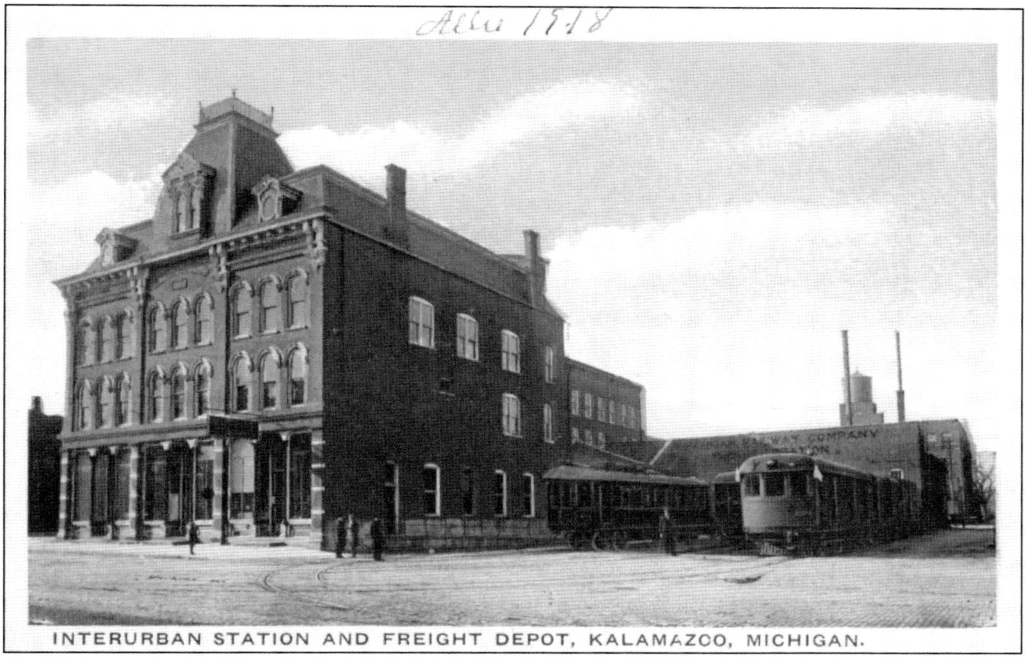


Before the rise of automobiles, electric short-range railroads, known as interurbans, served popular regional routes. Interurbans were so named because they connected neighboring towns and cities. One of Kalamazoo's interurban stations was located in this landmark building at Rose and Water Streets. Erected in 1870 as an ironworks, it has also housed a furniture store and offices.

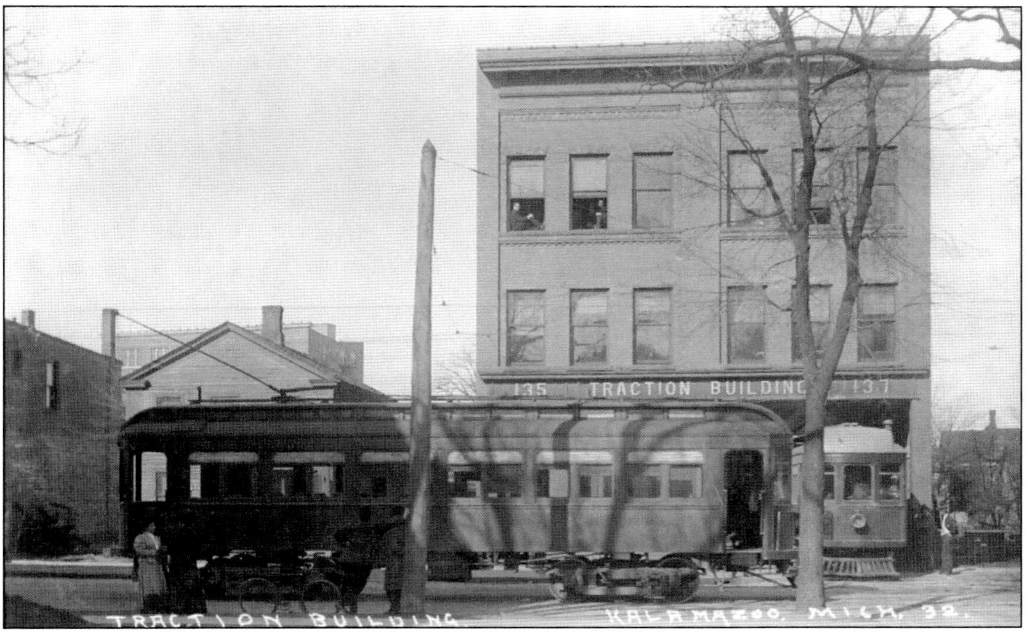


The Traction Building on Portage Street was Kalamazoo's other interurban station. This postcard provides an excellent view of an interurban train as well as how the trains entered the building itself. Interurbans peaked around World War I and quickly declined in the 1920s, as private automobiles and buses filled the need they once served. (From the Collection of the Kalamazoo Valley Museum.)

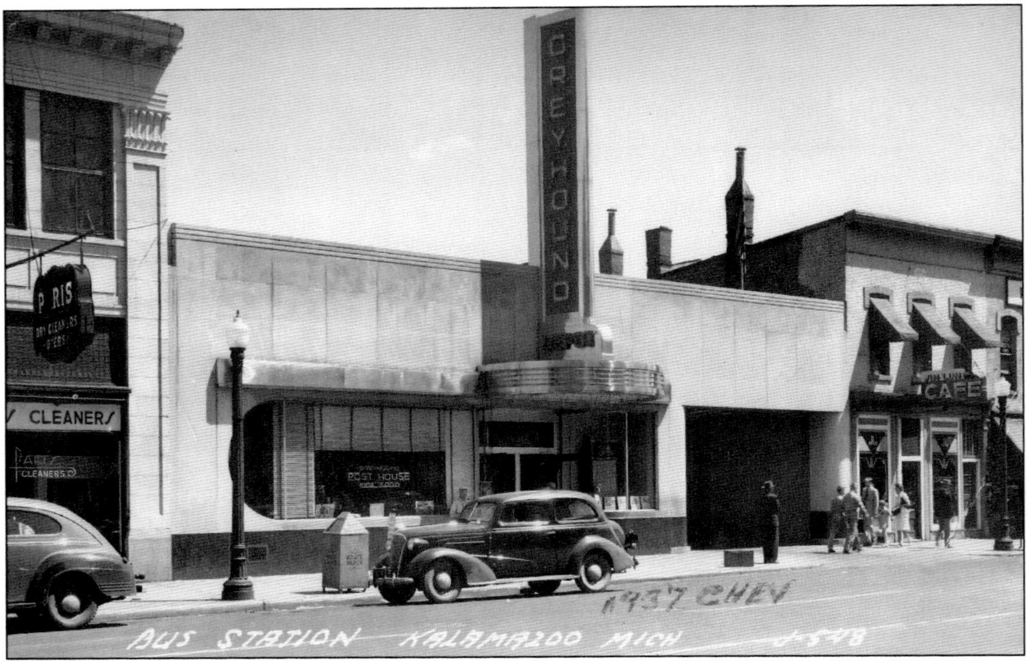


Buses provided a replacement for the interurbans. This 1944 view shows the handsome Art Moderne Greyhound station on West Michigan Avenue. The 1941 building still exists, although its 1979 conversion into a bank robbed it of its original facade.

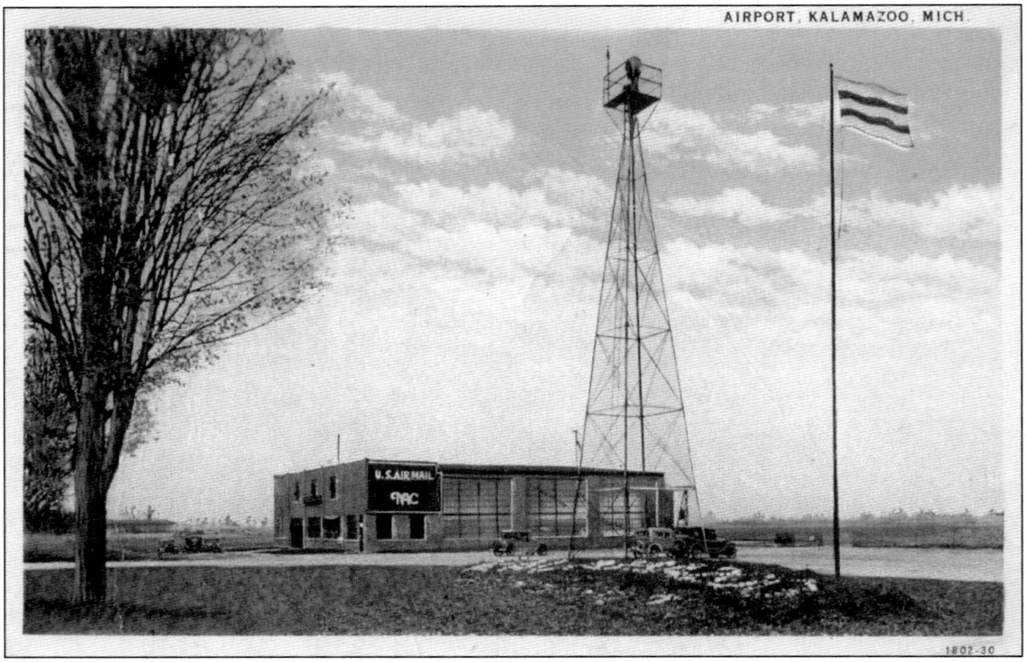


Kalamazoo's airport had humble beginnings. This 1920s postcard shows a simple hangar, a far cry from the complex that exists today. Aviation would not become a major form of public transportation until after World War II.

# *Three*

# Commercial Buildings

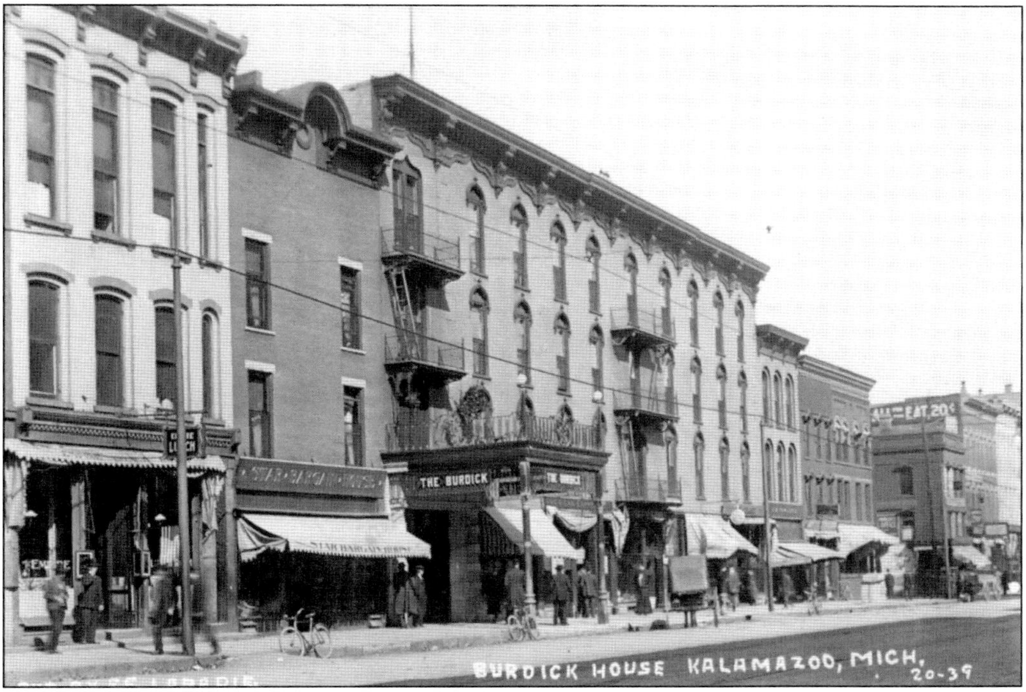


For over 117 years, the best hotel in the city bore the name Burdick. The Burdick Hotel first appeared on Main Street in the form of an imposing four-story brick building in 1855. Originally opened as the Cosmopolitan Hotel the year before, the grand structure was renamed after Gen. Justus Burdick, whose home had previously occupied the site. The hotel was expanded and renovated several times throughout the 19th century, including a new Italianate facade, additional wings of rooms, and horse stables for the use of guests.

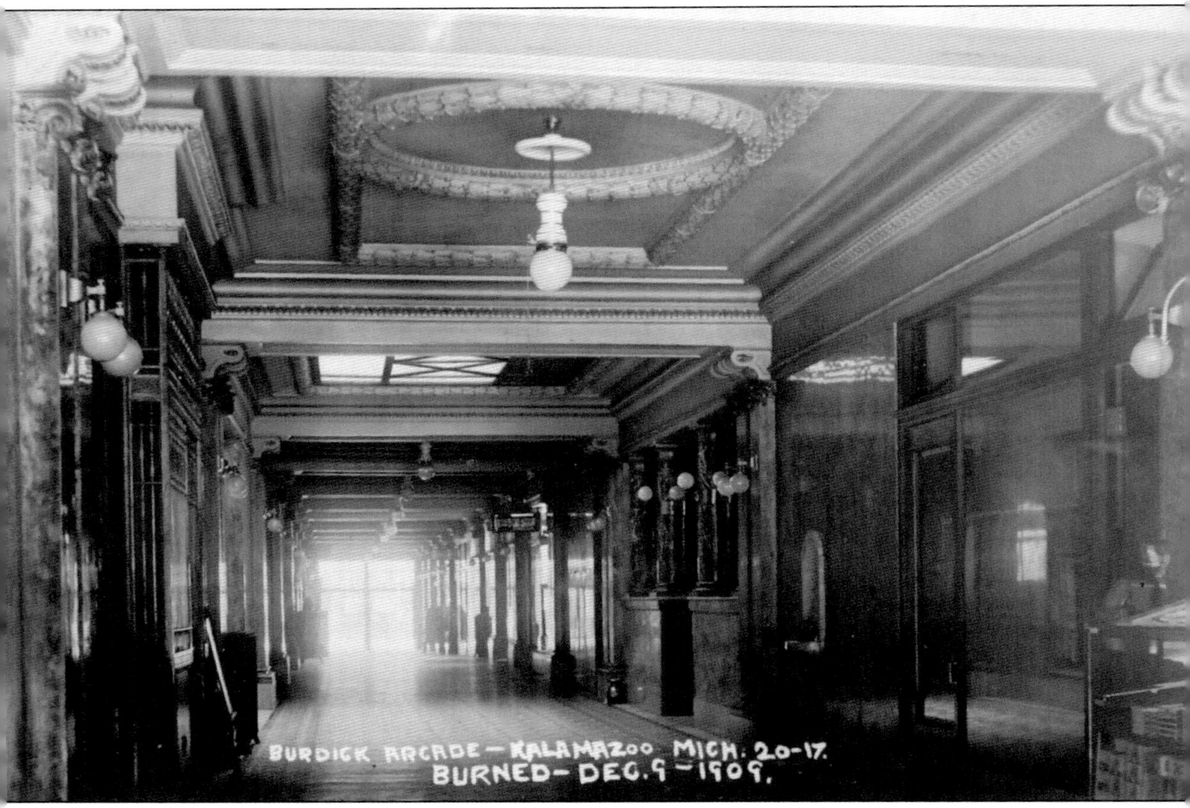


By the 20th century, Kalamazoo's existing hotels, including the Burdick, were considered out of date and an embarrassment. A group of civic boosters, led by John Henry Burke, was determined to give Kalamazoo a modern hotel. In 1905, their efforts to raise the necessary funds to build such a structure failed, and they purchased the old Burdick instead. The Arcade Company was organized, and the old structure was completely gutted and expanded until a virtually new hotel stood behind the familiar facade. This postcard showcases the elegant retail arcade that ran the length of the hotel from Main to Water Streets. Sadly, the new Burdick would not last long. The hotel was destroyed along with much of the block in a dramatic fire on the night of December 8–9, 1909.

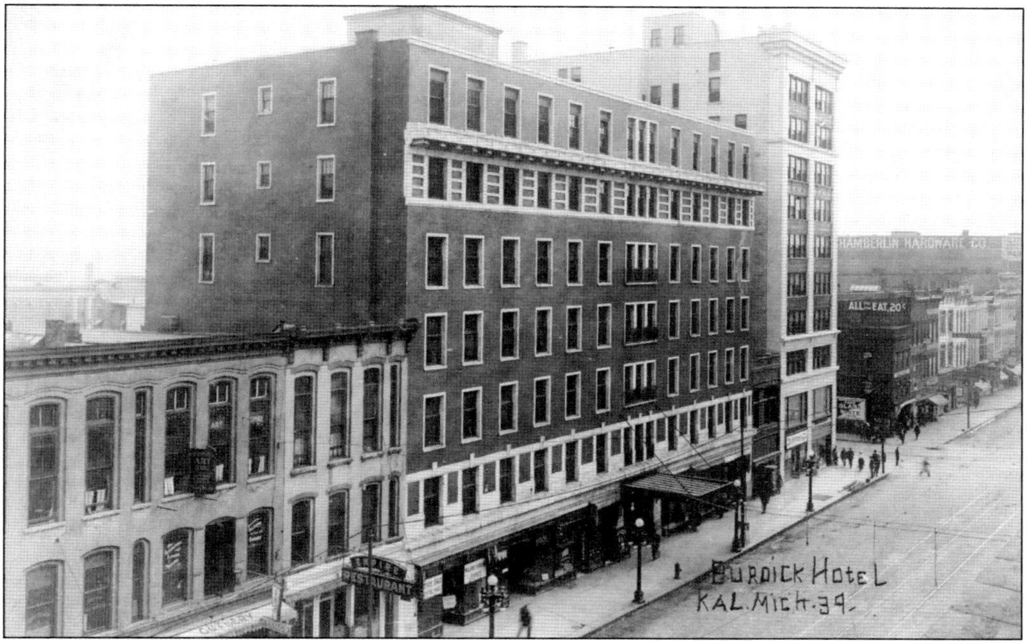


The fire provided a clean slate from which a new Burdick would rise like a phoenix. The rebuilt hotel was an enormous structure, with frontage on three streets. It was formally opened in 1911, with Pres. William Howard Taft registering as the first guest. The Burdick copied the retail arcade from its predecessor, and had 250 guest rooms. The well-stocked cigar stand (below) was located in its lobby. The hotel housed the city's first radio station, WKZO, from 1931 to 1958. However, with the rise of the interstate highway system and roadside motels, downtown hotels went into decline. The Burdick closed in 1971 and was demolished the following year to make room for the new Kalamazoo Center.

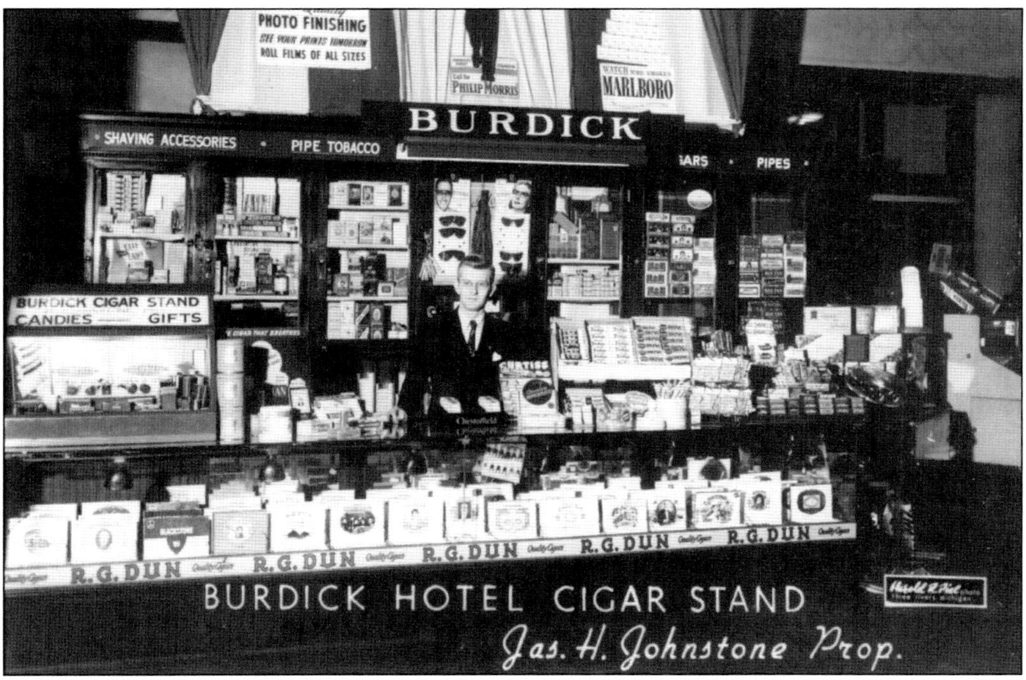

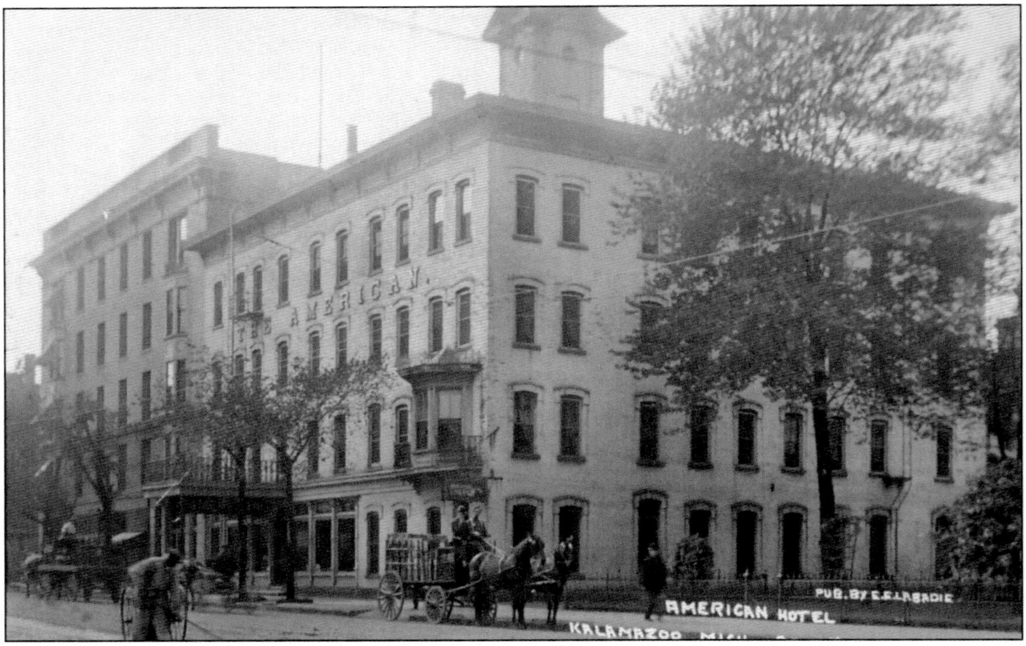


The American Hotel was one of the city's finest hostelries at the dawn of the 20th century. Its original building, erected in 1869, is seen here, along with a 1905 addition (at left). The hotel benefited from its location across East Main Street from the Grand Rapids & Indiana Railroad. It further benefited from the reputation of its dining rooms.

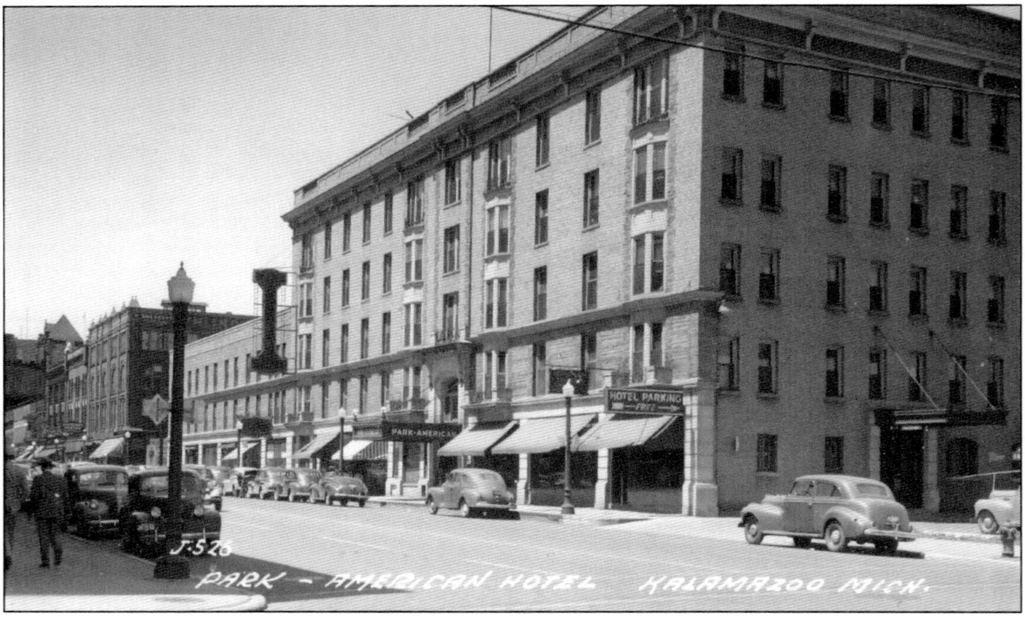


The hotel was renamed the Park-American in 1910 to advertise a private park built next door for the use of the hotel's guests. The original building came down four years later and was replaced with a new wing matching the 1905 building. Further expansion in 1929 meant that the hotel occupied the entire city block. However, prosperity was fleeting, and decline came in the years following World War II. It was renamed the Hotel Harris in 1947, but it closed in 1968 and was soon demolished. The downtown YWCA occupies part of the site today.

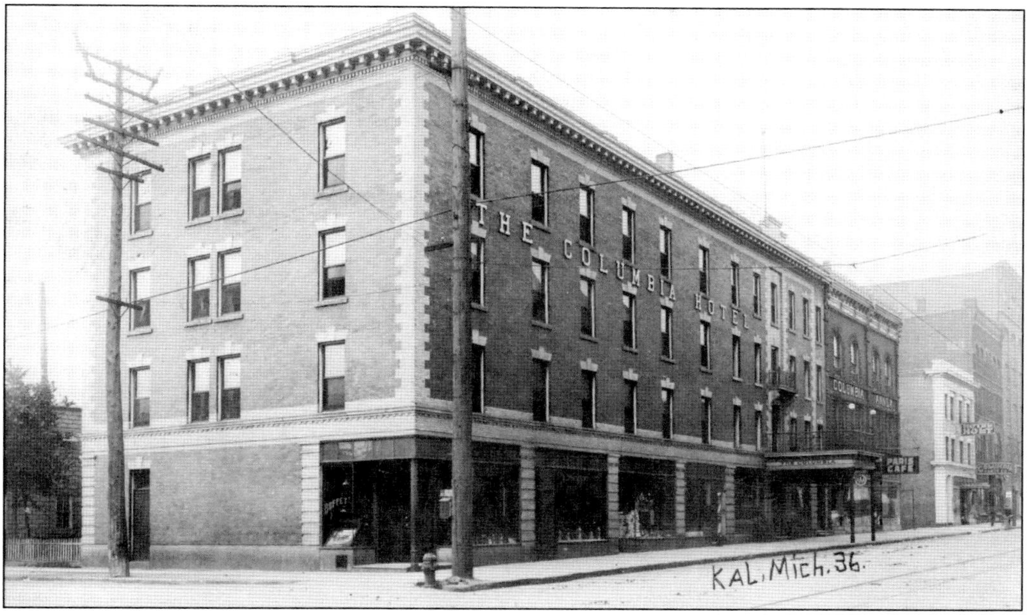


The nearby Columbia Hotel fared somewhat better than the American. It, too, was the product of steady expansion. It first opened in 1873 as the Pacific Hotel and became Burke's Hotel in 1889. Then, 10 years later, the modest structure was purchased by Adam Ehrman, who renamed it the Columbia and began a series of improvements that resulted in the structure seen here by 1909.

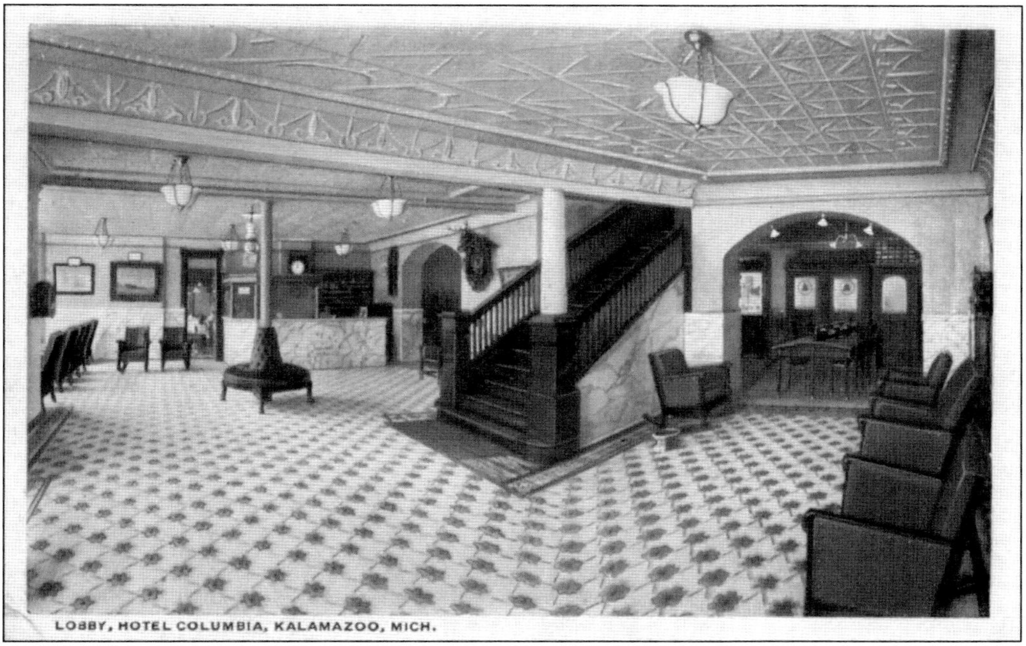


Adam Ehrman was a German American who raised his family in the hotel business. His son, Frank, worked alongside his father and took over management of the Columbia when his father retired in 1920. Frank continued the tradition of expansion, adding new wings and a redone lobby (pictured). When Frank died in 1942, his family sold the hotel. It continued to operate until it was finally shuttered in 1982. In 1985, work began on converting the vast structure into an office complex, the Columbia Plaza.

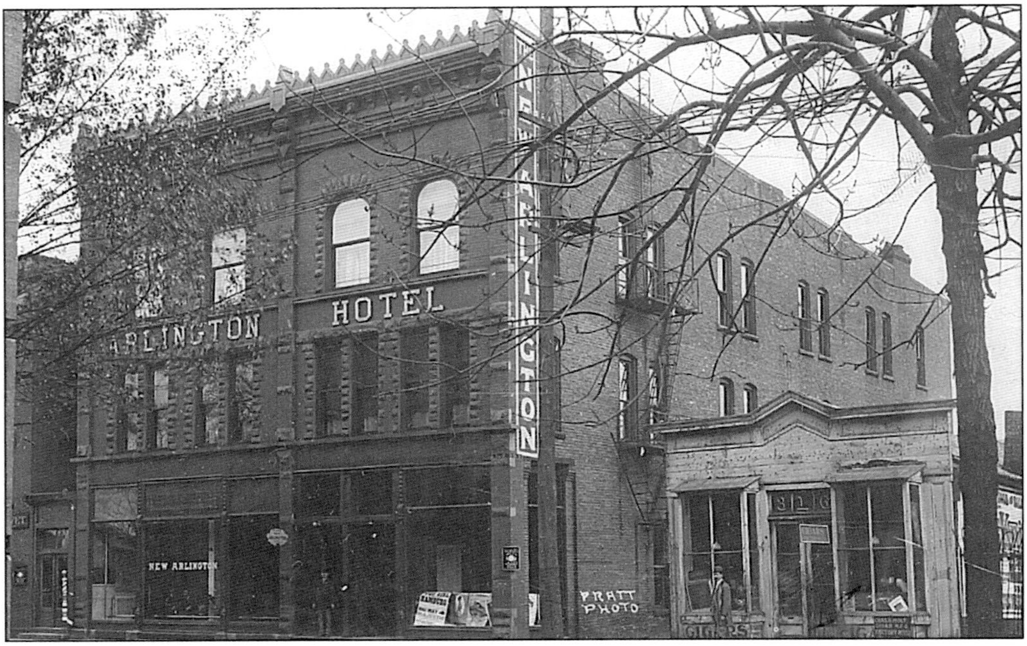


In 1911, Adam Ehrman purchased the neighboring Arlington Hotel (pictured) and incorporated it into his ever-growing Columbia as the Columbia Annex. Initially, the Arlington provided additional rooms, but in the late 1920s, it was mostly gutted, and a new ballroom was built within its shell. That space was recently uncovered during the Arlington's present conversion to apartments. (From the Collection of the Kalamazoo Valley Museum.)

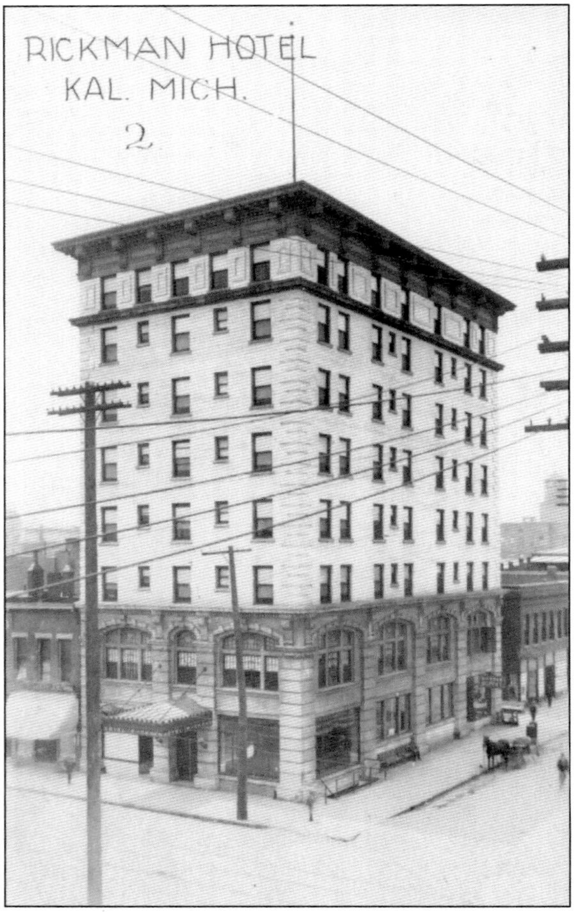


In 1907, the Rickman family erected a beautiful eight-story hotel at the southwest corner of Kalamazoo Avenue and Burdick Street. It was an advantageous location for a hotel, with the Michigan Central Railroad and the steady supply of potential overnight guests just a block away. The Rickman family patriarch, George, had founded a profitable construction business. His sons saw the construction of a hotel as a fitting monument to their father. In its later years, it was known as the Milner, Reid, and St. Regis. It ceased hotel operations in the 1970s and became a low-income housing facility known as the Rickman House. It was renovated in 2012.

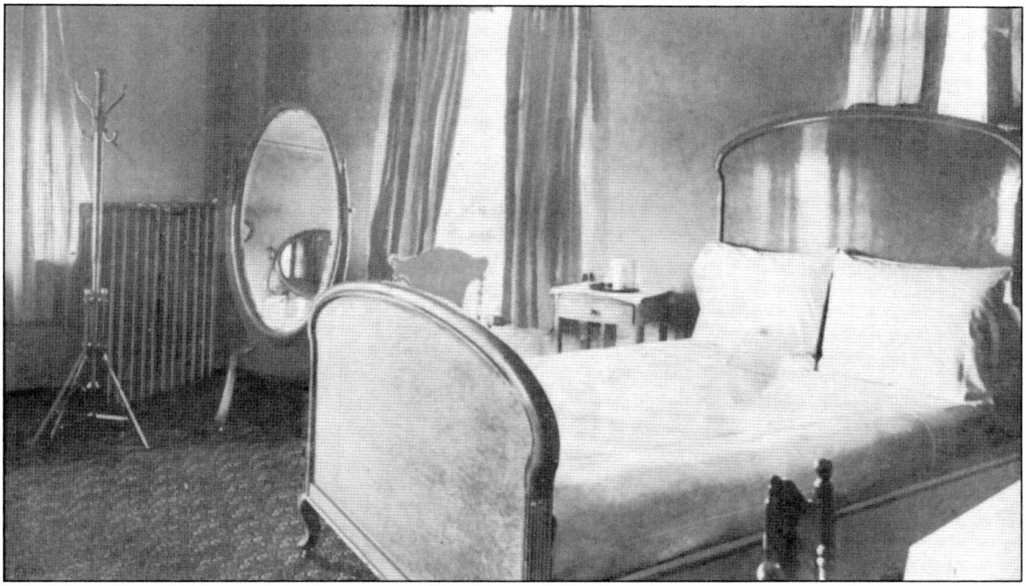

This is one of the Rickman Hotel's 75 guest rooms. These rooms were the scene of misfortune during the hotel's grand opening. The building was opened to the public for tours prior to registering the first guests later that evening. Unfortunately, a number of these tourists took hotel furnishings home with them as souvenirs. Management had difficulty replacing the lost items in time for their first occupants.

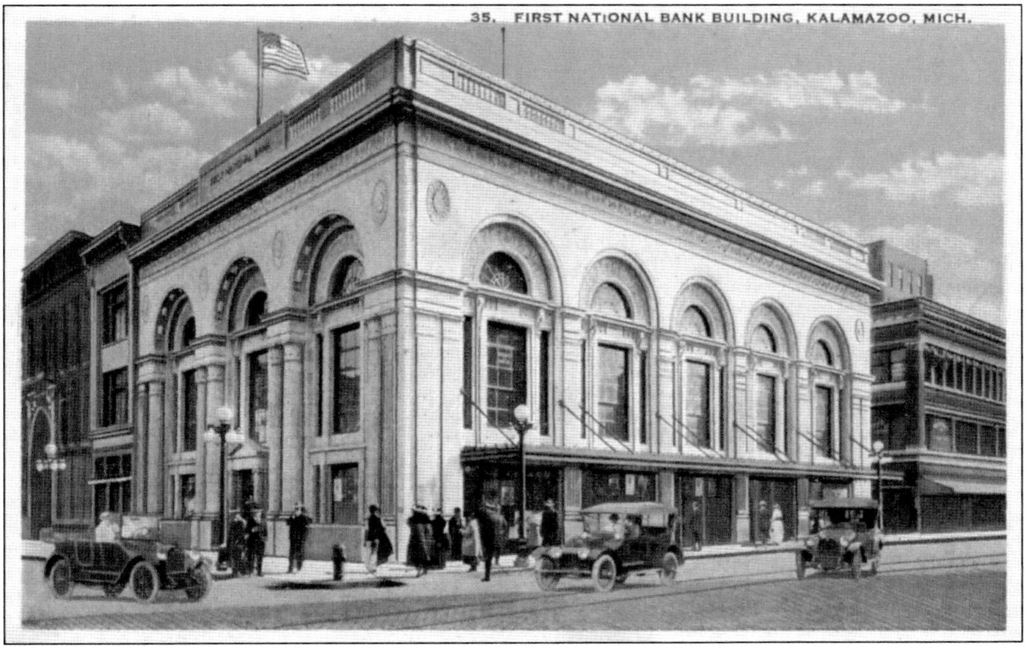


The First National Bank's origins date to 1856, and its longtime home was the House Block at the corner of Burdick and Main Streets. In 1915, the bank announced plans to erect a new skyscraper on the site, but, when the building was completed two years later, the upper floors were omitted. Still, the design was impressive. The building was later expanded with an additional wing along Main Street. But, in 1974, the original exterior was obscured with plain marble. PNC, the successor to First National, vacated the building in 2013.

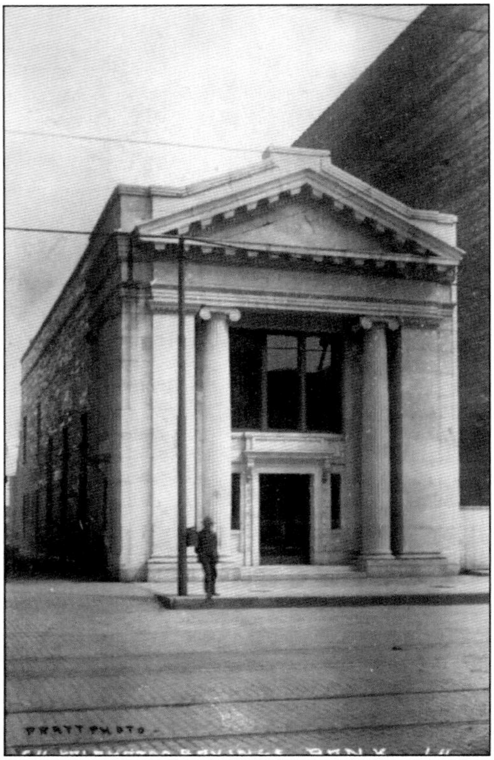


The Kalamazoo City Savings Bank opened in this classical building in 1909. The structure replaced the venerable Kalamazoo House, the city's premiere 19th-century hotel. Shortly after this 1914 photograph was taken, a new wing was added to the east side of the bank, doubling its size. It remains a downtown landmark.

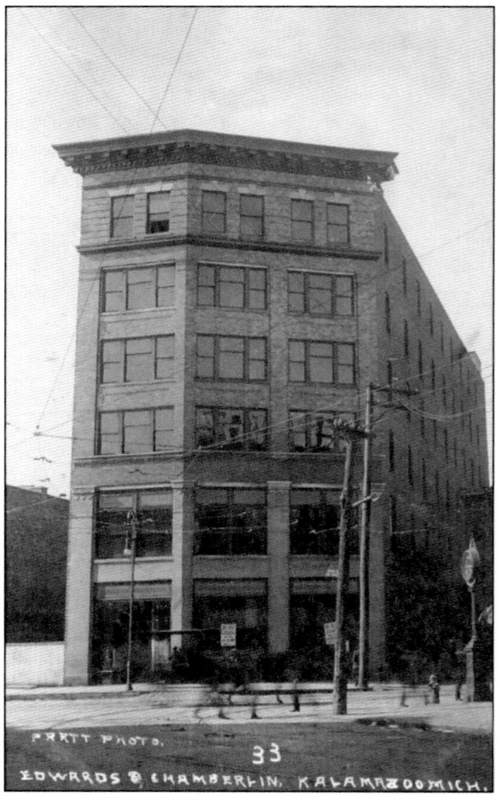


The 1908 Edward and Chamberlin Hardware Store occupied a key location, where Portage Street terminates at Main Street. The six-story building represented the latest in 20th-century retail design. Large windows flooded the open floors with natural light. In later years, the structure housed the local branch of Sears. The building was renovated into offices in the 1980s and is known today as the Haymarket Building.

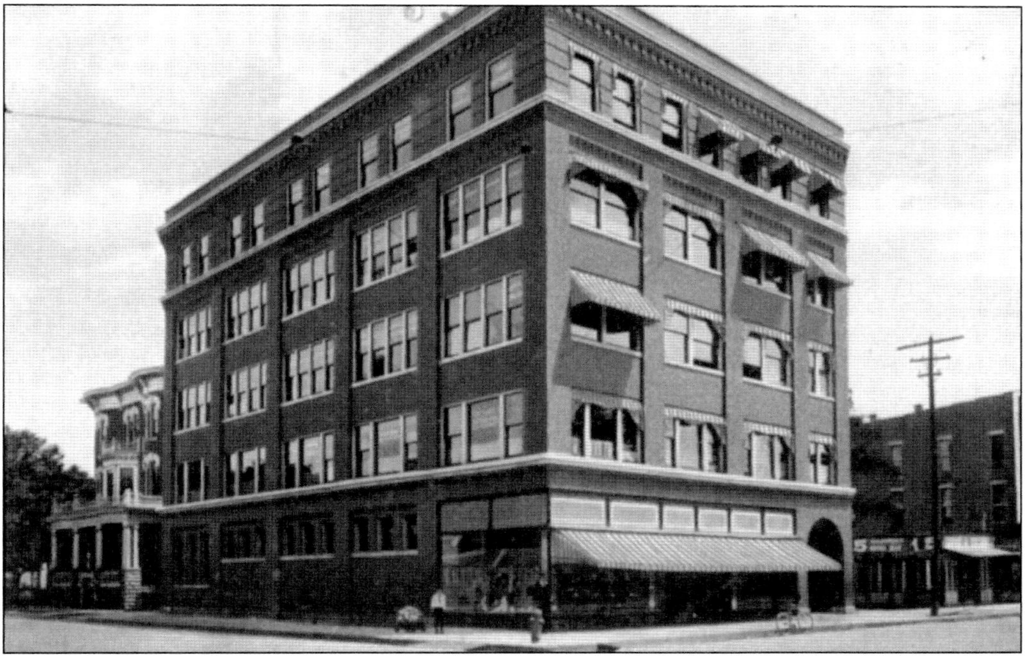

The Brown Block, later known as the Peck Building, opened in 1905 as one of Kalamazoo's first modern office buildings. With five floors, it was one of the tallest buildings in the city at the time. The simple facade and large windows were a contrast to earlier 19th-century buildings. Located at the corner of South and Burdick Streets, it was demolished in 1975.

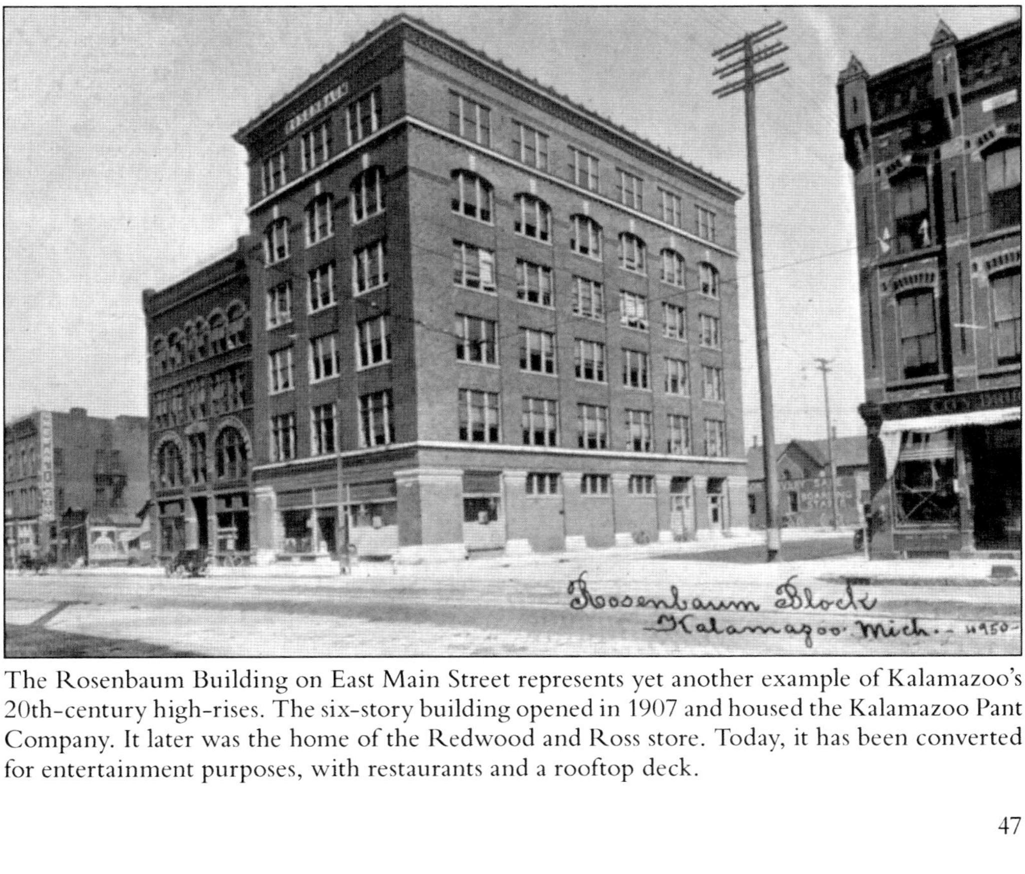


The Rosenbaum Building on East Main Street represents yet another example of Kalamazoo's 20th-century high-rises. The six-story building opened in 1907 and housed the Kalamazoo Pant Company. It later was the home of the Redwood and Ross store. Today, it has been converted for entertainment purposes, with restaurants and a rooftop deck.

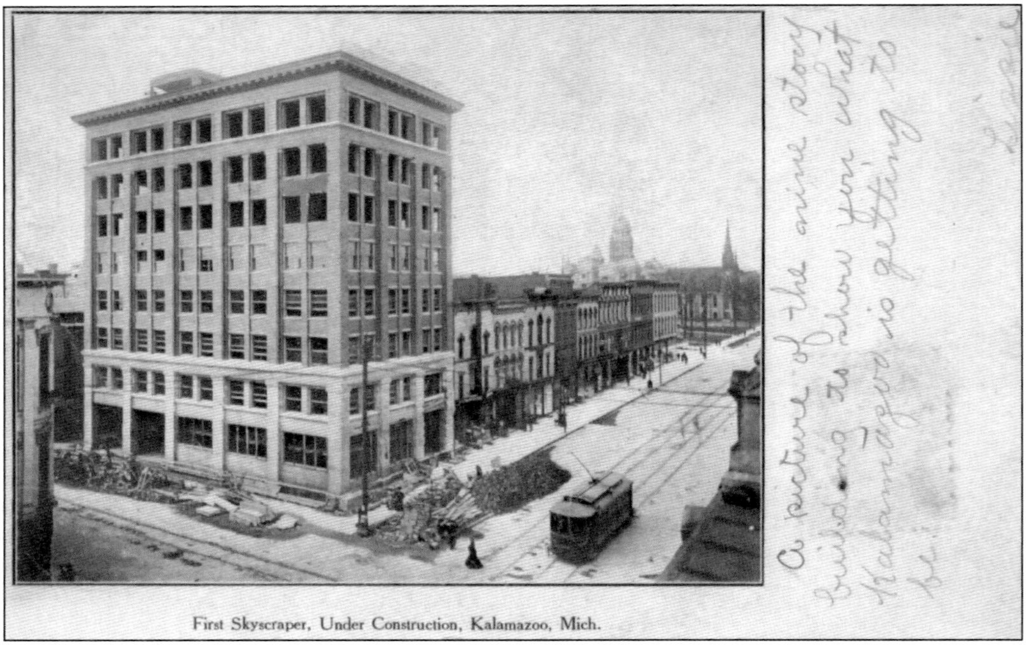


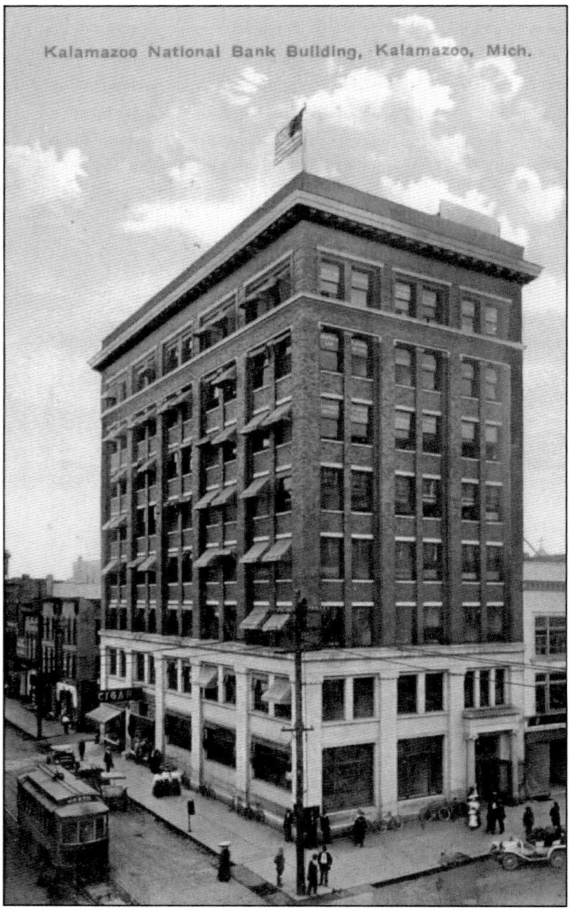


Few construction projects generated as much excitement as the Kalamazoo National Bank Building, announced in 1906. At eight stories, it was to be the city's first skyscraper. Residents saw it as proof that Kalamazoo was truly modern. Postcards of its construction are common. The sender of this 1907 card wrote, "A picture of the nine story building to show you what Kalamazoo is getting to be."

When the skyscraper opened in 1907, it overshadowed everything else around it. The building's namesake, the Kalamazoo National Bank, occupied the ground floor and basement. The *Kalamazoo Gazette* described the upper floors as a "colony up in mid-air" consisting of professional offices. A special rooftop penthouse was constructed to house J.M. Reidsema's photography studio. The Kalamazoo National Bank did not survive the Great Depression; the structure is known today as the Kalamazoo Building.

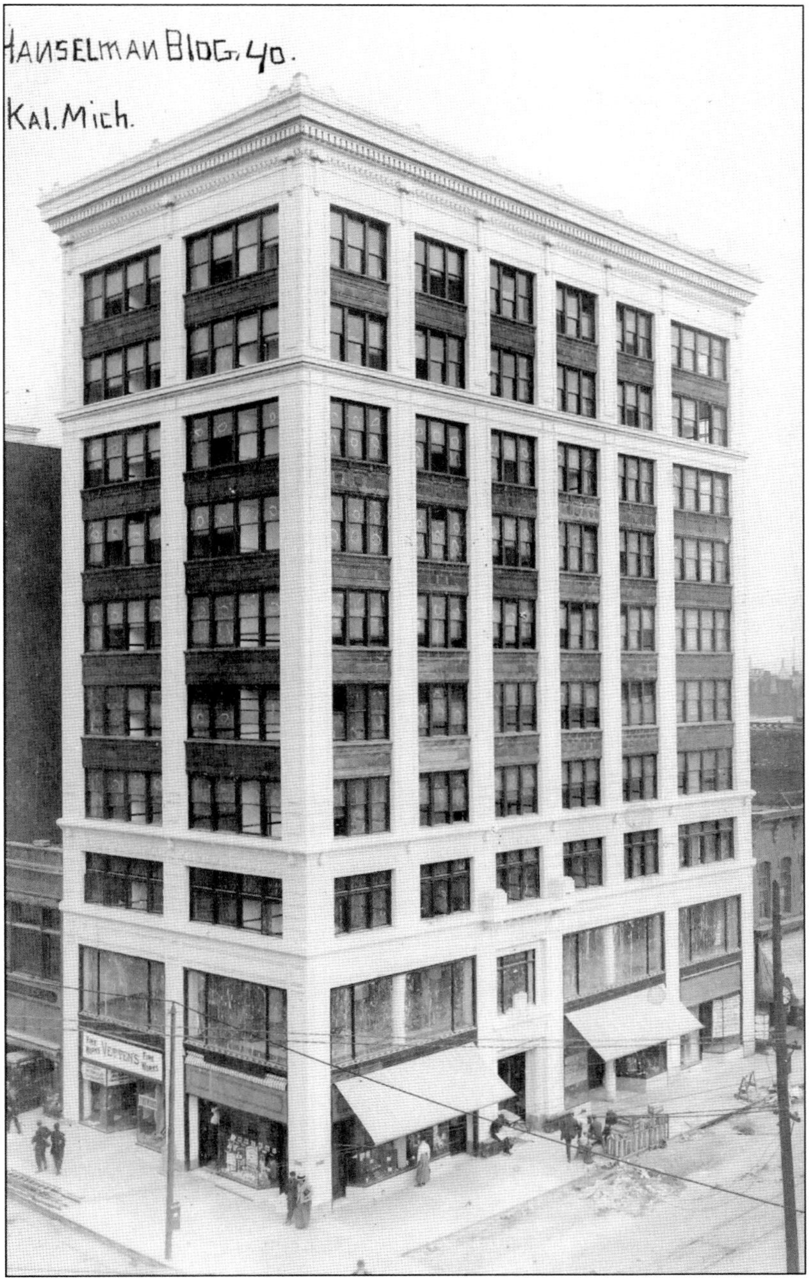


George Hanselman built his Hanselman Building in 1912. Local lore has it that a young Hanselman vowed to buy the northwest corner of Main and Burdick Streets after officers of the City National Bank, which stood there, forced him to remove his peanut stand. His vow resulted in laughter, but, years later, the successful Hanselman Candy Company enabled him to acquire vast real-estate holdings. The 10-story office building was the jewel in the crown. The tallest building in Kalamazoo, it featured marble in the stairways and corridors. Offices were leased to various professionals, with the top floors reserved for doctors and dentists. Sadly, the building was in the wrong place at the wrong time. It was imploded in 1973 to make room for the Kalamazoo Center.

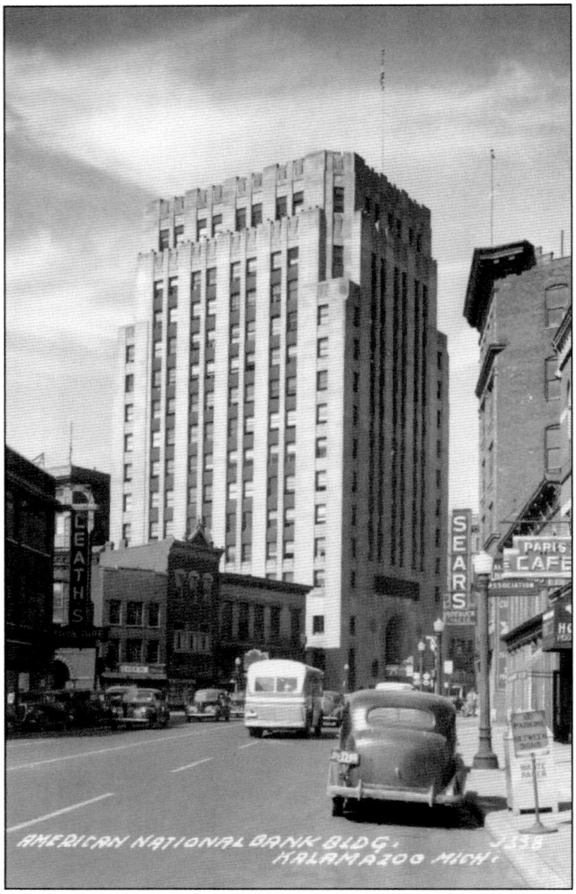


The Hanselman Building was finally overshadowed by the 1929 construction of the 15-story Bank of Kalamazoo. However, that bank never occupied its splendid Art Deco home. The bank failed in the Depression, and the American National Bank became the tower's occupant. The building's location on East Main Street dominates the view in this 1944 card. The building is the home of the Fifth Third Bank today.

The *Kalamazoo Gazette* has been the city's most successful and enduring newspaper. In fact, it is the oldest published paper in Michigan outside of Detroit and the oldest business in Kalamazoo. This postcard shows its new headquarters building at the corner of South Burdick and Lovell Streets. The paper, now part of the Mlive Media Group, has moved its operations a block from its former home. This building was recently sold for redevelopment.

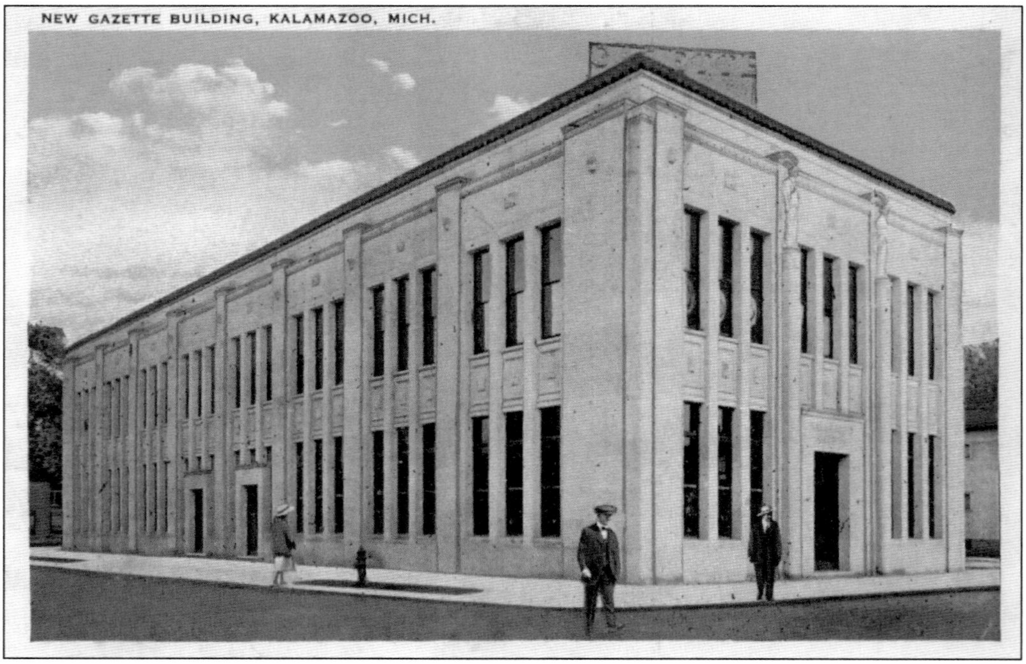

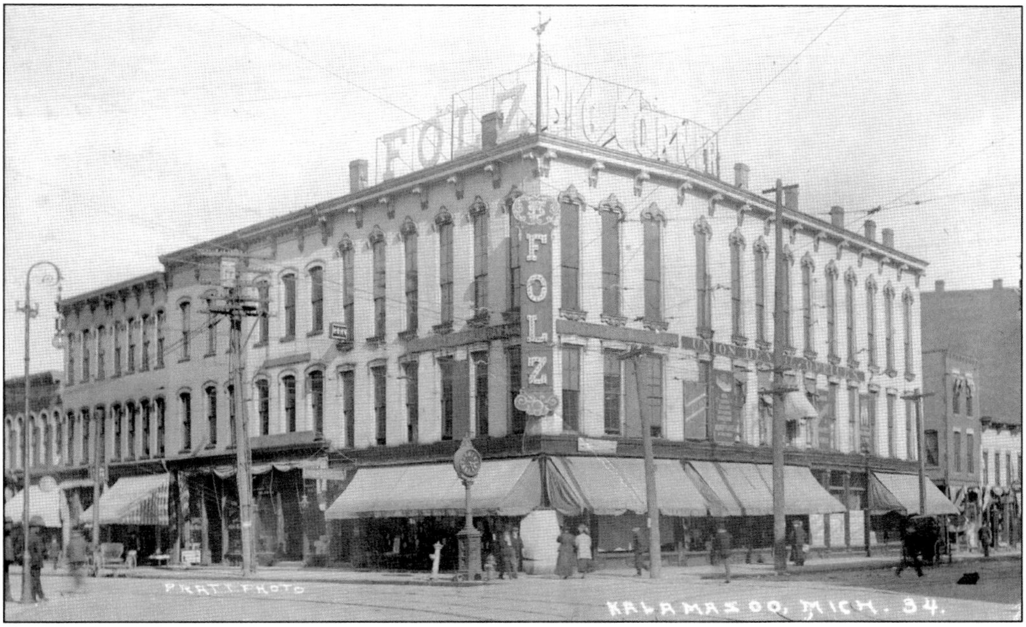


Downtown has had a number of notable retail establishments over the years. For collectors of postcards, the most visible of these was Samuel Folz's "Big Corner." Folz's clothing store occupied a key corner of East Main and Portage Streets, making it visible in most street views. This building still stands, although the exterior was altered beyond recognition in the 1920s. It currently houses the popular Olde Peninsula restaurant.

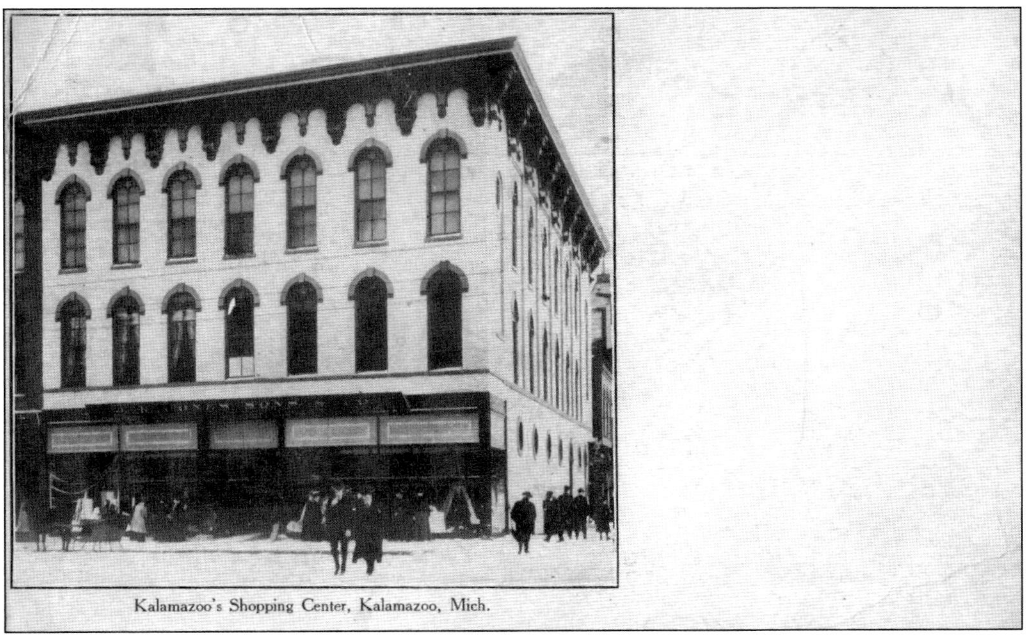


J.R. Jones Sons & Company was another longtime landmark on Kalamazoo's retail scene. The department store opened in 1872 and first occupied this building at West Main and Rose Streets in 1902. The firm suffered a disastrous fire in 1945 that completely leveled the building. It continued to do business at other locations on the block, until an even larger fire in 1964 leveled what was left of the block.

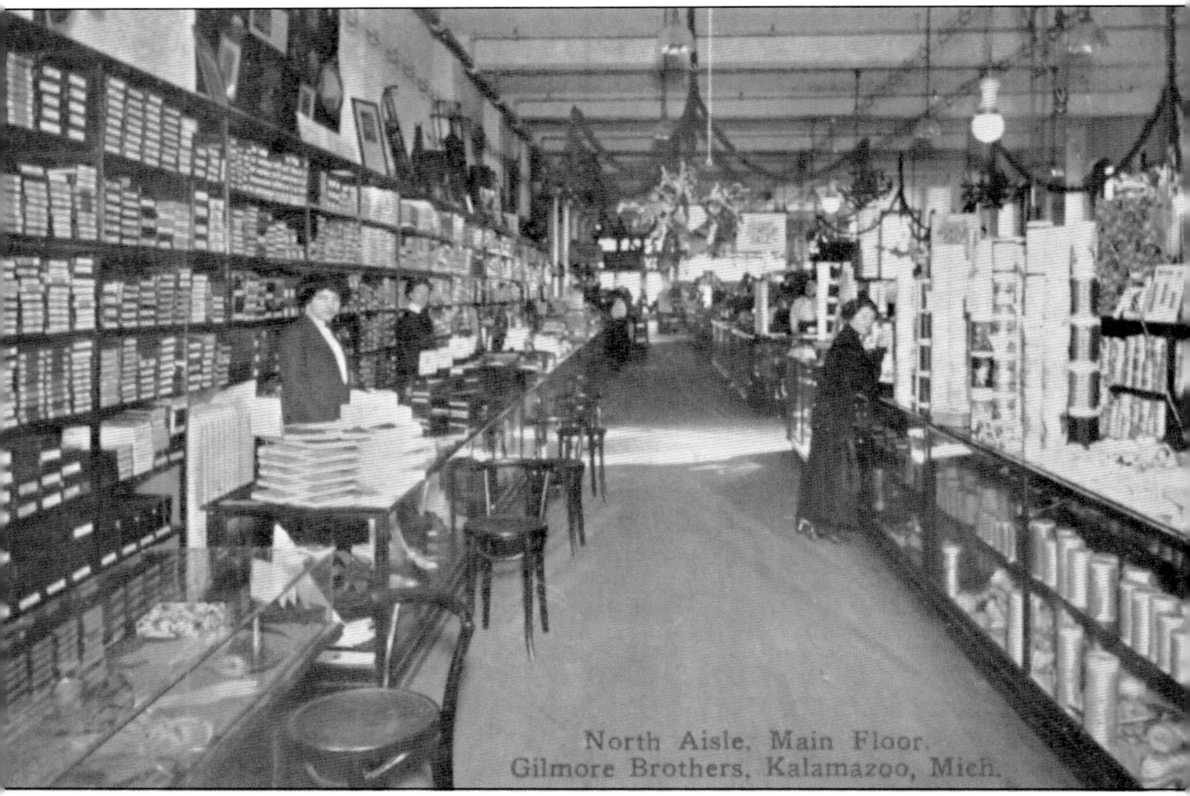


In many respects, the Gilmore Brothers Department Store was the heart of Kalamazoo. No other merchant could compare. The business, founded in 1881 by John and James Gilmore, occupied a handsome, three-story building on Burdick Street. The construction of a massive, six-story wing behind the original building in 1909 testified to the firm's success. This postcard shows the vast interior of that structure, as well as the wide range of goods offered. Gilmore Brothers came to dominate the city's retail scene in the 20th century. In addition to the flagship store, Gilmore's operated two branch stores in the new postwar suburban shopping malls. However, the firm struggled in the 1990s and closed in 1999. The downtown building has been redeveloped.

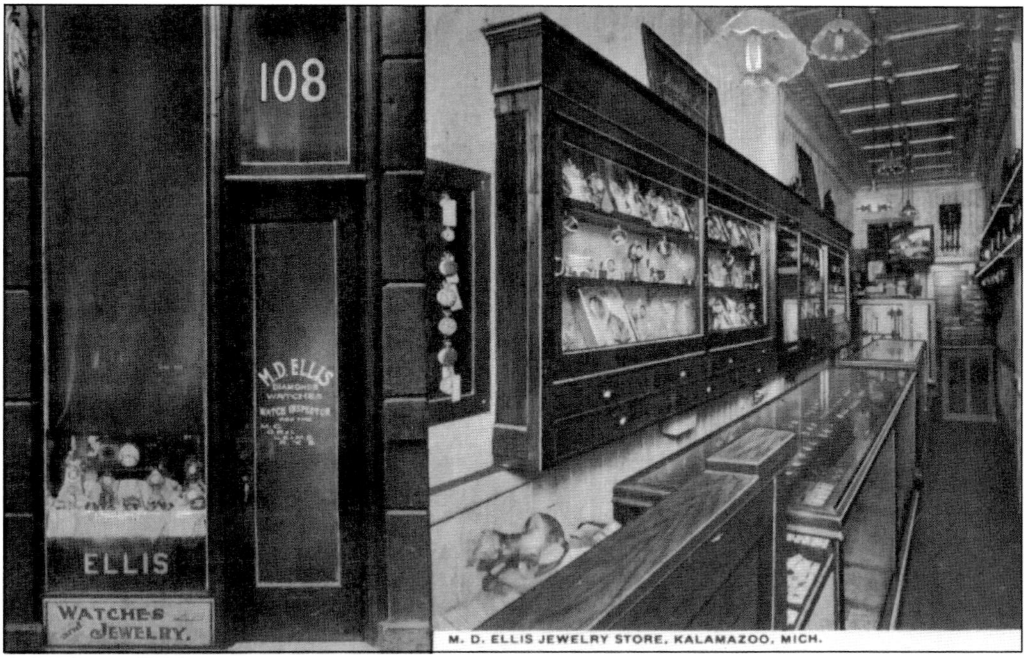


At times, tight property boundaries, peculiar lot shapes, and owners desiring to maximize profits resulted in unusual spatial arrangements. This postcard shows how one business managed to squeeze into a rather tight space. Miron D. Ellis opened his jewelry business at this location on Portage Street in 1906. He remained here until the late 1920s, when he moved his shop to a new address on West Main Street. Ellis passed away in 1961, after 55 years as part of Kalamazoo's business community.

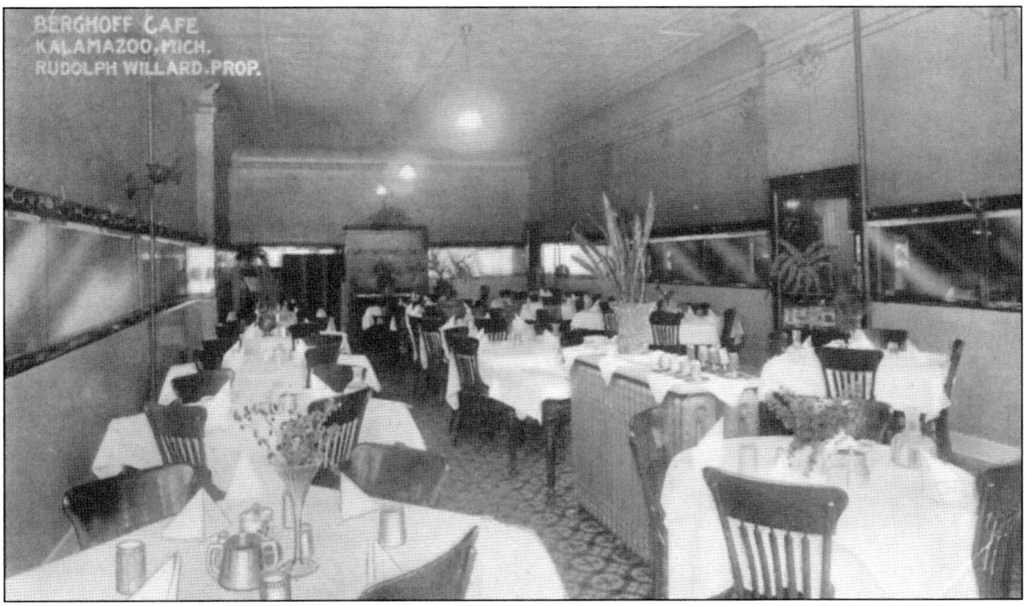


This interior view shows Berghoff Café on East Main Street. The restaurant was located within the Berghoff Hotel, which opened in 1910. At the time, East Main Street was Kalamazoo's German district, and the names of many of the surviving buildings testify to that fact. However, the Berghoff is not among them.

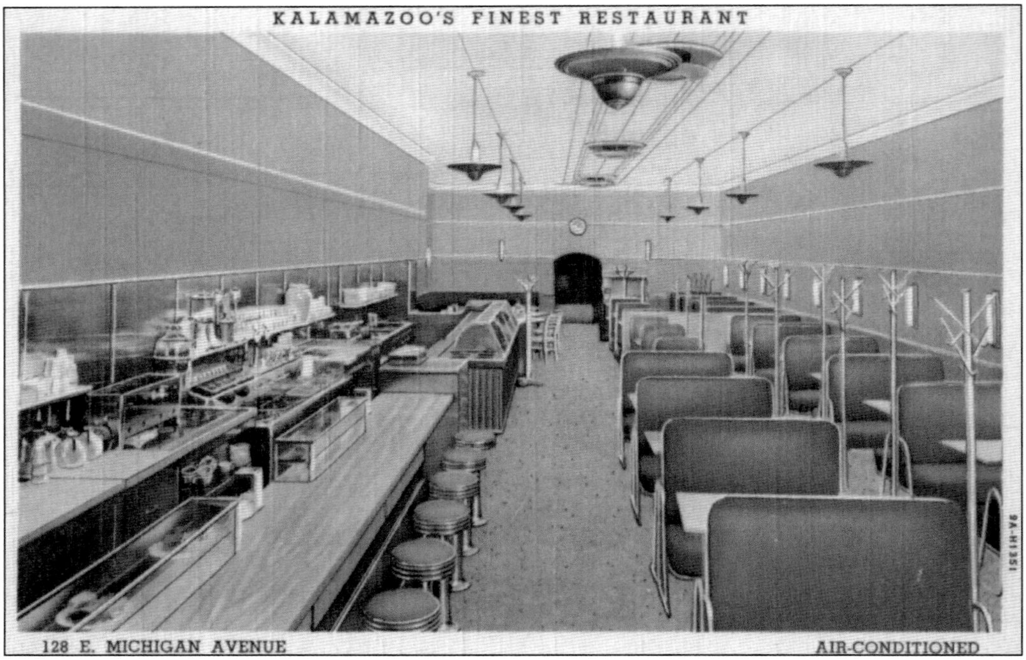


This linen postcard shows the sleek interior of the new Holly's Restaurant, which opened in 1939. It was part of a regional chain founded in South Haven in 1924 by Ward and Hollis Webster. In 1938, Hollis moved the firm's base of operations to Kalamazoo and soon operated three restaurants in the city. At the chain's height, it also had establishments in South Haven, St. Joseph, Grand Rapids, Lansing, and South Bend. The last Holly's closed in Kalamazoo in 1996.

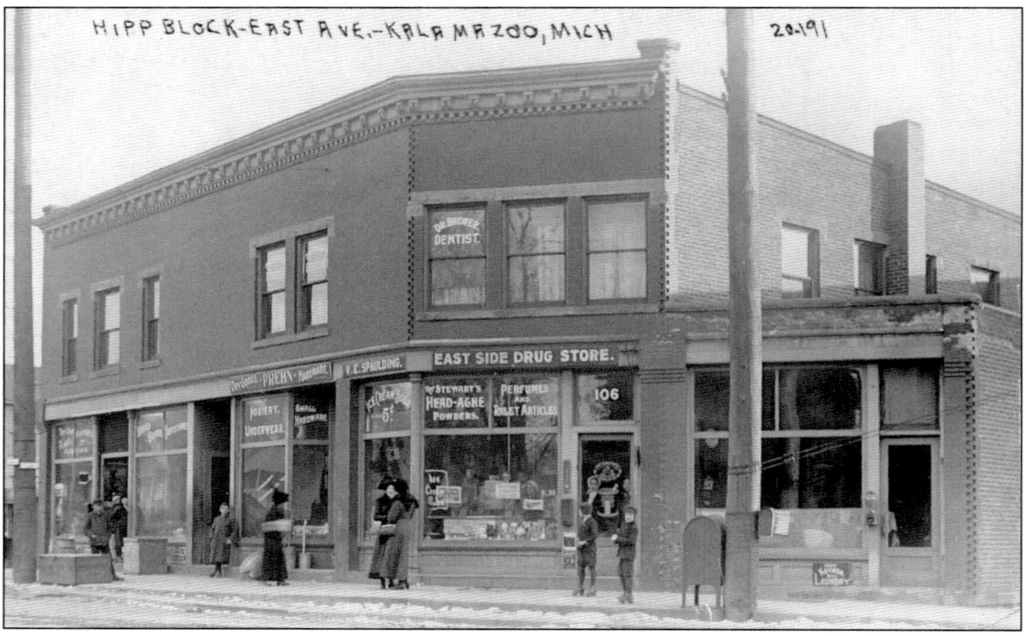


As the city grew, small business districts and corner shops began to appear in the neighborhoods. This photo postcard shows one such neighborhood business block. The modest, two-story structure houses a drugstore, hardware store, and dentist office. It served the east-side neighborhood just beyond downtown. The building still exists, but its appearance has been somewhat altered.

*Four*

# Religious and Social Institutions

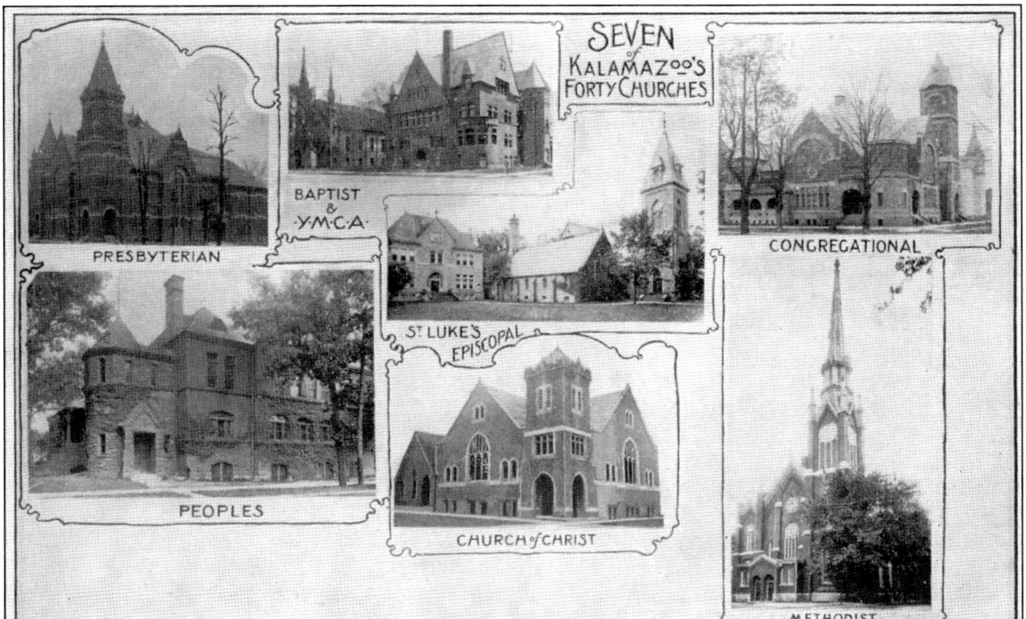


Religious and social institutions have played an important role in the life of Kalamazoo, just as they have in the nation as a whole. From the village's earliest days, plots were reserved for churches adjacent to Bronson Park. By the time this c. 1910 postcard was produced, Kalamazoo had over 40 congregations as well as a large number of social clubs and other institutions.

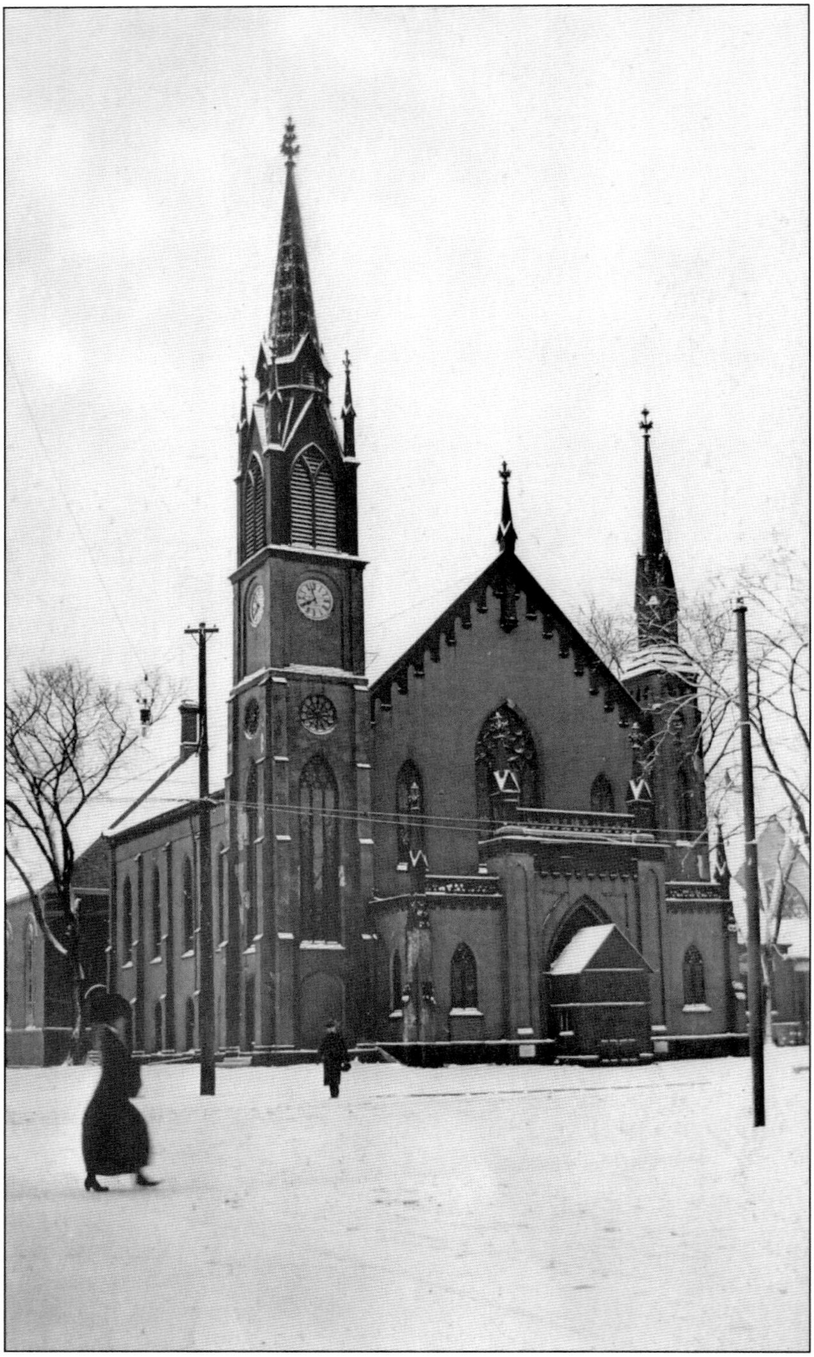

The congregation of First Baptist Church has the distinction of worshiping in the oldest religious building in Kalamazoo. The congregation, founded in 1834, occupies a building completed in 1855 on the village's original "church square." The size of the building suggests the popularity of the Baptists. This winter view shows the church as it appeared after an 1871 renovation gave it a new spire and roofline. The church's clock tower served as Kalamazoo's unofficial timepiece; the village paid to have a fire alarm installed to provide warning throughout the community in the event of emergencies.

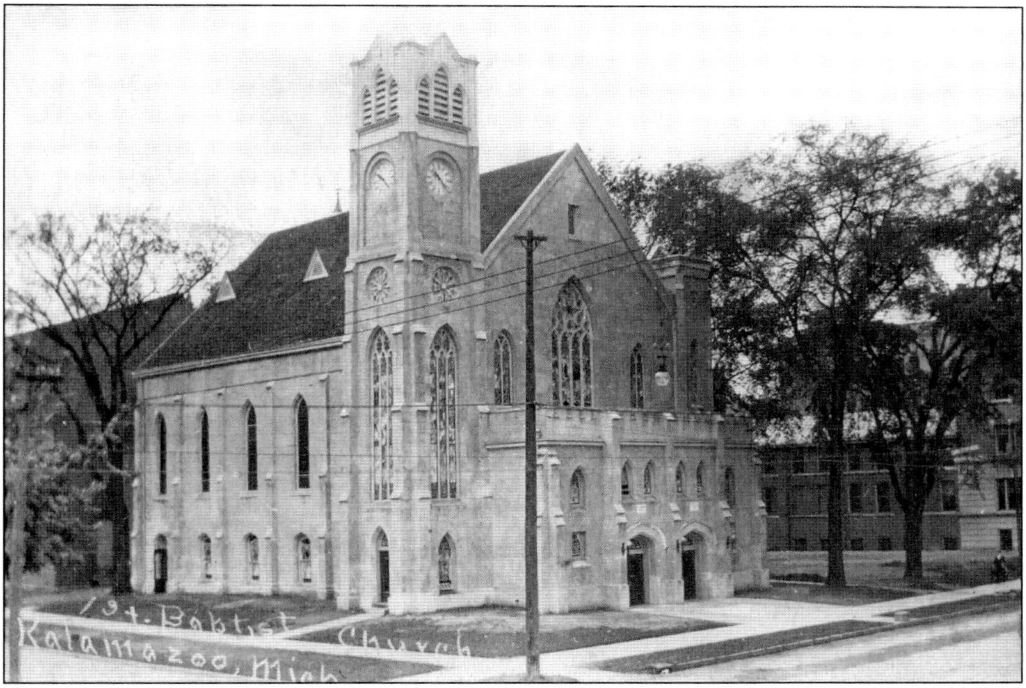


First Baptist Church is seen here after an extensive 1912 exterior renovation gave the church much of its current appearance. Among the notable changes were the removal of the spire and the construction of a new entrance. An expansion in 1931 added an education wing.

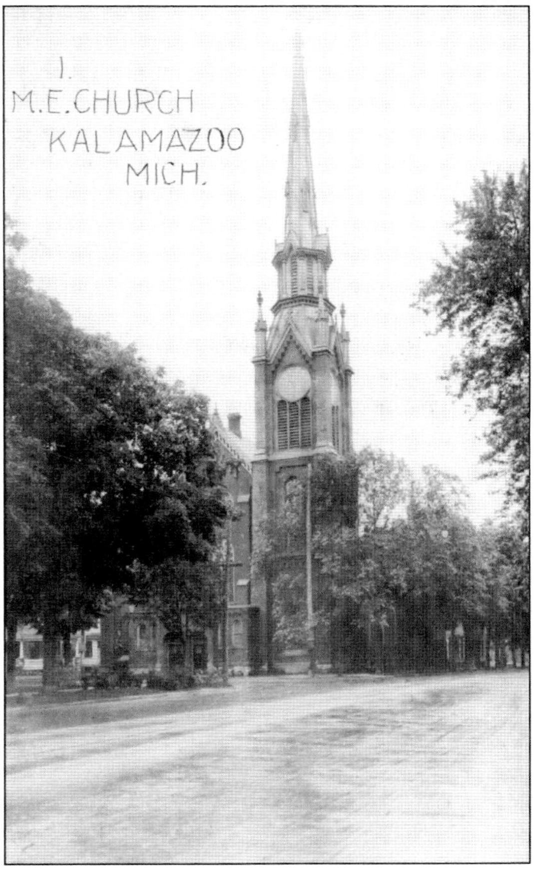


The First Methodist congregation is Kalamazoo's oldest. Founded in 1833, its members met in private homes, including the log cabin of village founder Titus Bronson. This building was erected at the corner of Rose and Lovell Streets between 1865 and 1869. It served the Methodists well, but, by the 1920s, plans were in the works to build a larger structure facing Bronson Park. These plans were accelerated when the building was destroyed in a fire on March 13, 1926. It was just one in a series of suspicious church fires that plagued Kalamazoo in the 1920s.

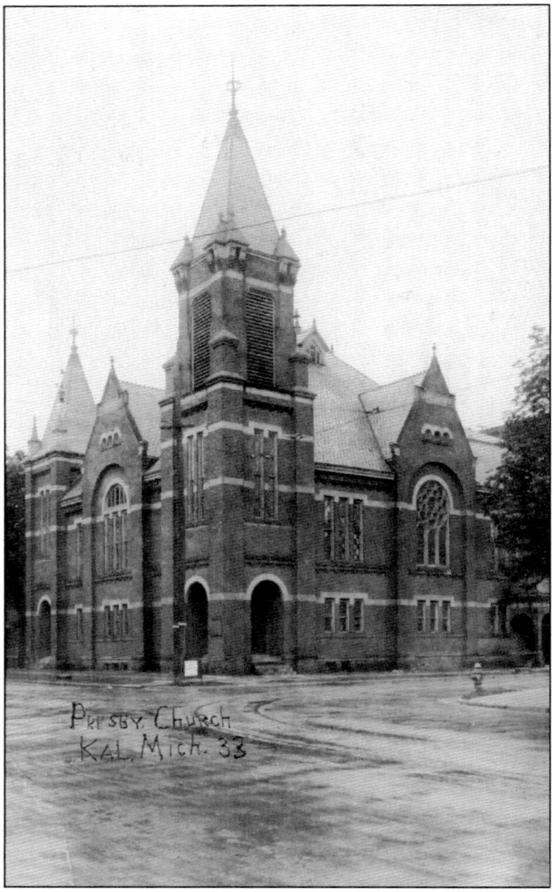


The Presbyterians organized in 1834 and occupied a handsome church on Rose Street, facing Bronson Park. That building burned down in 1883 and was replaced by this structure in 1885. The story of the Presbyterians is similar to that of the Methodists. The congregation grew to the point that the old building was no longer sufficient. Work had already started on the congregation's current home on South Street when the old building burned down on July 6, 1926.

The First Congregational Church built this handsome structure in 1889 at the corner of Park and Academy Streets. But, like many of its contemporaries, it fell victim to a mysterious fire. A pair of young boys on their way to the neighboring YMCA discovered that the church was ablaze on the afternoon of December 29, 1925. The present building was dedicated on the same site in 1928.

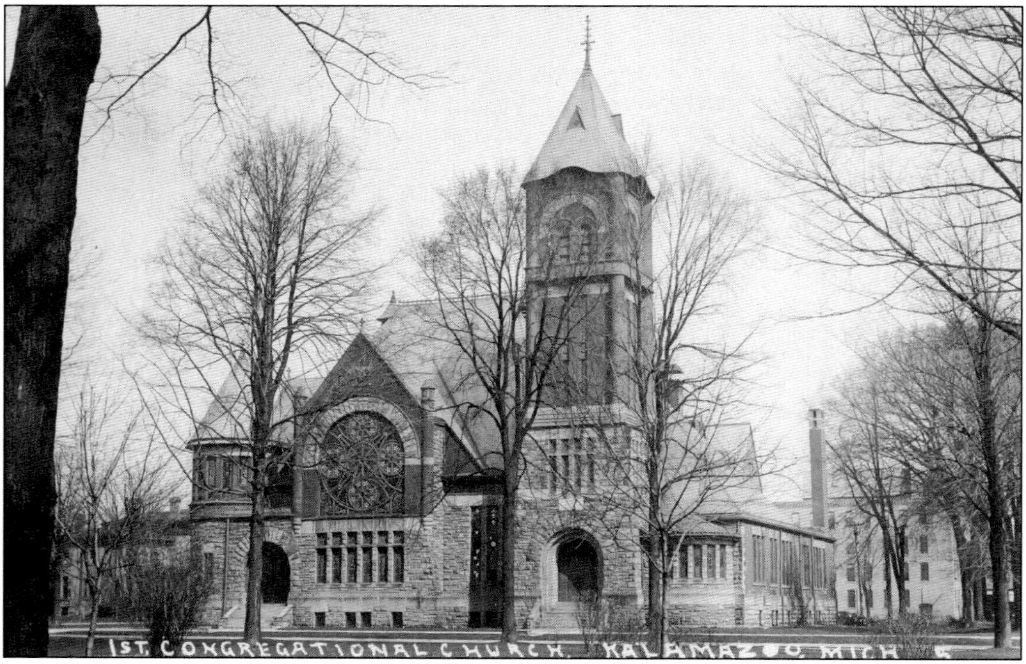

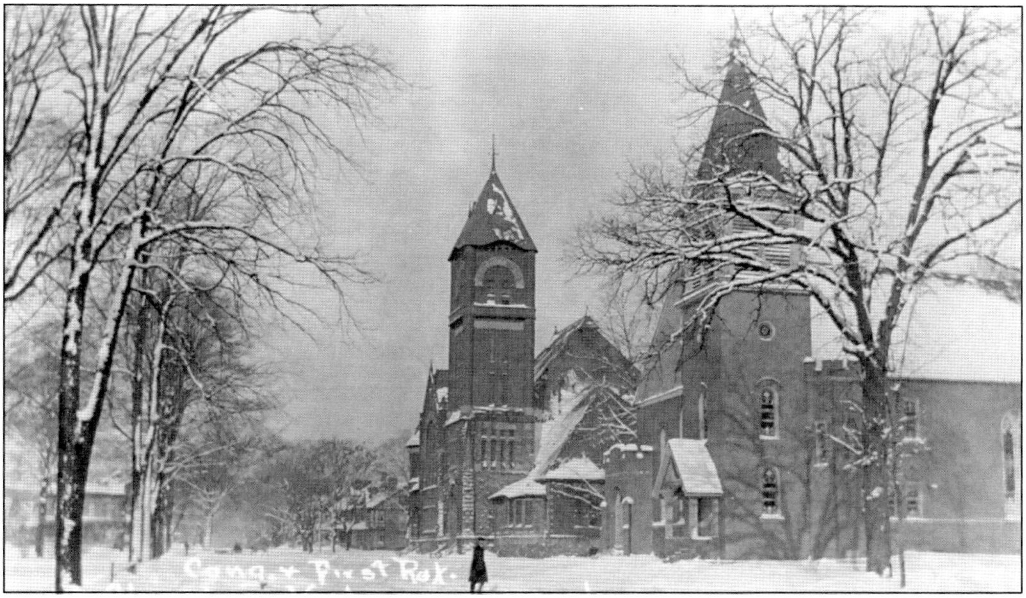

First Reformed Church (above right) stood adjacent to First Congregational on Academy Street. This wintertime view highlights this relationship, as well as the church's prime location on Bronson Park. The congregation was organized in 1850. This building was erected in the 1870s and renovated in 1910. First Reformed Church closed in 2004 due to declining membership. The building remains in use by other congregations.

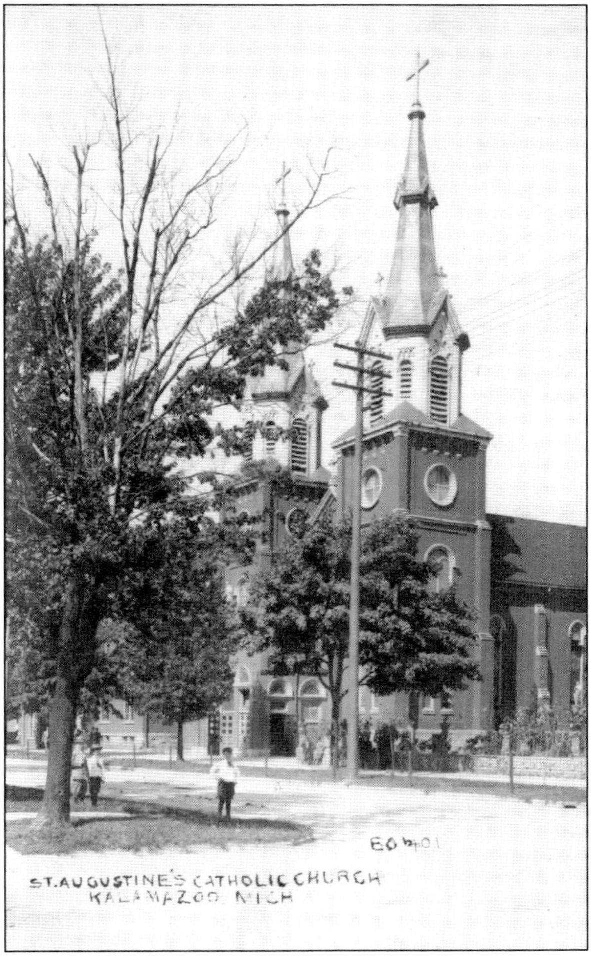


Unlike other Kalamazoo congregations, the town's Catholics established themselves far from Bronson Park. This handsome twin-spired church was built in 1869 on Kalamazoo Avenue, on the village's northwest side. It anchored a parish that included a parochial school, the Le Fevre Institute, as well as a rectory. The parish moved to a new complex on West Michigan Avenue in 1951, and these buildings were demolished.

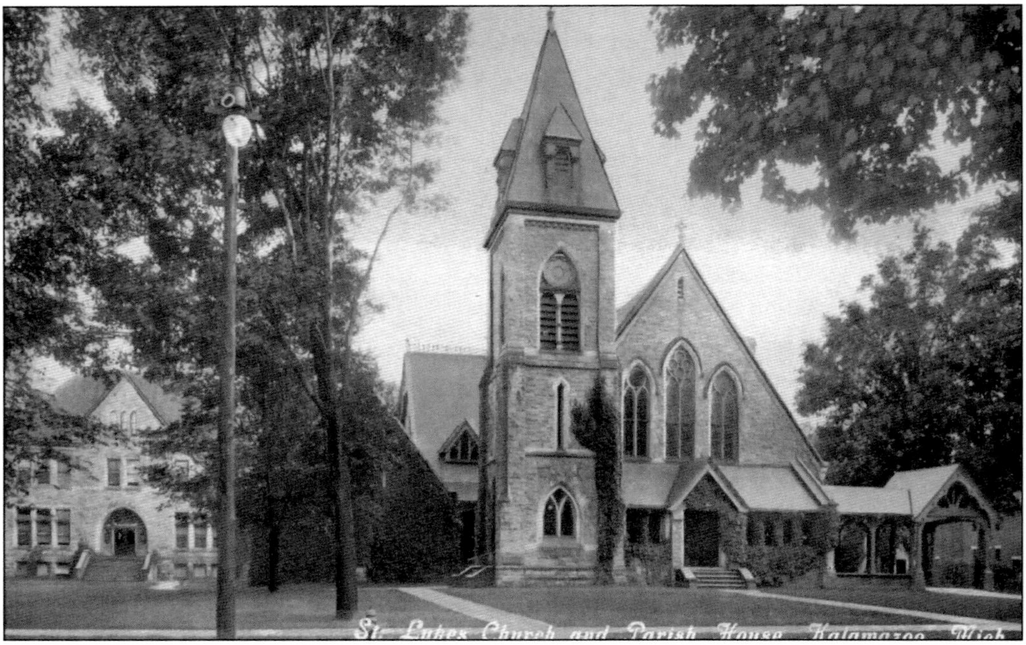


The Episcopalians still call this handsome stone Gothic church on Lovell Street home. The building was constructed in 1885, shortly after Kalamazoo's two Episcopal congregations, St. Luke's and St. John's, united. The church itself still appears much as it does in this image, but the school wing has been replaced by a larger structure.

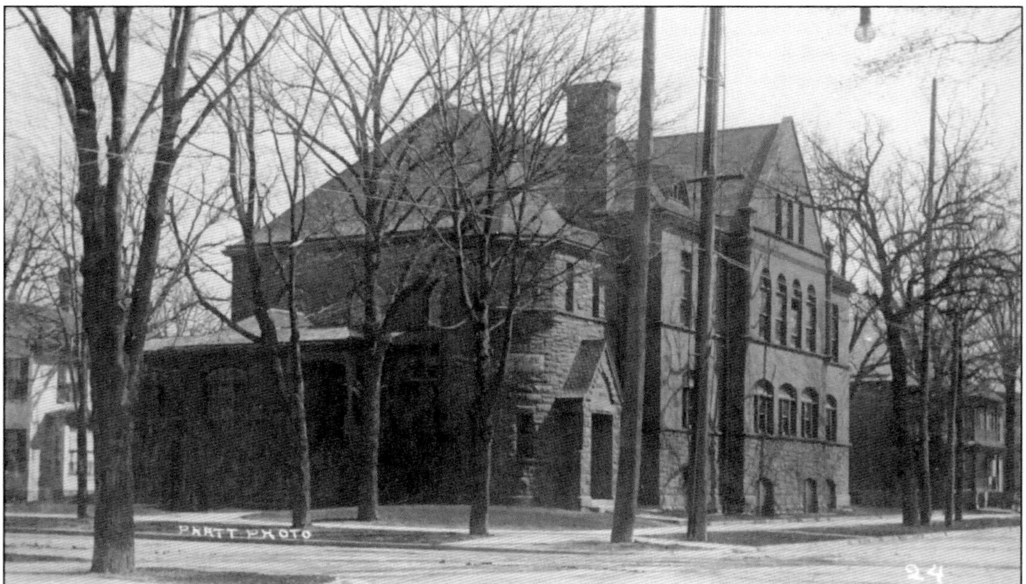


Kalamazoo's Unitarians built their church a few doors down Lovell Street from the Episcopalians. The 1894 building was perhaps the most distinct of the city's major churches, as it lacked a tower of any sort. But the congregation and its liberal version of Christianity were equally unique. The Unitarians opened the first kindergarten in the city and provided meeting space for an early African American organization, the Frederick Douglass Club. The church was razed in 1968 after the congregation moved out of the downtown area. The site is now a parking lot.

Kalamazoo's early Jewish residents organized the B'nai Israel congregation in 1866. They constructed their home (right) on South Street in 1875. The structure was small but handsome and fit well into its residential surroundings. However, by the 20th century the city's expanding commercial district caught up to the congregation. In 1910, work began on a new building (below) located on South Park Street, farther away from downtown. This Neoclassical building continued to serve B'nai Israel until 1946, when dwindling membership caused its sale to another Jewish congregation, the Congregation of Moses. The original temple on South Street was taken over by commercial enterprises, heavily altered, and finally razed in 1976. The Park Street temple served the Congregation of Moses until the early 1960s. It was torn down shortly afterwards.

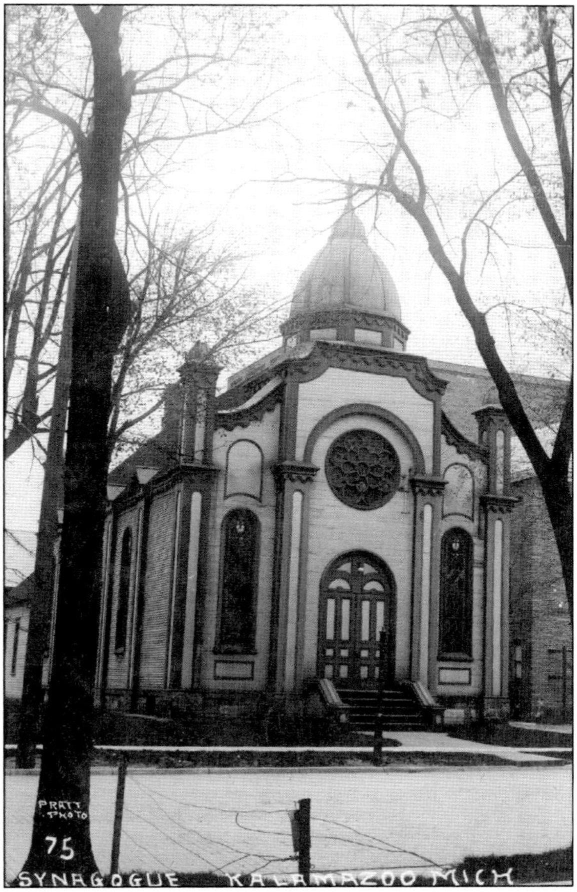


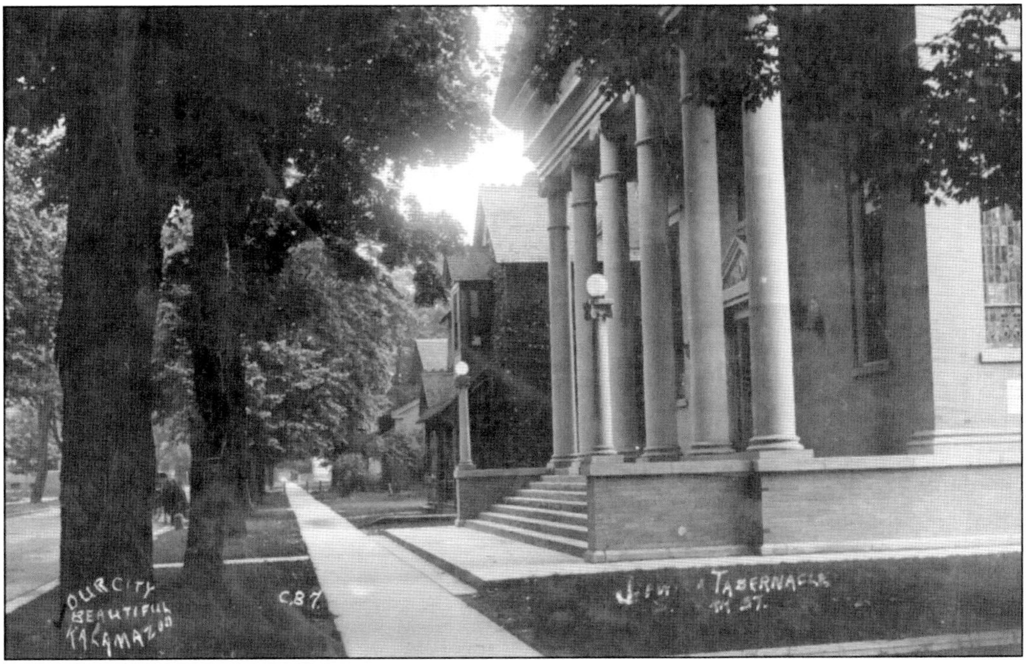

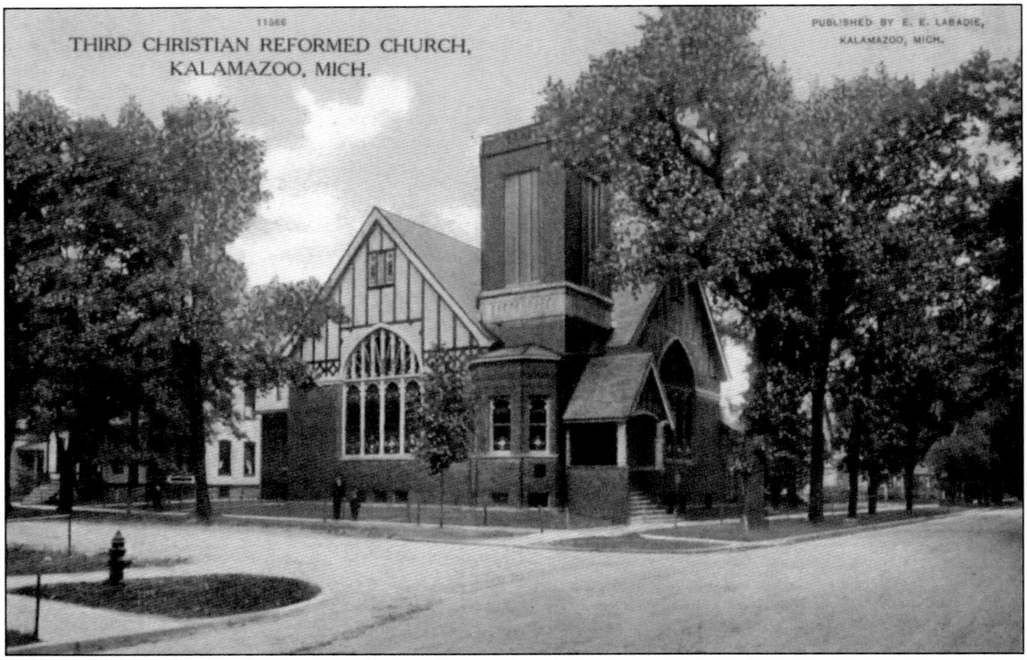


The Third Christian Reformed Church served Kalamazoo's south side. The congregation was organized in 1907, and the church was dedicated in 1908. The building was razed in 1975 after the congregation moved away from downtown.

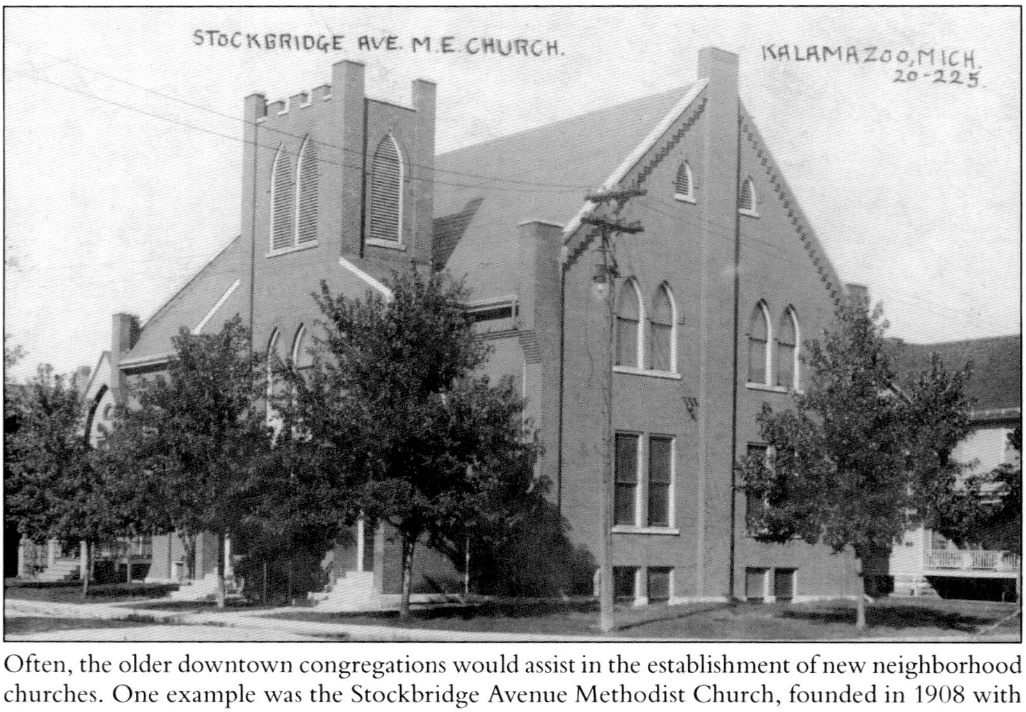


Often, the older downtown congregations would assist in the establishment of new neighborhood churches. One example was the Stockbridge Avenue Methodist Church, founded in 1908 with the assistance of First Methodist. The congregation remains, but this building was destroyed in a fire in 1979.

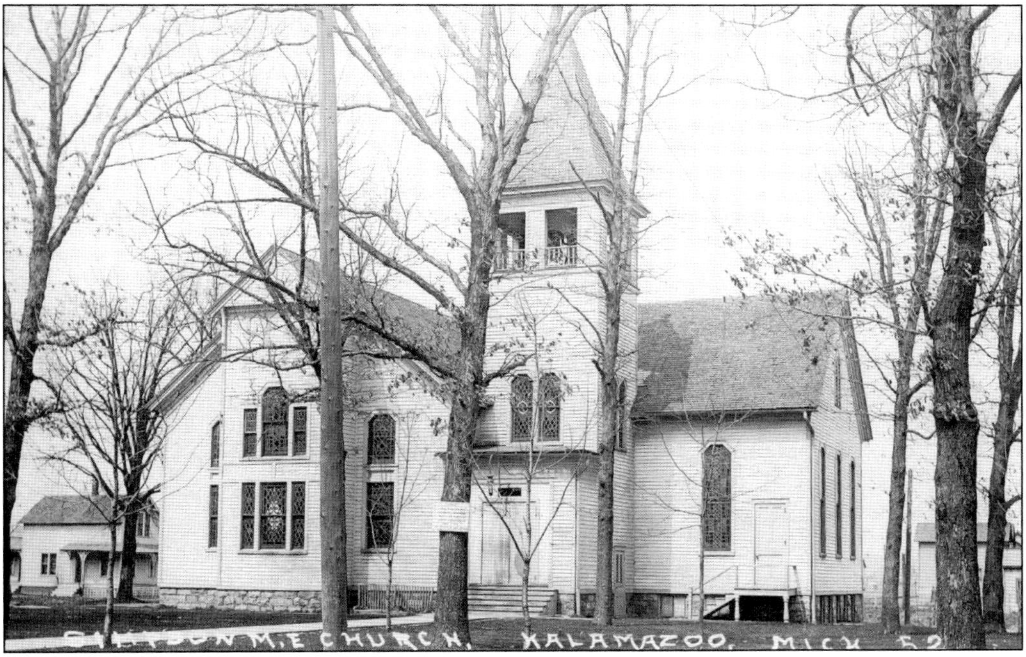


The Simpson Methodist congregation was another that got an early boost from the older downtown congregation. This postcard shows its first wooden building on North Street and Cobb Avenue. A brick building replaced it in 1913. That building still stands, but the congregation is gone.

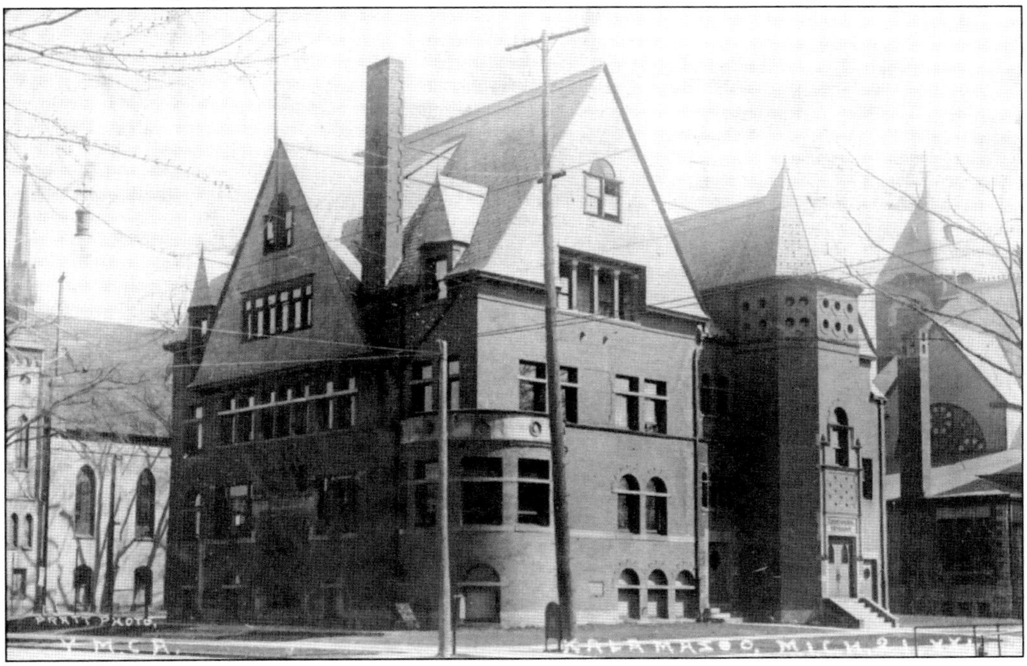


The Young Men's Christian Association was part of a national movement to provide urban youths a wholesome place for lodging, social programs, and sport. The Kalamazoo YMCA occupied this impressive building at the corner of West Main and Park Streets beginning in 1892. Sadly, this impressive castle-like structure was relatively short-lived. It burned to the ground in January 1911.

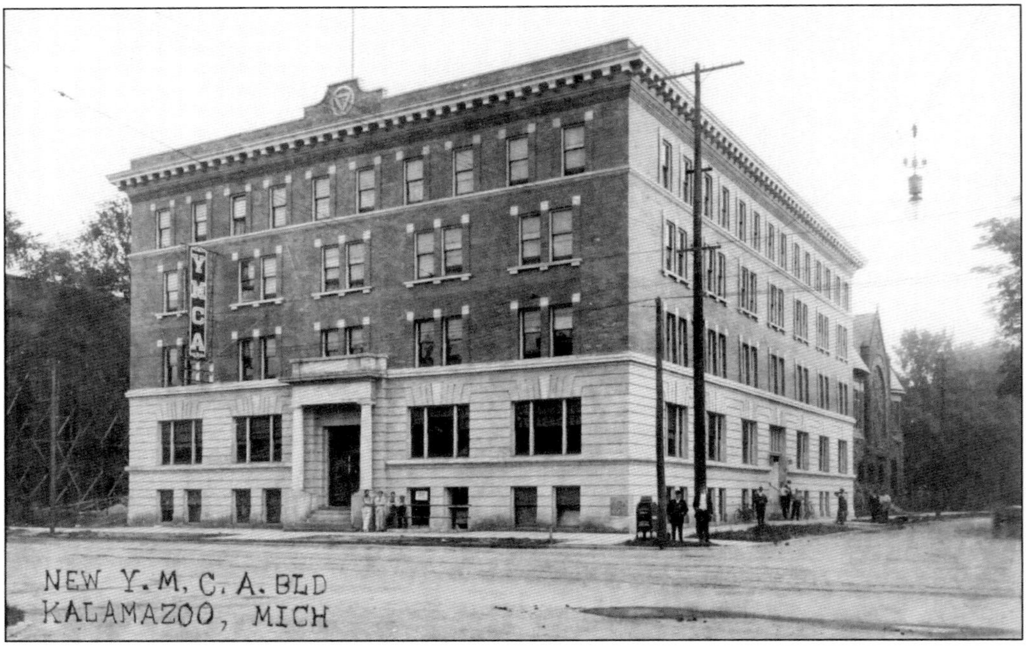


The YMCA promptly raised funds for a replacement structure on the same site. This new building, completed in 1912, was certainly less fanciful than its predecessor. But it served its purpose well, and was expanded in 1941, with a new wing with matching architecture. Even with this new wing, the organization joined the postwar flight of so many others out of the downtown area. It was vacated in 1970 for a new YMCA on Maple Street.

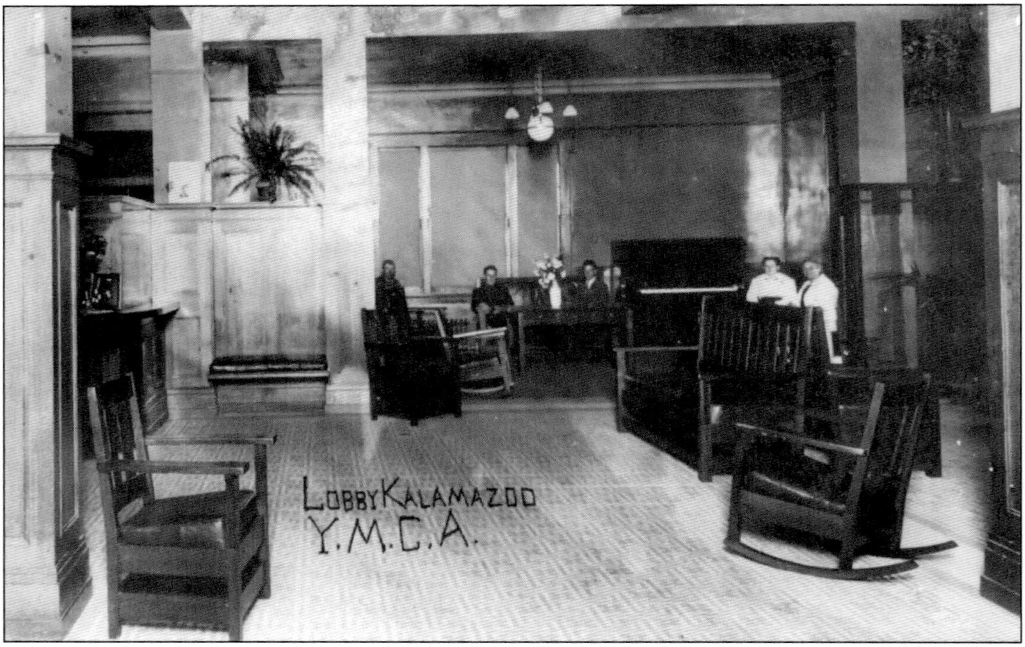


This interior view shows the lobby of the 1912 YMCA building. The wood paneling and Arts and Crafts furniture are very much in keeping with the taste of the time. The building was razed in 1971 for a parking lot.

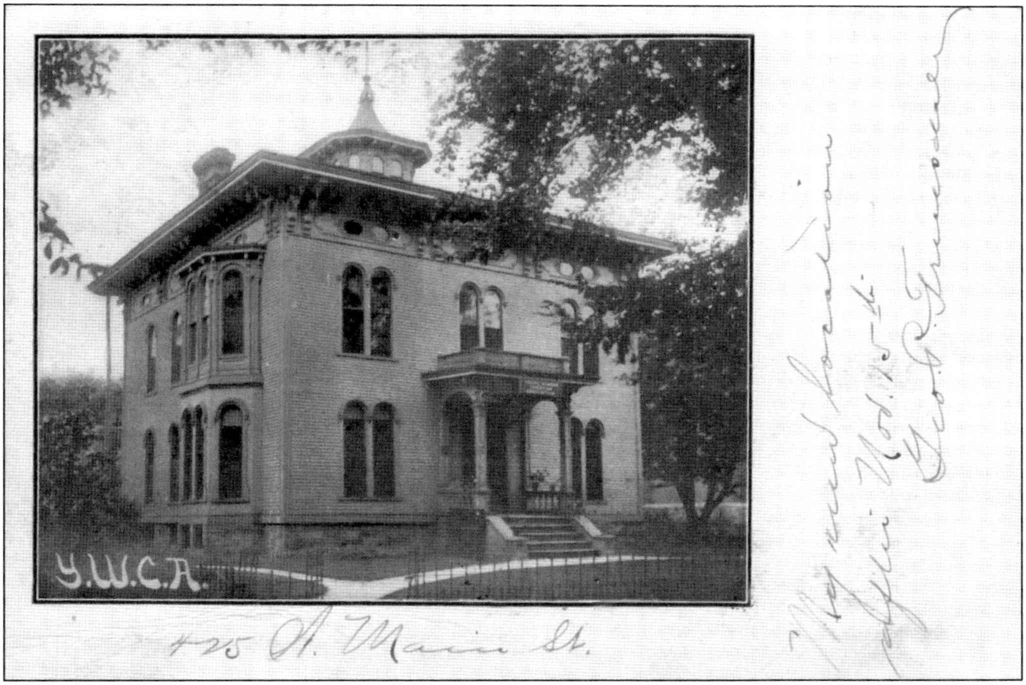


The YWCA provided similar services as the YMCA, but for women. The organization purchased this 1861 home, originally built by William House, in 1895. It remained here until 1908, when the building was sold to the Truesdale Funeral Home, which remained until the structure's demolition in 1986. It was the last home along the former "Mansion Row" to be leveled.

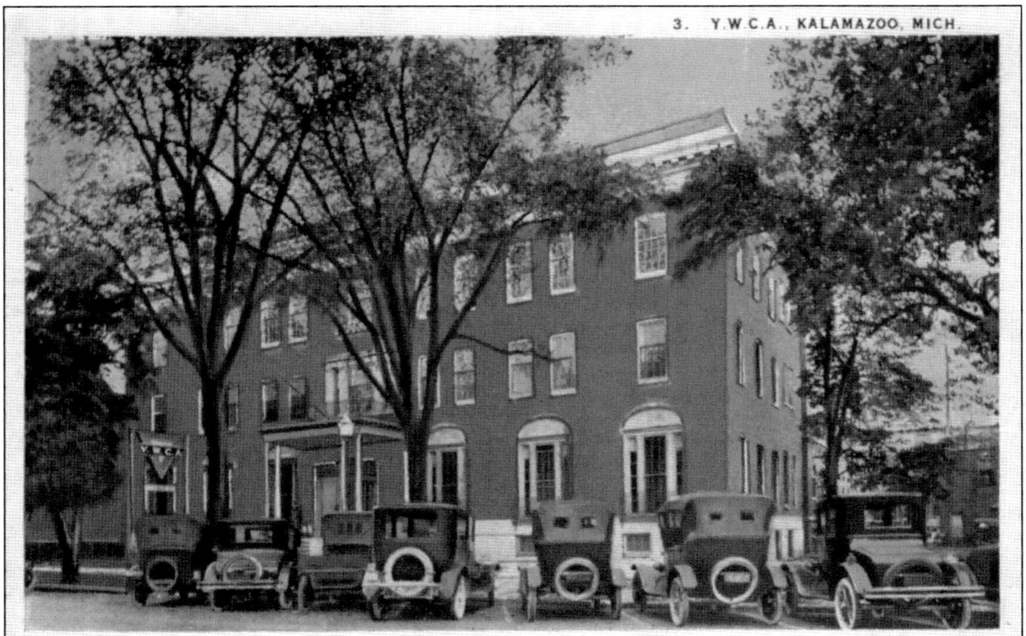


The YWCA opened this new facility on Rose Street, facing Bronson Park, in stages from 1918 to 1923. It contained lodging, a cafeteria, and a swimming pool. The Georgian building was sold in 1985 and renovated into offices a few years later.

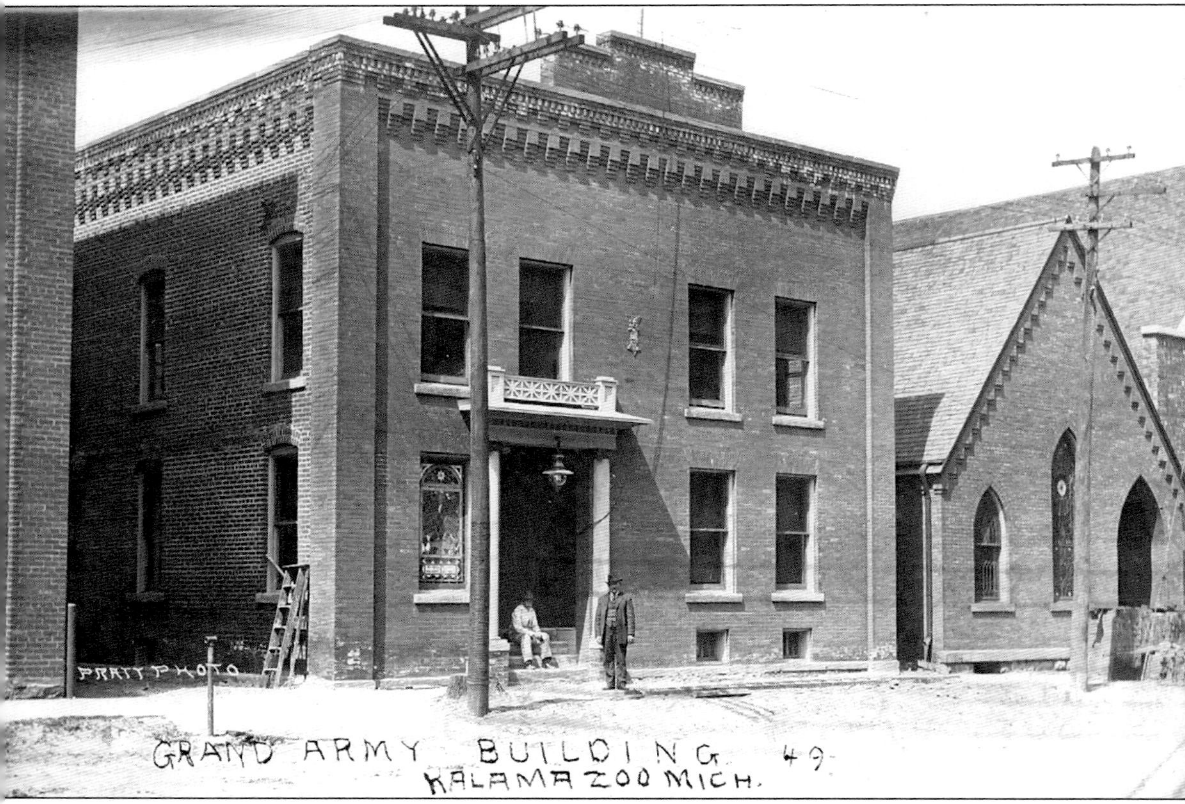


The Grand Army of the Republic (GAR) was a fraternal organization of Union veterans of the Civil War. It became a powerful force for political advocacy, supporting veterans' issues and Republican politics. At the organization's peak, around the turn of the 20th century, one would find GAR halls in nearly every Northern community. Kalamazoo's GAR hall was located on Park Street. (From the Collection of the Kalamazoo Valley Museum.)

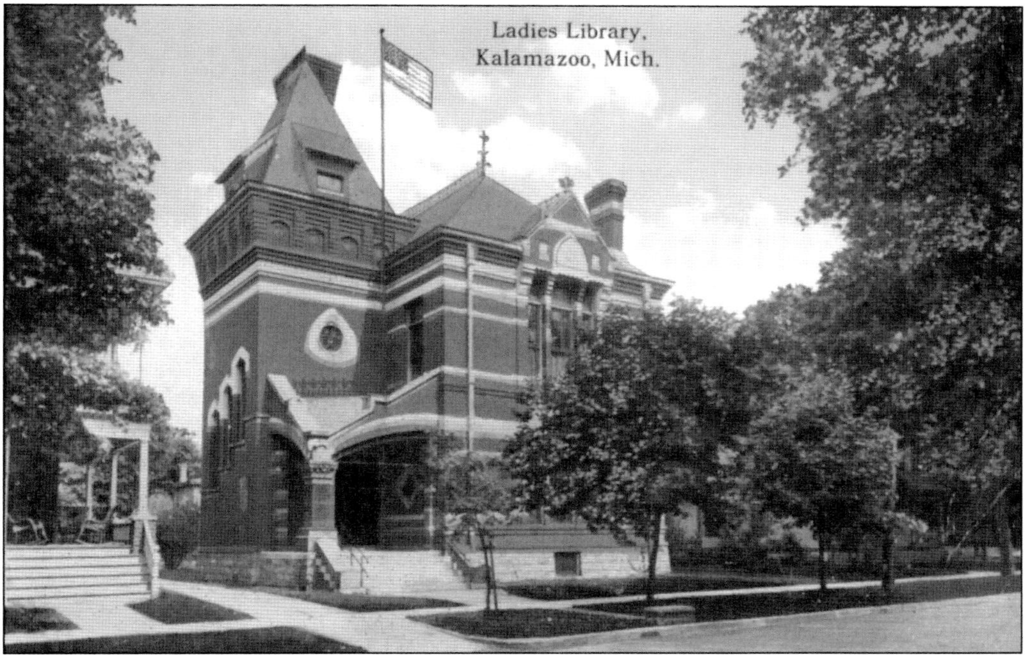


This postcard shows the first building constructed for and by a women's organization in the United States. The Ladies Library Association was one of the first groups of its kind, organizing in 1852 to provide Kalamazoo's women with a place to meet for literary and cultural events. The association erected this building in 1878; its beautiful architecture remains a landmark on Park Street.

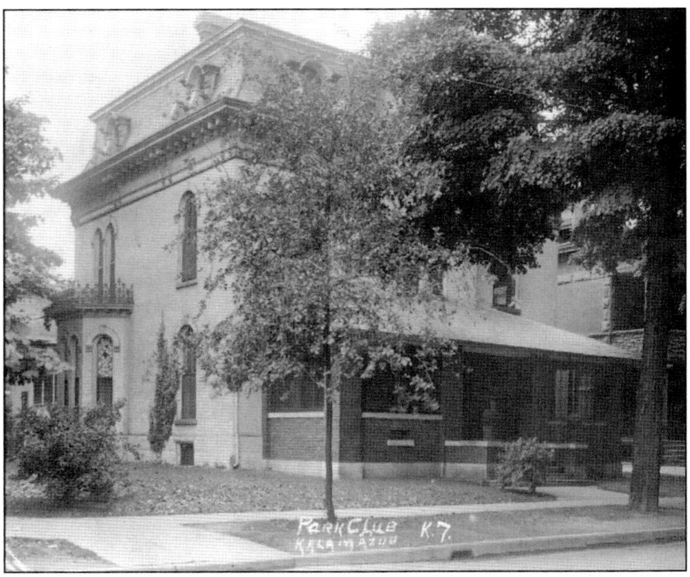


In 1904, Kalamazoo's three men's social clubs merged. The new club purchased the former Nathaniel Balch home, at the corner of Rose and South Streets. Because the home faced Bronson Park, the club was named the Park Club. The club continued to occupy this clubhouse until 1924, when it purchased the neighboring William Lawrence home. The old Balch house (pictured) was then removed for parking. (Courtesy of the Kalamazoo Public Library's Local History Room.)

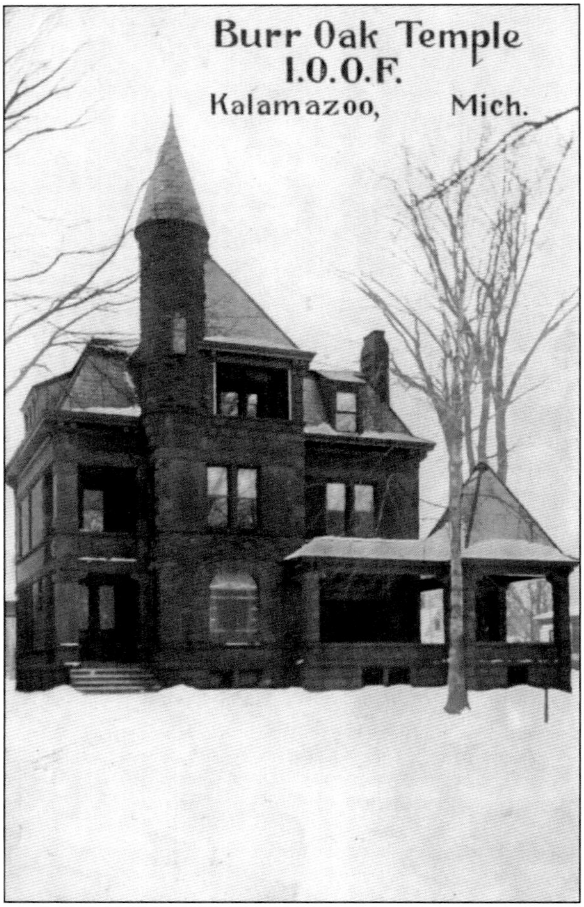


This postcard shows the William Lawrence home when it was occupied by the Independent Order of Odd Fellows. The 1889 house was converted to the uses of the IOOF by 1909. The Odd Fellows was only one of several fraternal organizations that were immensely popular in the late 19th and early 20th centuries. The Park Club moved into the home in 1924 and has remained there ever since.

The Knights of Pythias first occupied this "Pythian castle" on West Main Street in 1912. In fact, the core of the building was one of the splendid 19th-century mansions that contributed to "Mansion Row." Close examination reveals a boxy addition behind the original house.

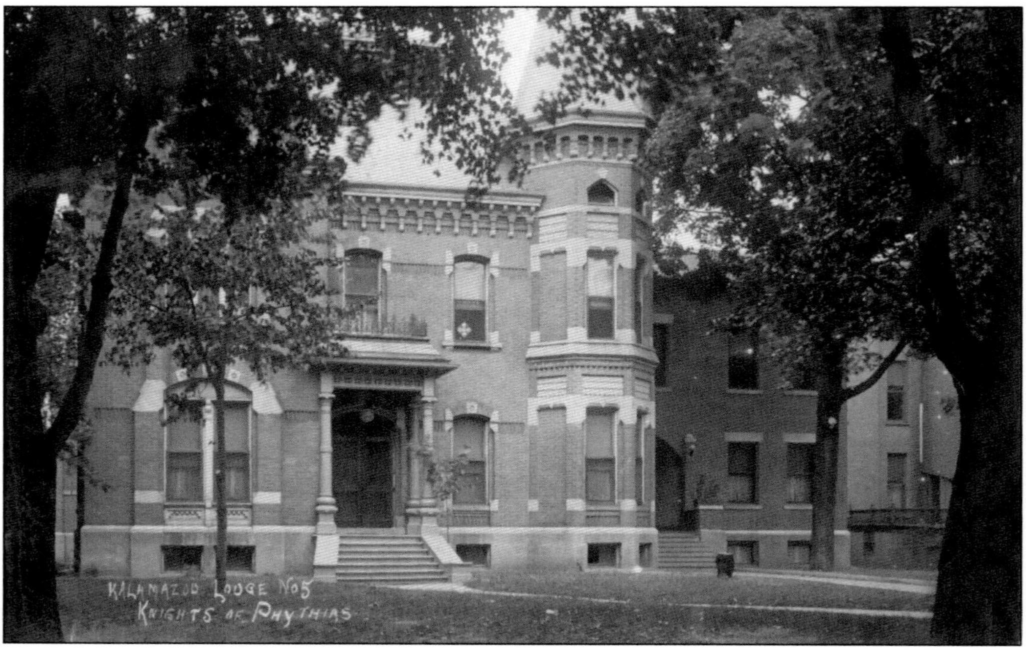

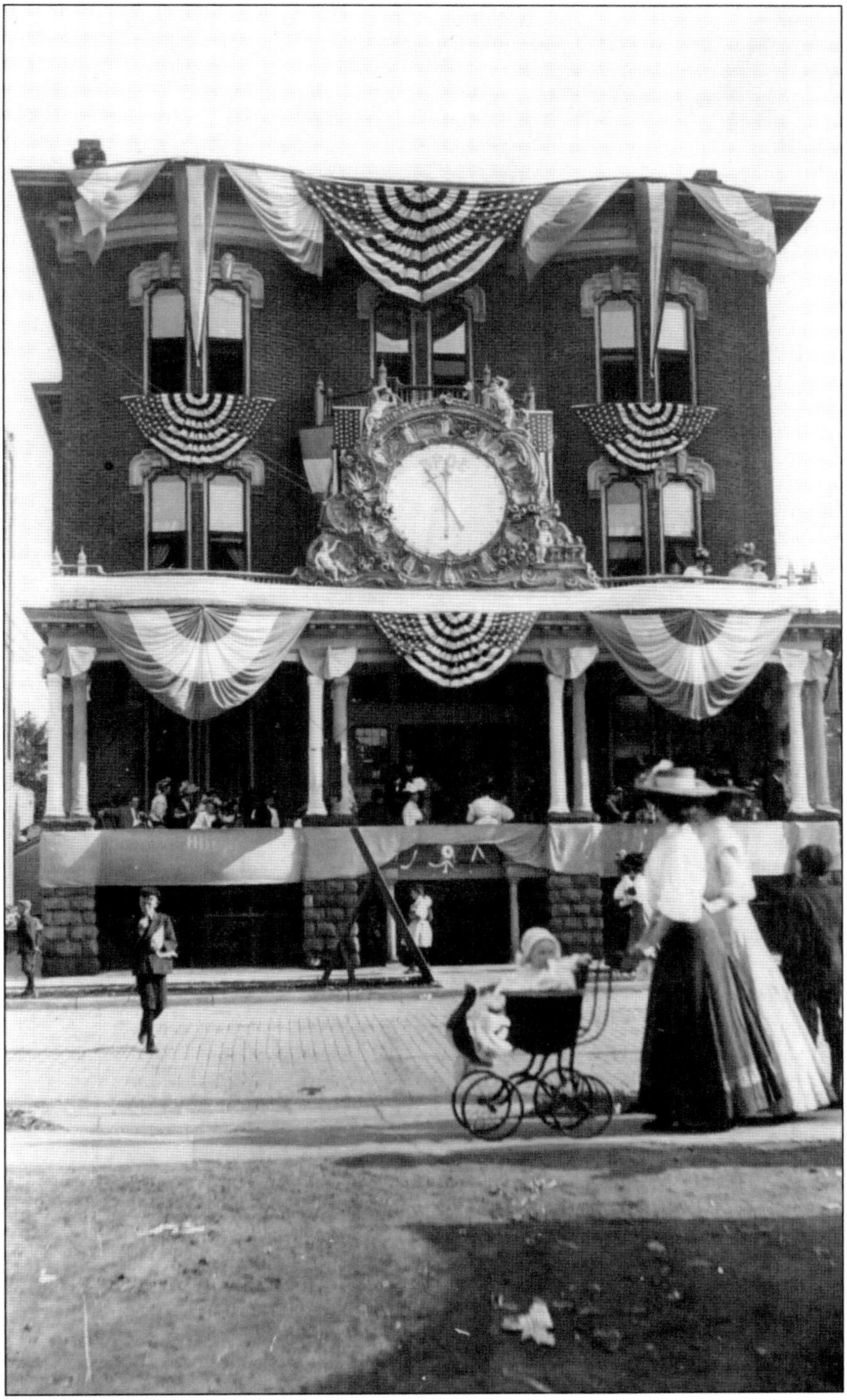

Kalamazoo's lodge of the Benevolent and Protective Order of the Elks purchased this Italianate building on South Street to serve as its clubhouse in 1902. Three years later, the building was expanded, providing the Elks with proper meeting rooms. In this postcard, the building is patriotically decked out for the city's 1909 "Silver Annie" celebrations. (Courtesy of the Kalamazoo Public Library's Local History Room.)

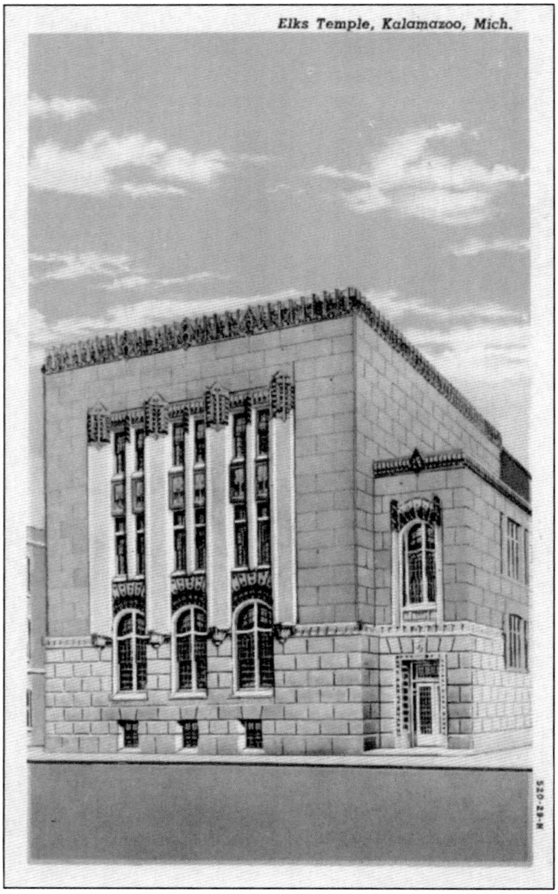


The Elks further expanded and modernized their lodge in 1928. The building received this modern facade, which completely obscured the original, as well as updated facilities. The Elks vacated this property in 1959, and it was demolished three years later. The site is occupied by a parking garage.

Without a doubt, the Masons built Kalamazoo's most spectacular fraternal facility: the Masonic Temple on Rose Street. The cornerstone was laid with great fanfare in 1913. Once completed, the building contained three auditoriums, meeting rooms, offices, and stores. The Masons called this building home until dwindling membership and neighborhood decay led them to vacate it in the early 1970s. It fell into disrepair, but was resurrected in the 1980s as the Rose Street Market.

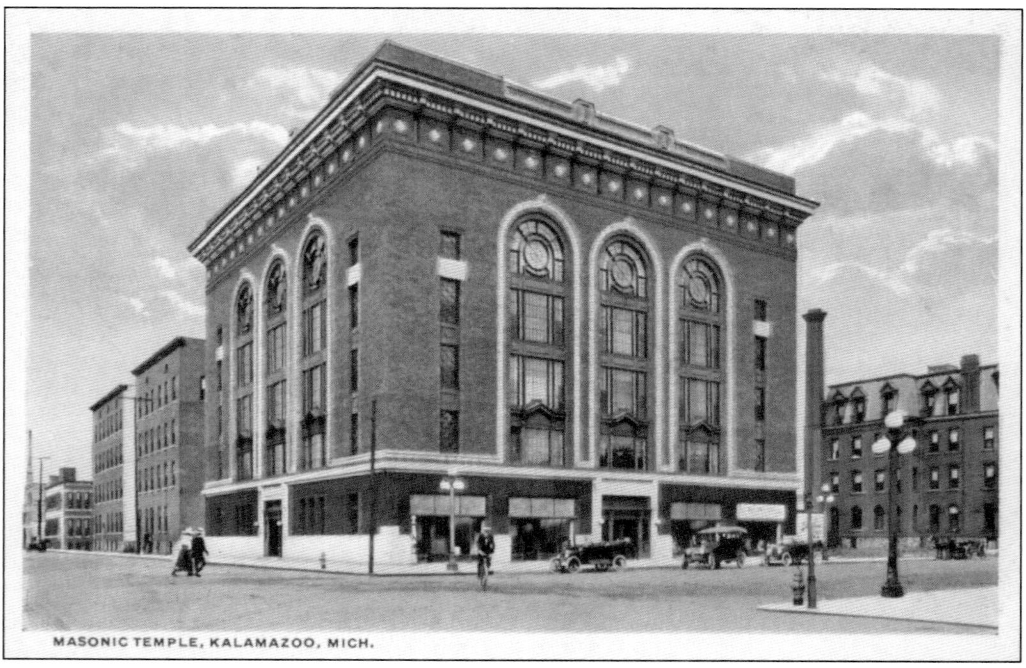

# *Five*

# Recreation

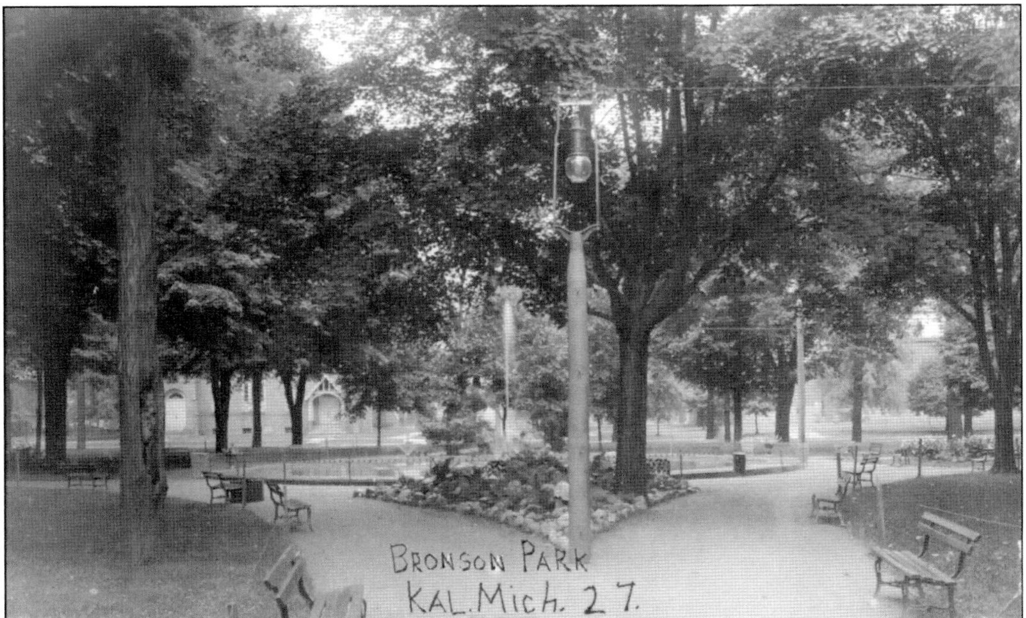


When Titus Bronson first laid out the new village, he set aside a central square for a public park. Today, that park remains and bears his name. Its central location has made the park an important feature of the downtown landscape. Homes, theaters, churches, and government buildings have all surrounded it. The park itself has served as a gathering spot for the community and as an escape from the busy urban streets around it. This photo postcard shows the large trees and paths that defined the park a century ago.

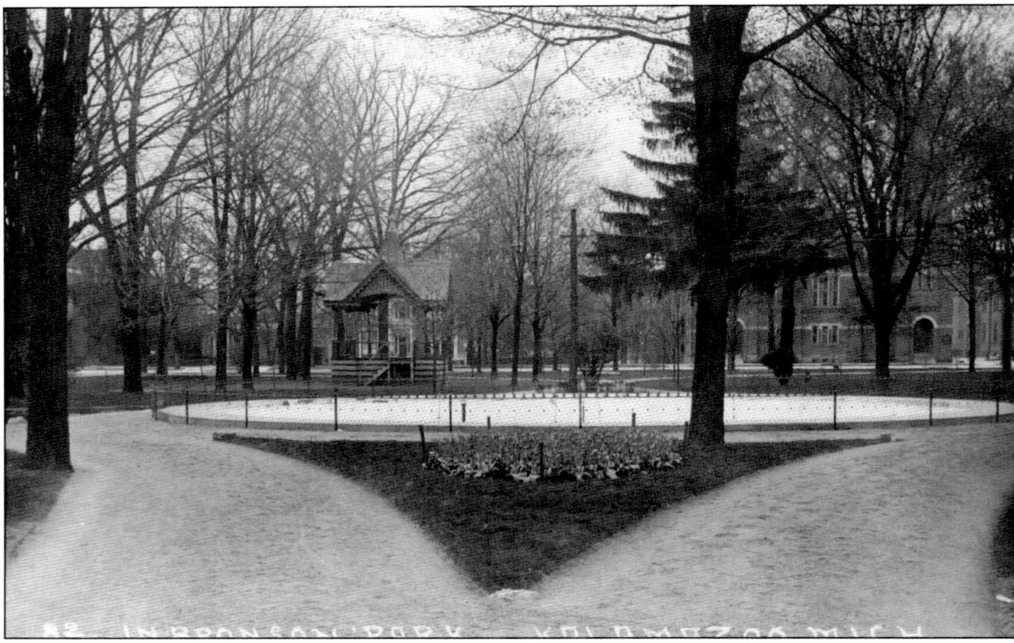

In 1879, the center of Bronson Park received its first fountain. This water feature was circular in design and served as the focal point for the curving paths that made their way throughout the park. These photo postcards show the fountain when it was turned off (above) as well as when it was on (below).

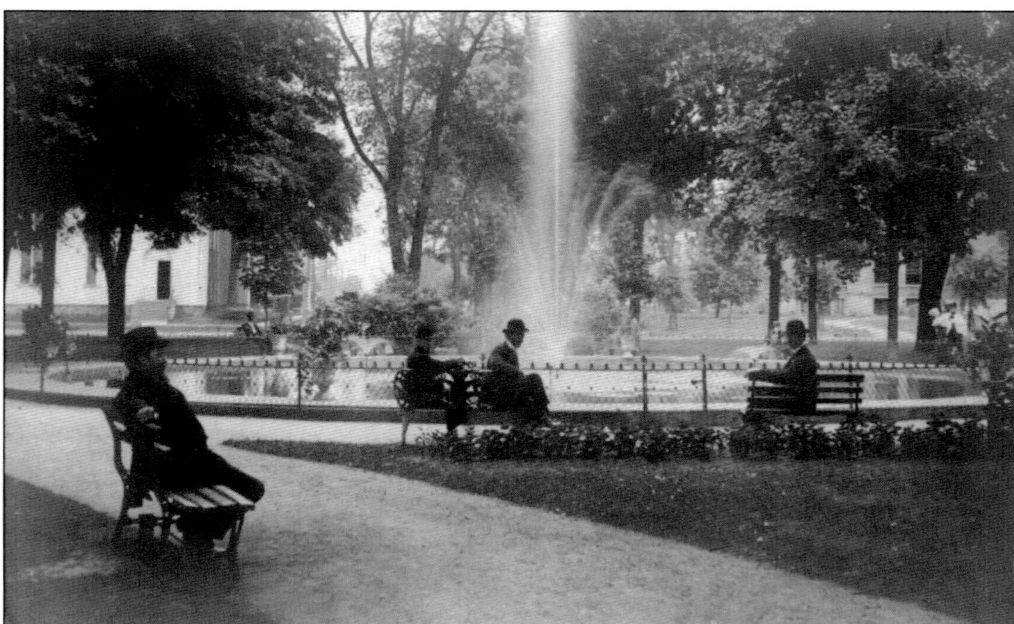

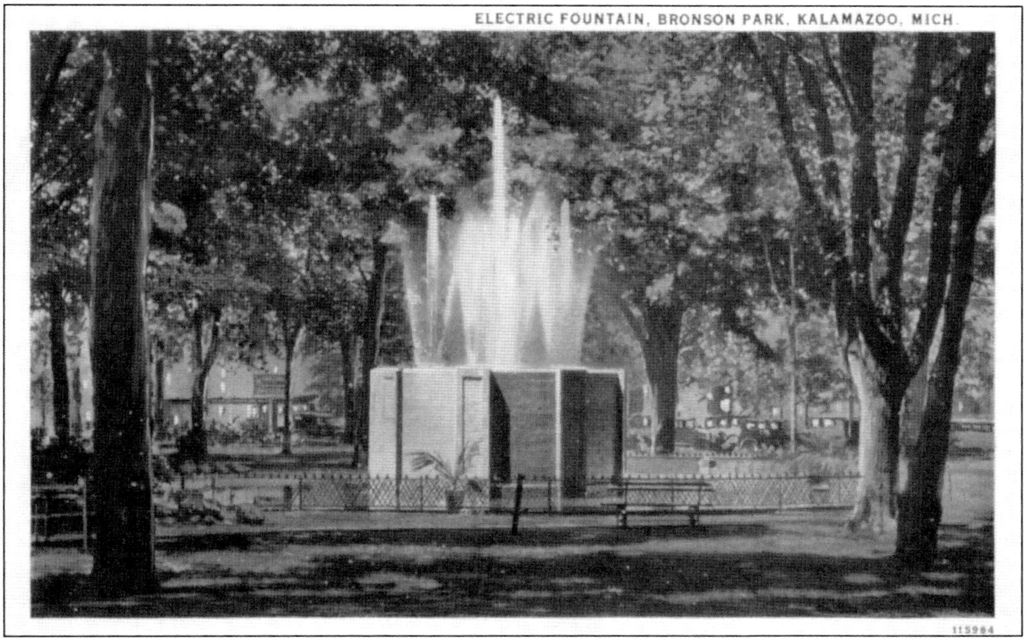


The original fountain gave way to this electric model in 1926. Its lighted-color effects dazzled park visitors, but the bulky appearance of the concrete base left much to be desired. Before long, calls were made to replace it with a more visually appealing structure.

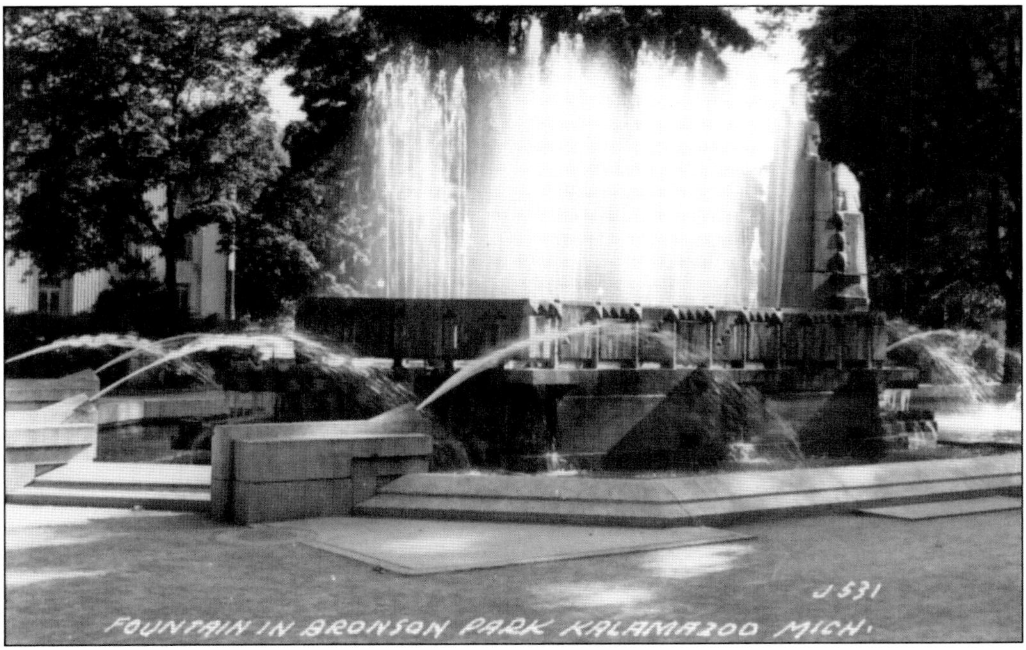


In 1939, the electric fountain was removed, and the Fountain of the Pioneers took its place. The new fountain utilized its predecessor's lighted effects, but improved on its lack of physical beauty. Artist Alfonso Iannelli designed the elaborate structure, which featured the highly stylized figures of a pioneer and a Native American. Its construction marked the 100th anniversary of the removal of the natives from Kalamazoo. Iannelli also added a reflecting pool to Bronson Park's layout.

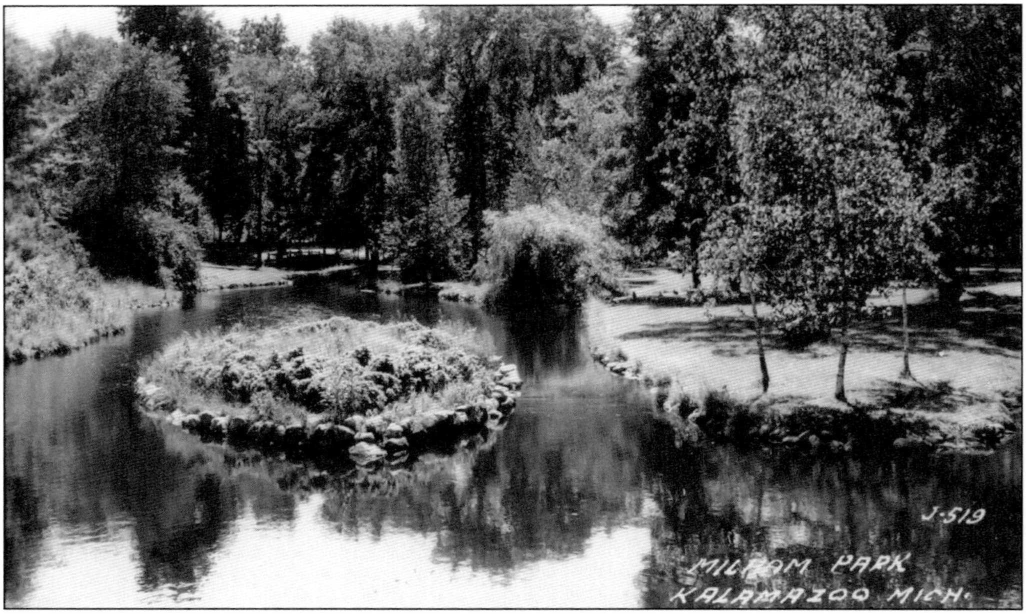


In 1911, the City of Kalamazoo opened John A. Milham Park on property purchased from the estate of John Milham, one of the region's early pioneers and a successful farmer. The 60-acre property was transformed into a natural escape from urban life. Roads, playgrounds, and picnic areas were added to the land, which already boasted large trees and waterways. The park was expanded in 1929, and an 18-hole public golf course was added. Further improvements came during the Great Depression, when WPA money was used to add stone bridges, a pavilion, and other structures.

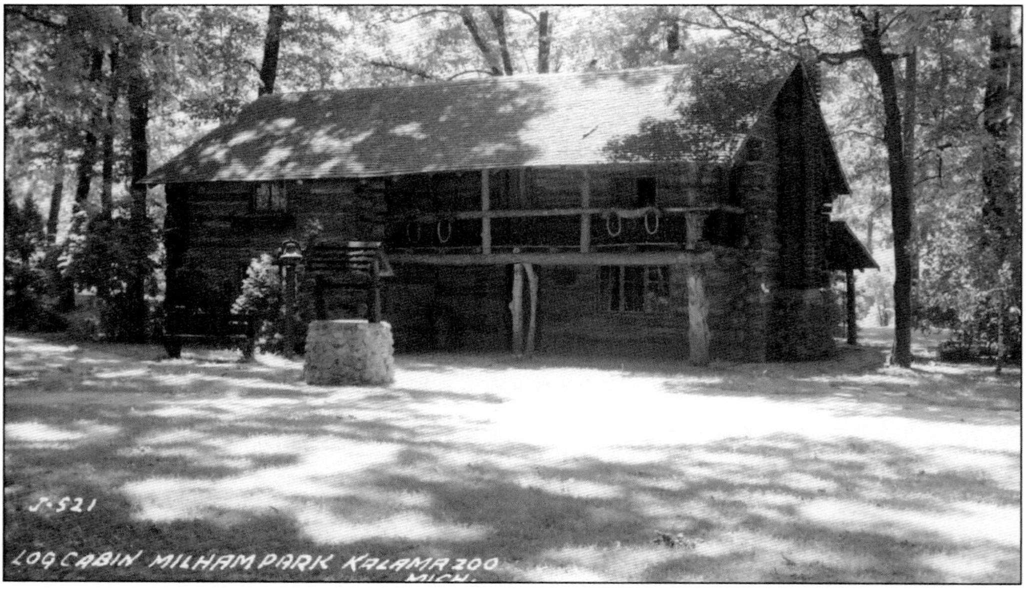


Another interesting feature of the park was a two-story log cabin, built in 1930 to commemorate the centennial of Kalamazoo County. The cabin, the project of the Southeastern Community Club, featured logs and stones taken from every pioneer-era farm in the county. Over the years, the cabin functioned as a museum, reptile house for the zoo, meeting space, and storage. It fell victim to deterioration and was razed in 1964.

Milham Park's zoo was added in 1926. It featured buffalo, peacocks, foxes, owls, swans, monkeys, and raccoons. The most popular animals were the black bears, seen here in their WPA-era enclosure. The animals delighted generations of Kalamazooians. The zoo came to a sad end. The animals fell victim to cruel attacks in the 1970s. The peacocks were stoned to death, and the bears were subjected to abuse by visitors, who threw bottles and rocks into the enclosure. The last bear was put to sleep in 1977.

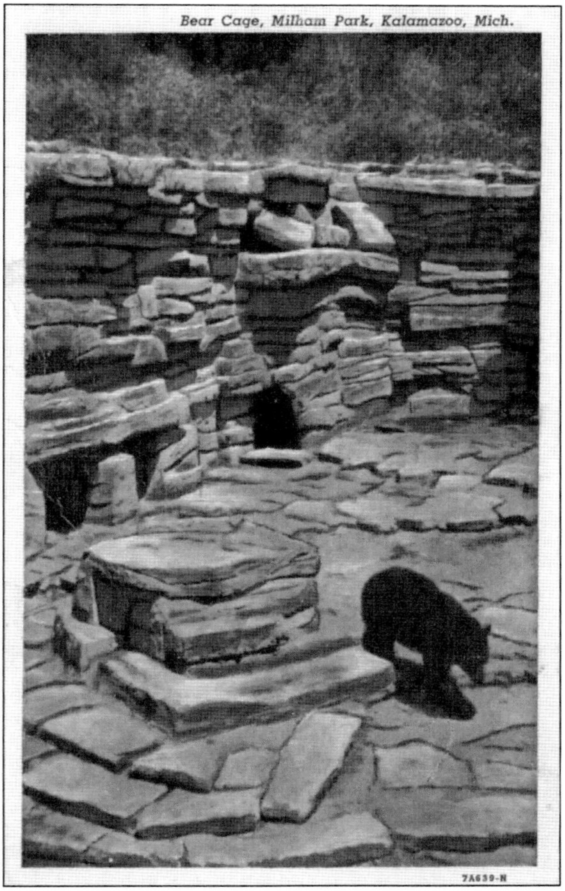
Bear Cage, Milham Park, Kalamazoo, Mich.

During the first two decades of the 20th century, Kalamazoo residents could find entertainment and relaxation on the shores of Wood's Lake. Oakwood Amusement Park occupied that lake's southern bank, at the terminus of the city's streetcar lines. The park offered dancing, music, a roller coaster, water sports, and an escape from city life. It peaked during the 2010s, but declined in the 1920s. Most of the park was disassembled in 1925, with the remainder disappearing by the 1940s.

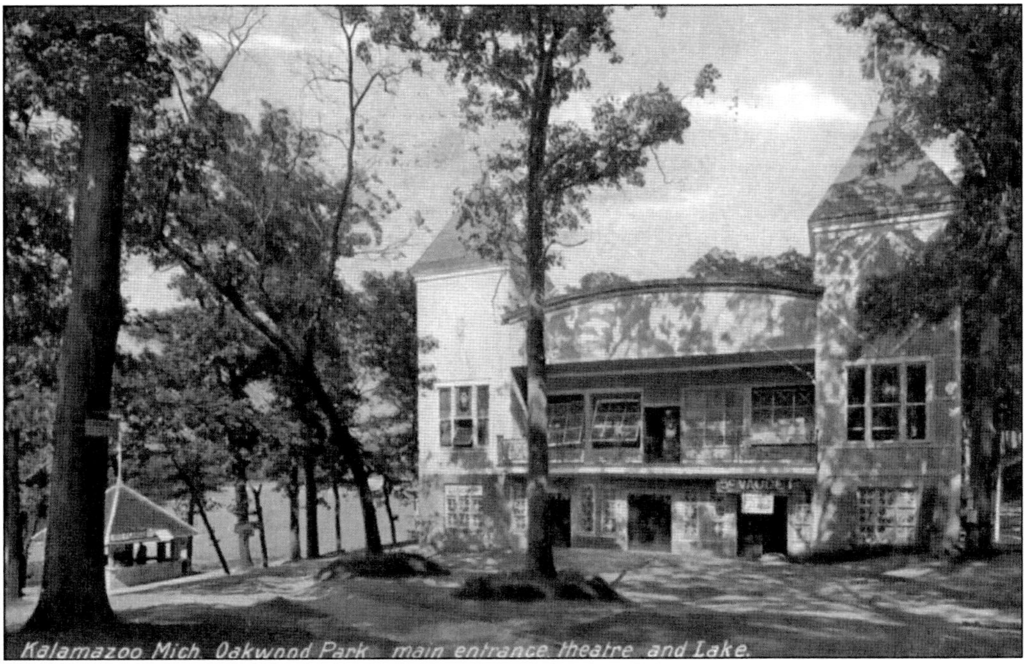
Kalamazoo Mich. Oakwood Park main entrance theatre and Lake.

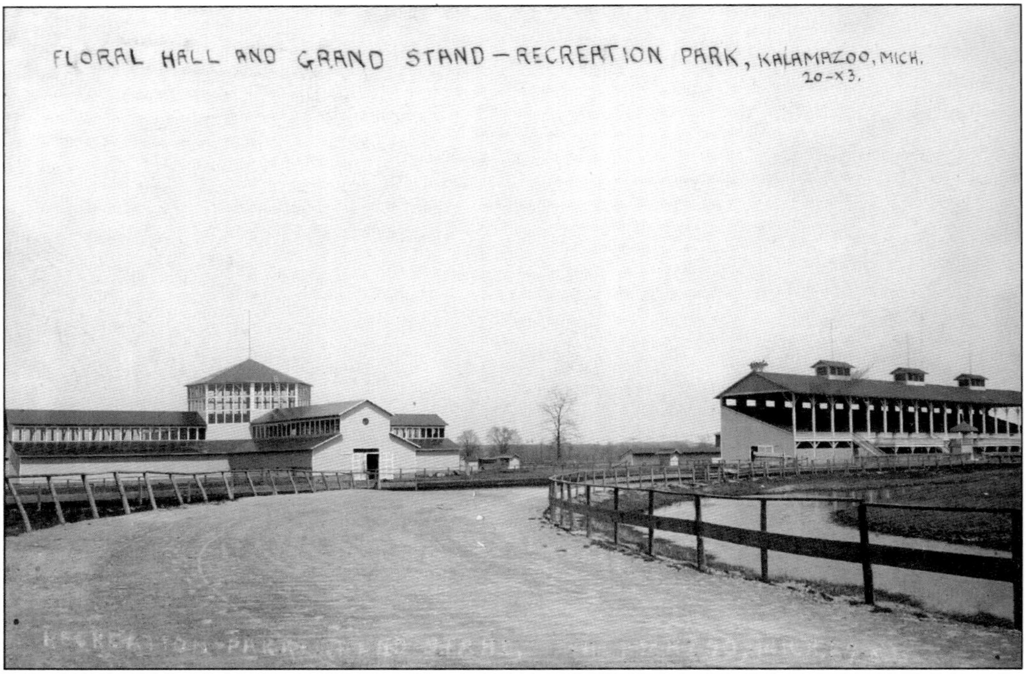


Recreation Park, at Lake and Olmsted Streets, provided ample facilities for fairs and horse racing. The above photograph shows the display hall, as well as the grandstand and track used for sporting events, such as horse racing. The postcard below provides a closer view of the grandstand, this time filled with spectators. These wooden structures are all a memory, but Recreation Park lives on today as the Kalamazoo County Fairgrounds.

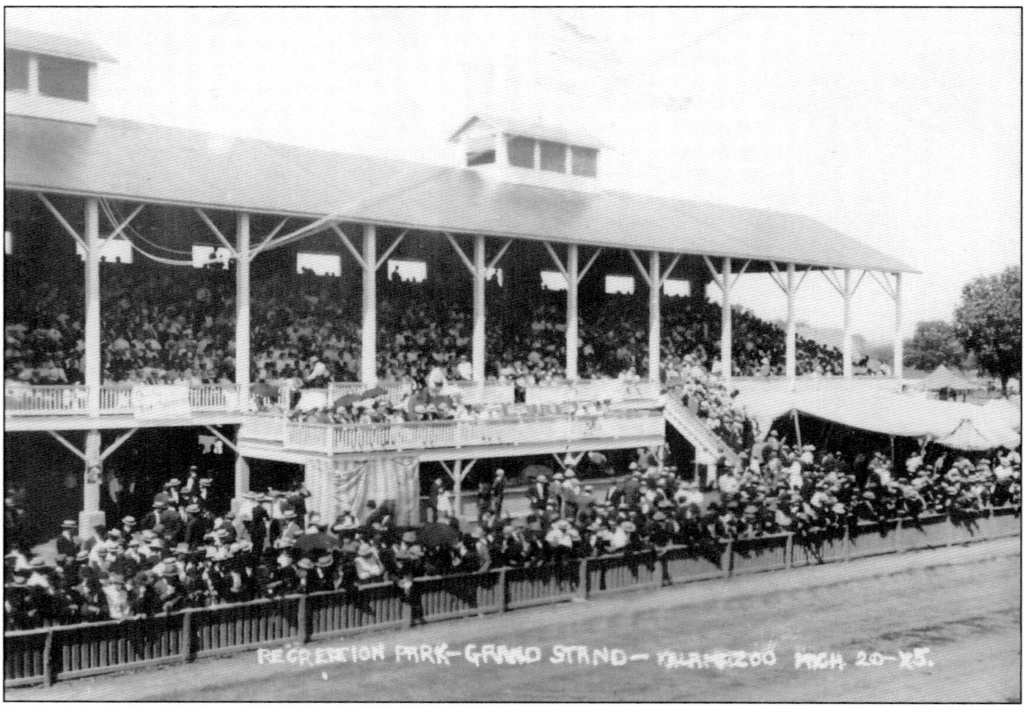

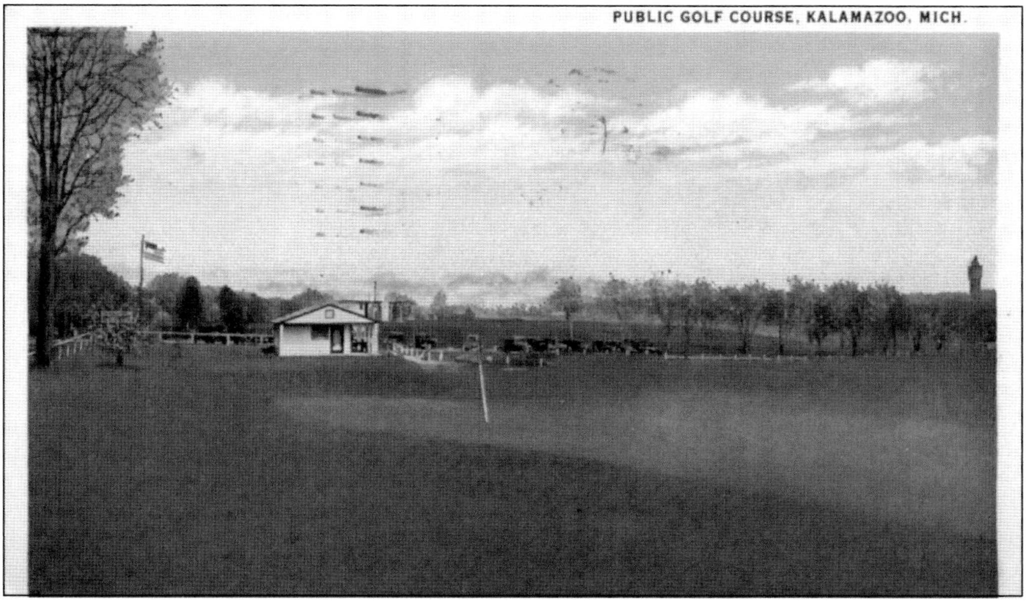


Most current students of Western Michigan University probably have no idea that the campus once looked like this. The Arcadia Brook Golf Course was opened to the public in 1928 by developer Charles Hays. At that time, the course's location along Stadium Drive was remote. But its existence was short-lived. The university purchased the property in 1943; by the 1950s, the course disappeared into the rapidly expanding west campus.

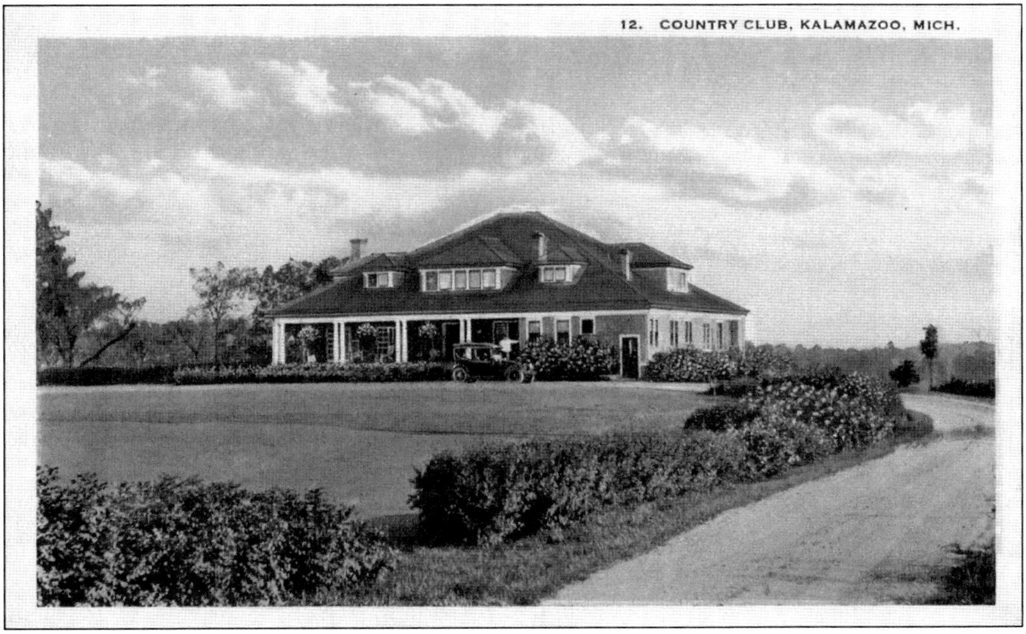


The Kalamazoo Country Club was organized in 1906. In 1909, the club purchased the White farm, located along White's Road and Oakland Drive. Construction began on a nine-hole golf course and tennis courts. Architect A.E. Rose drafted plans for a clubhouse. When the new building was announced, the *Kalamazoo Gazette* made note of the beautiful landscaping, some of which is evident here. The club, which today features an 18-hole course, has remained a landmark in Kalamazoo for over a century. However, the original clubhouse was replaced in 1988.

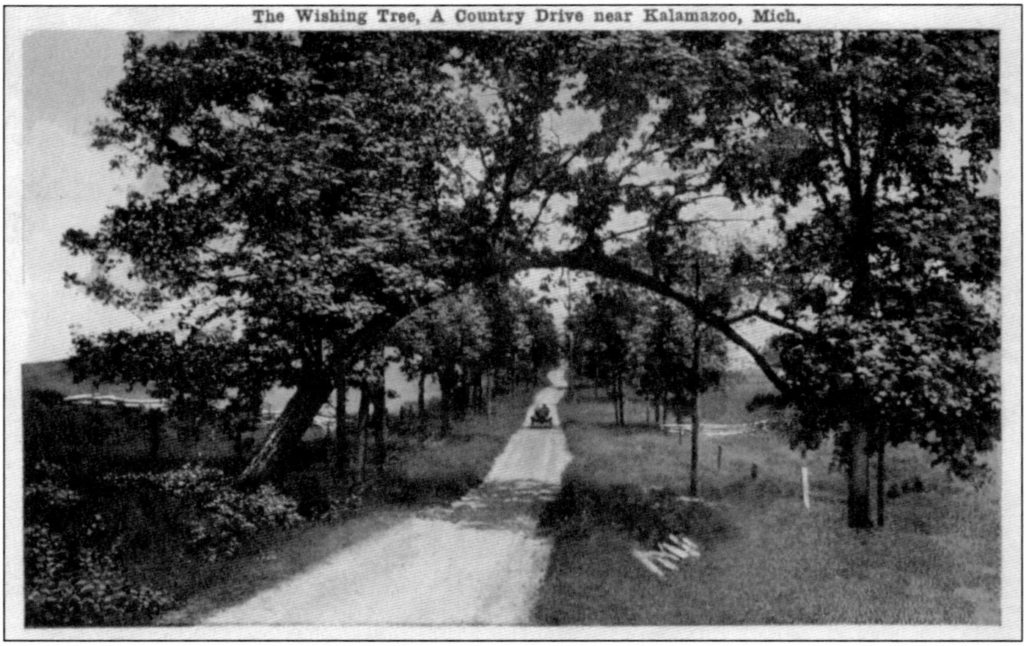


Automobiles did more than just provide people with transportation. They served as a means for entertainment, as well. Suddenly, the countryside became more accessible, and recreational drives and roadside picnics became increasingly popular pastimes.

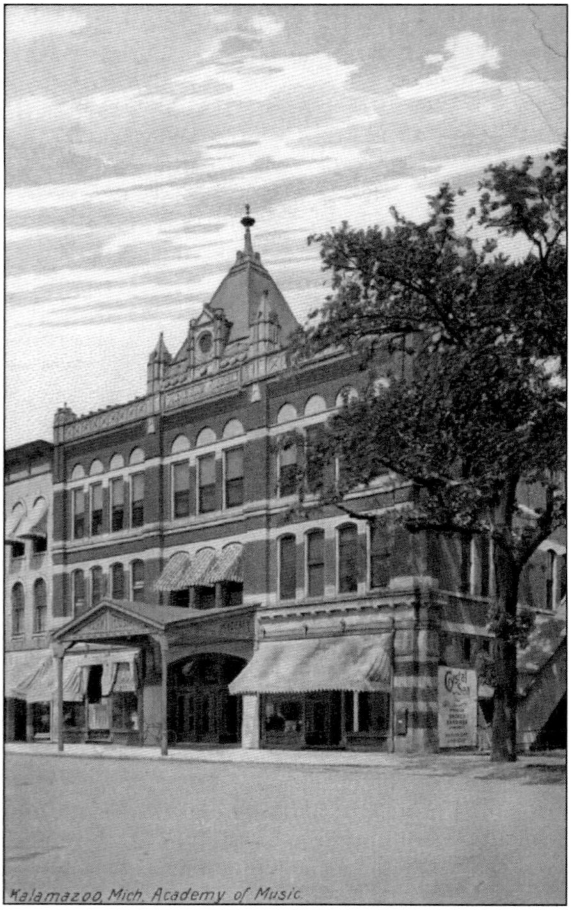


The Academy of Music was Kalamazoo's venerable legitimate stage. It was built in 1882 and designed by noted Chicago architects Dankmar Adler and Louis Sullivan. The theater was converted into a vaudeville house and movie theater named the Regent in 1916. It continued to serve the city's entertainment needs in this capacity for another 14 years. In 1930, the auditorium was destroyed in a fire. The rest of the structure came down in 1967.

This real-photo postcard shows several individuals standing in front of the Bijou Dream on South Burdick Street. The 680-seat theater opened in 1906 as the Bijou, a vaudeville venue. In 1908, it was renamed the Bijou Dream and began offering patrons the newest craze, motion pictures. However, its existence as a movie house was short-lived. The theater closed in 1910, by which time several larger and more impressive movie houses had opened nearby.

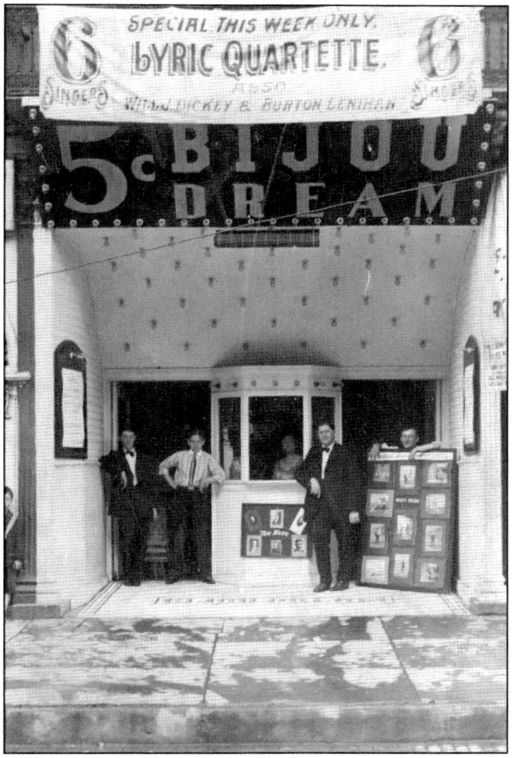


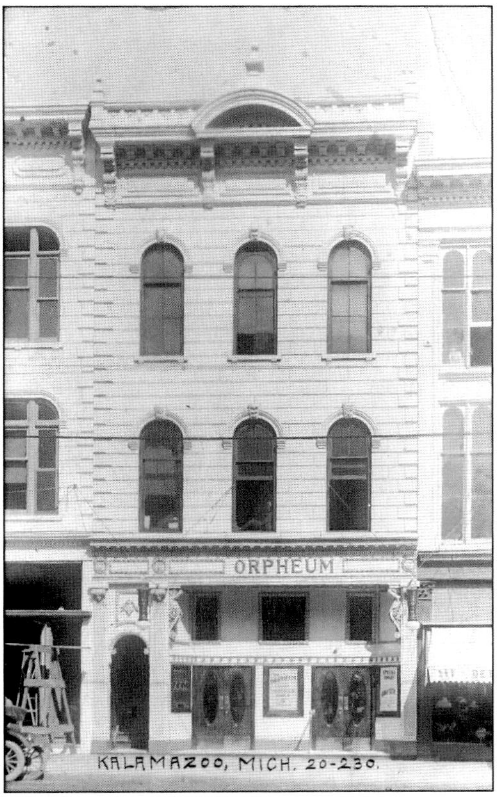


The Orpheum Theater operated out of this 19th-century Italianate business block located on East Main Street starting in 1911. It was relatively modest, offering seating for only 300. Despite that, it endured until 1949. The theater is long gone, but the building still stands and was recently restored. (From the Collection of the Kalamazoo Valley Museum.)

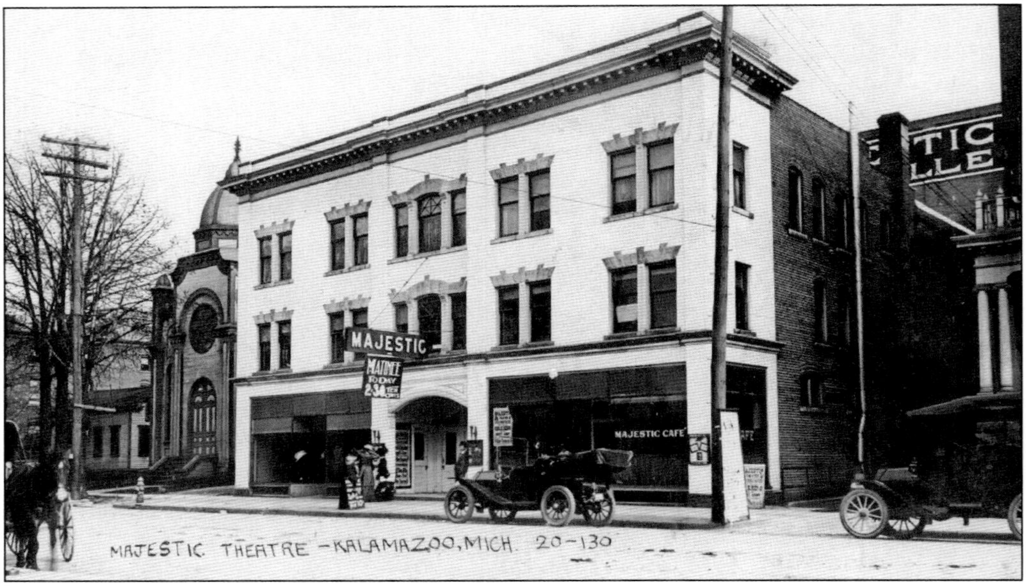


When it opened on South Street in 1907, the 1,100-seat Majestic Theatre was far larger than the city's earlier vaudeville and movie houses. It was one of the first theaters built by Walter S. Butterfield, who would eventually own most of the movie theaters in the region. The Majestic was renamed the Capitol Theater in 1926. It declined after the advent of television and was replaced with a parking garage in 1976.

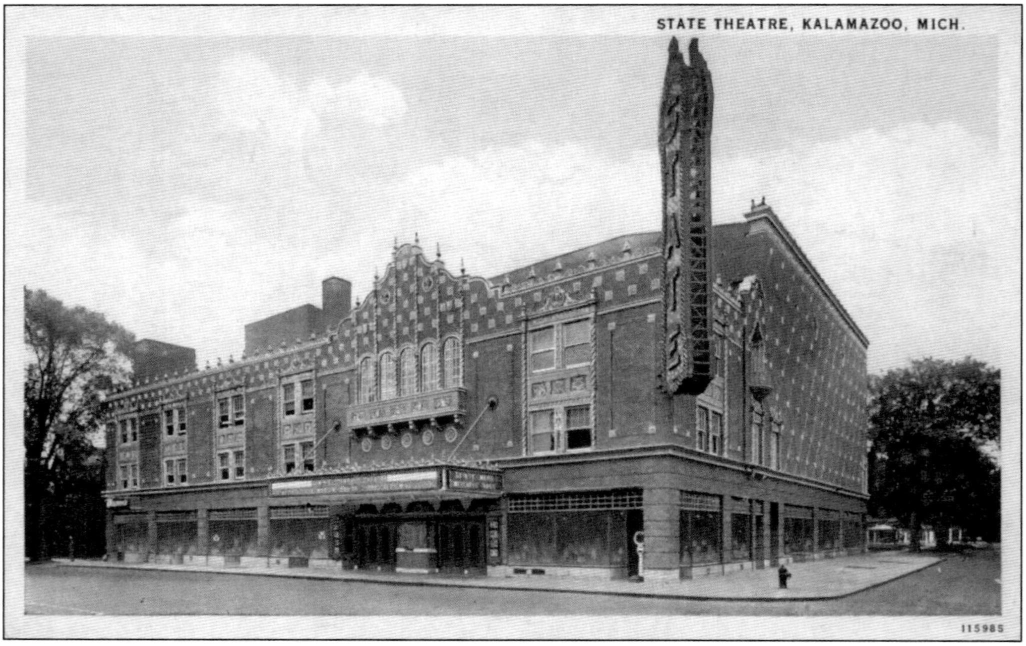


The 1,300-seat State Theatre was built in 1927 as the jewel of W.S. Butterfield's theater chain. It is a true movie palace. Butterfield brought in noted theater architect John Eberson, who created one of his trademark "Eberson atmospherics." Theaters in this style featured an interior designed to resemble an exotic courtyard. The ceiling was treated like a night sky, complete with drifting clouds and sparkling stars. The State served as a first-run movie house until 1982. It survives today as a performance venue.

# Six

# INDUSTRY

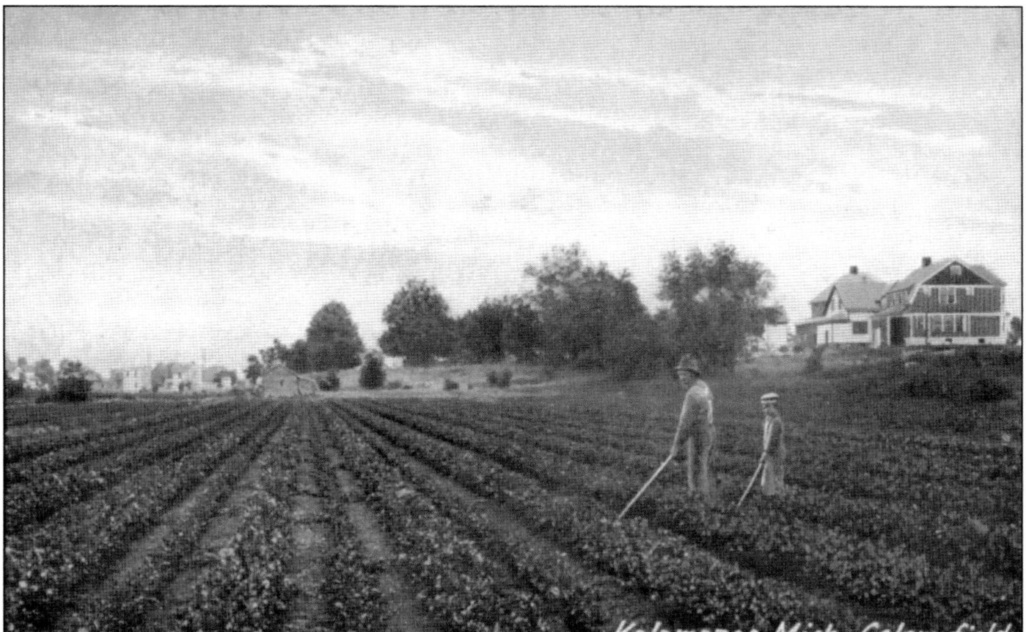


Kalamazoo has had a number of nicknames over the years. At the dawn of the 20th century, most people would have recognized it as the "celery city." The soil and climate in the surrounding countryside proved ideal for the cultivation of white and yellow celery that was sweeter than that grown elsewhere. In terms of economic impact and jobs, celery farms outdid every other industry by a significant margin. But, the industry disappeared after the 1930s, the victim of extensive labor requirements and a lowered water table. Many of the former celery growers switched to cultivating flowers.

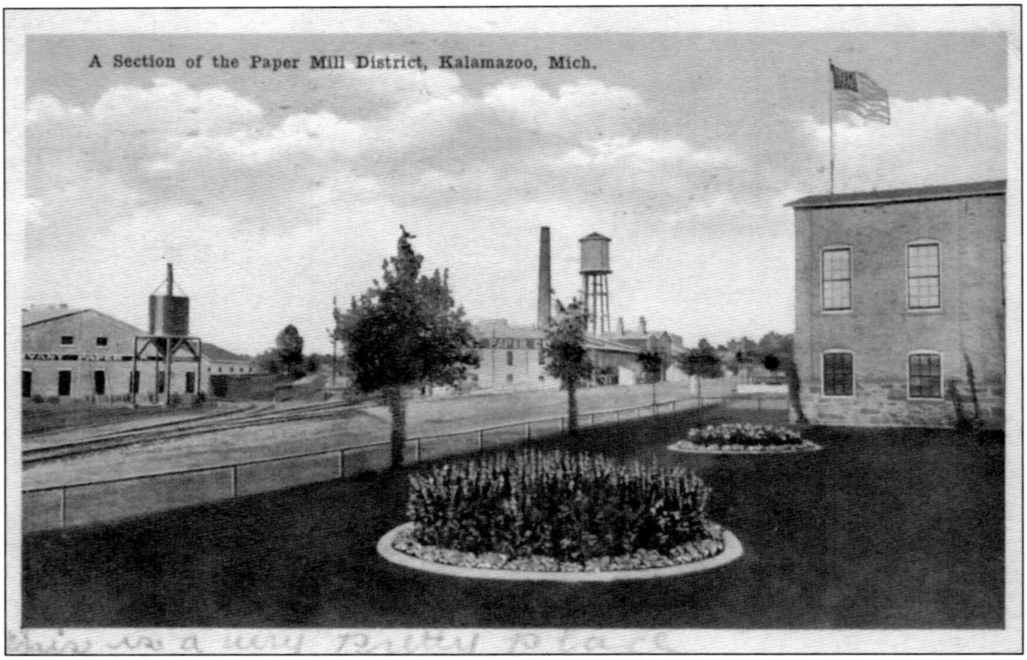


Paper was the dominant industry in Kalamazoo for much of the 20th century. Between the 1890s and World War I, over a dozen paper mills opened in Kalamazoo and surrounding communities. They were drawn to the region's rivers, access to raw materials, and the growing numbers of experienced papermaking executives and workers. The industry became so important that Kalamazoo increasingly became known as the "paper city." The sender of this postcard was obviously impressed with one of the early mills.

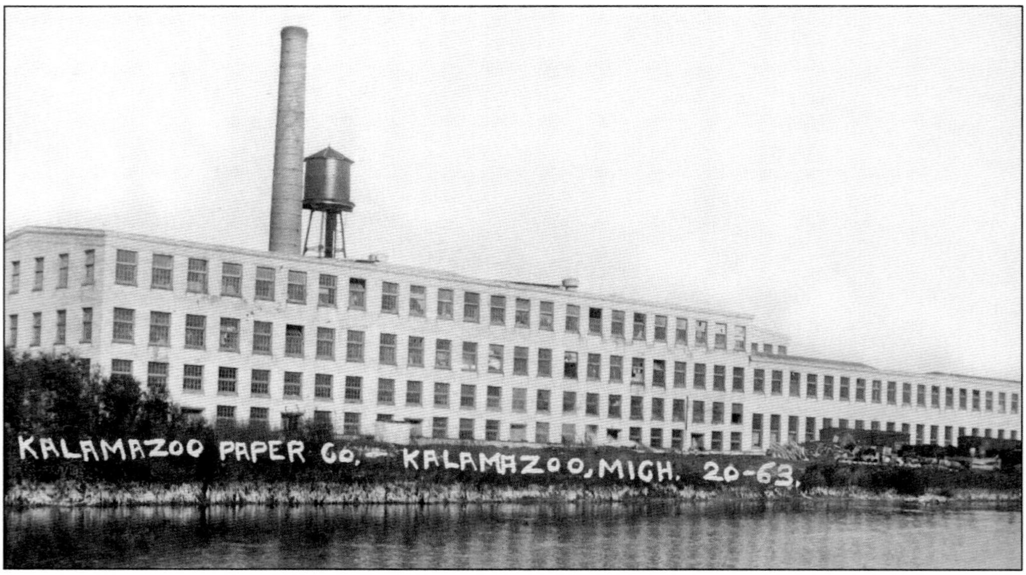


Although the paper industry really did not take off until the 1890s, the first mill to be established, the Kalamazoo Paper Company, opened in 1867. For its first several decades, it was a relatively small operation, barely a blip on Kalamazoo's business landscape. But, it helped to establish the foundation for future papermaking in the region and provided a training ground for the second generation of Kalamazoo papermakers, many of who would start their own companies.

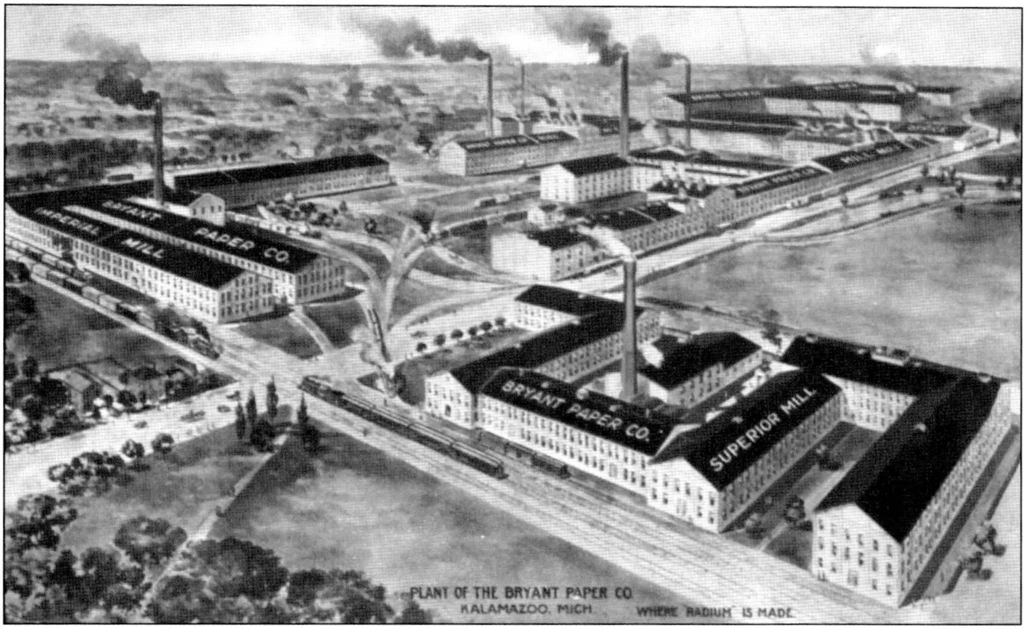


This somewhat exaggerated artist's rendering of the Bryant Paper Company provides an overview of the type of architecture paper manufacturers employed. Noah Bryant established the mill in 1896 on the city's south side. It quickly became one of the most successful in the city and one of the largest manufacturers of book-grade paper in the world. In later years, the firm was known as the Allied Paper Company. It closed in the late 1990s and was razed in 2004.

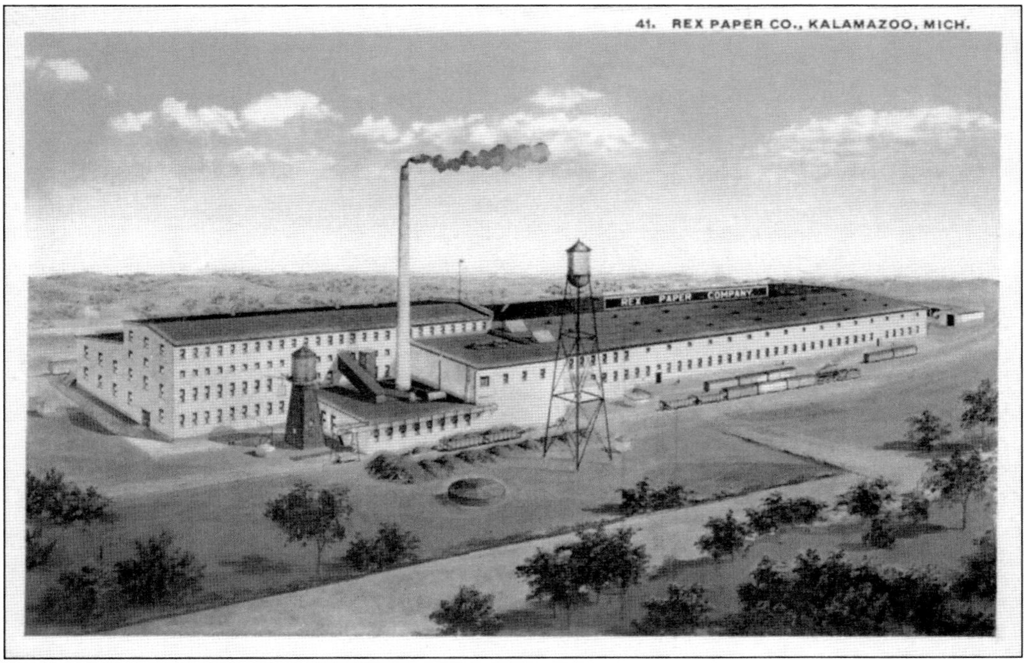


The Rex Paper Company was an example of a smaller mill that operated in the shadow of one of the city's larger operations. Rex opened in 1918 and was a late entry to the city's collection of mills. Located just south of the Kalamazoo Paper Company's vast complex, it produced specialty papers.

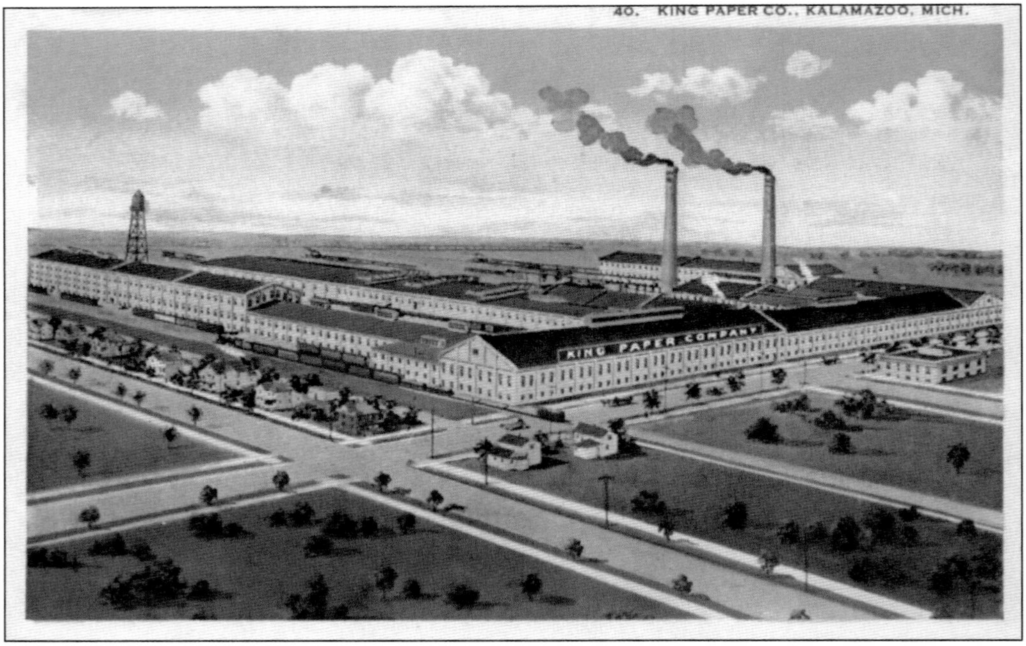


The King Paper Company, located on the city's east side, was a midsized manufacturer that, along with the Monarch and Bardeen Paper Companies, formed the Allied Paper Company in 1921. Allied grew into a powerful corporation, eventually including the former Bryant mills in 1956. The King complex was closed in the early 1970s and demolished shortly afterward.

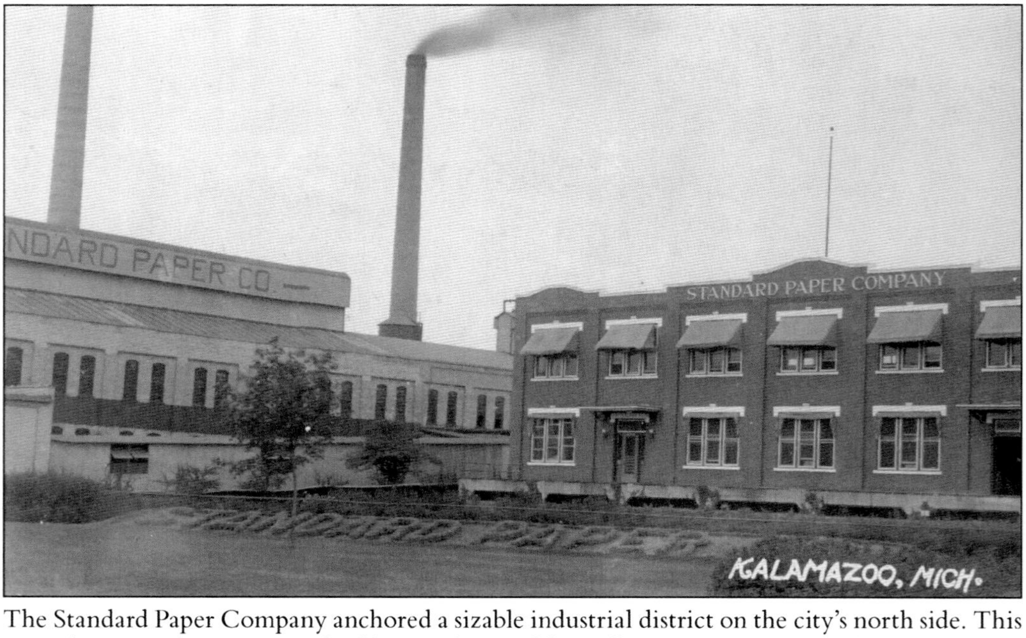


The Standard Paper Company anchored a sizable industrial district on the city's north side. This view shows its administration building and part of the mill on Paterson Street. The complex was later occupied by the Sutherland Paper Company. It remains active today as Graphic Packaging; both of these structures remain in use.

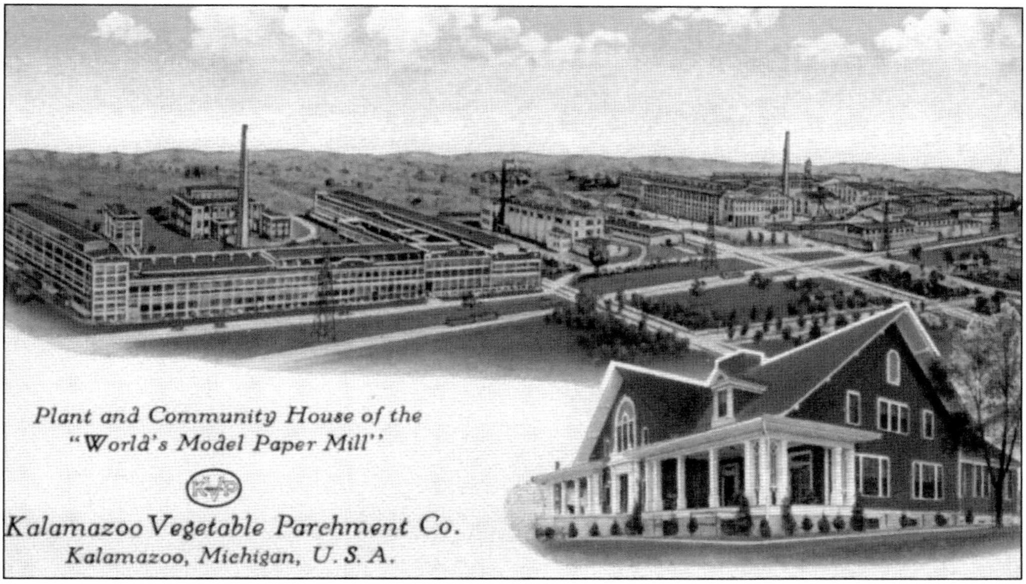


The Kalamazoo Vegetable Parchment Company opened in 1917 in an abandoned sugar-beet mill just north of the city limits. Under the leadership of its founder, Jacob Kindleberger, the producer of waxed papers became one of the largest mills in the region, operating the vast complex seen here. In the process, Kindleberger founded the town of Parchment to house his workforce. This postcard also shows Parchment's Community House, a social hall that was the center of the new town.

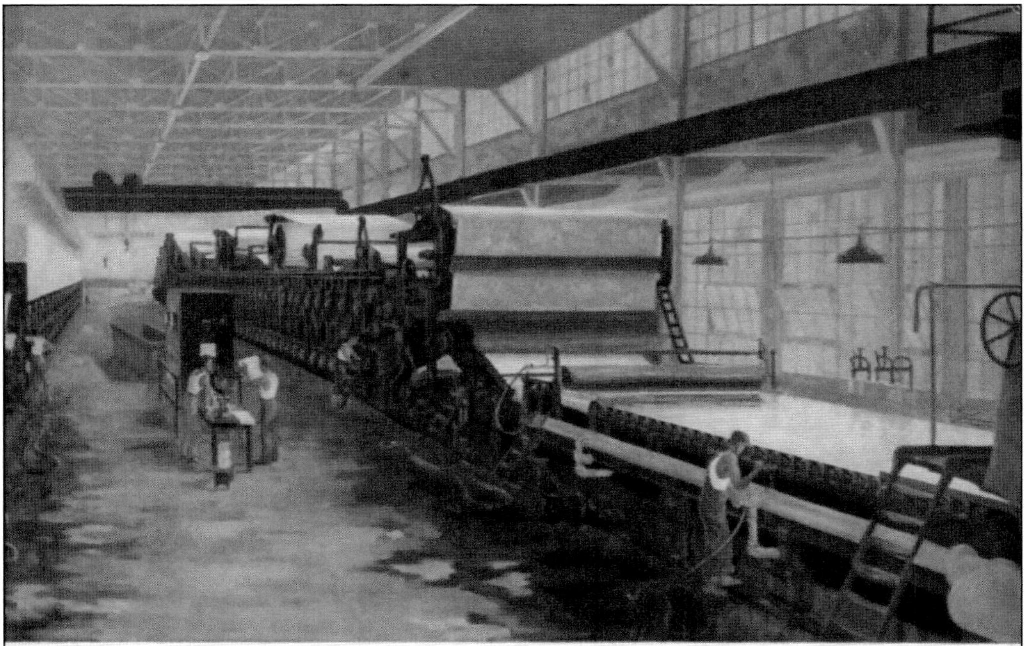


This artist's sketch depicts the interior of a paper mill. The paper machines were only one part of the process, although they were probably the most intriguing to someone unfamiliar with paper manufacturing. These machines could be over a city block long and two stories in height. They transformed pulp into rolled paper.

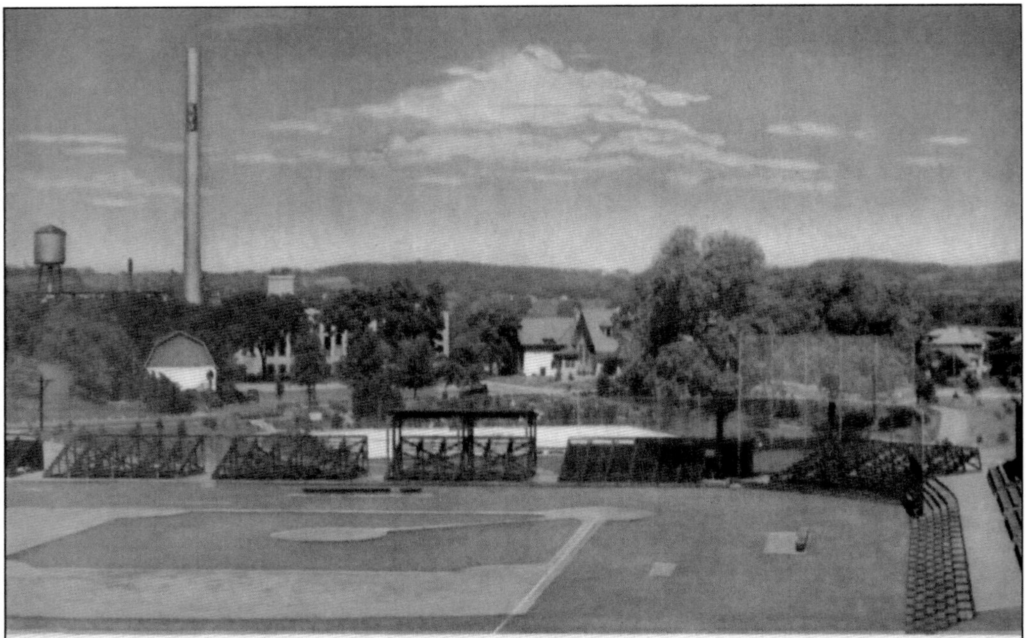

Base Ball Diamond, Kindleberger Park, Parchment, Michigan

Jacob Kindleberger took a paternalistic view toward his workforce. He set strict rules for how the town of Parchment was to appear, and even made visual inspections of workers' homes. He also provided plenty of recreation. Parchment's Kindleberger Park is testament to this. The park included sporting grounds for the use of the community as well as for the company's official teams, which competed in a citywide industrial league.

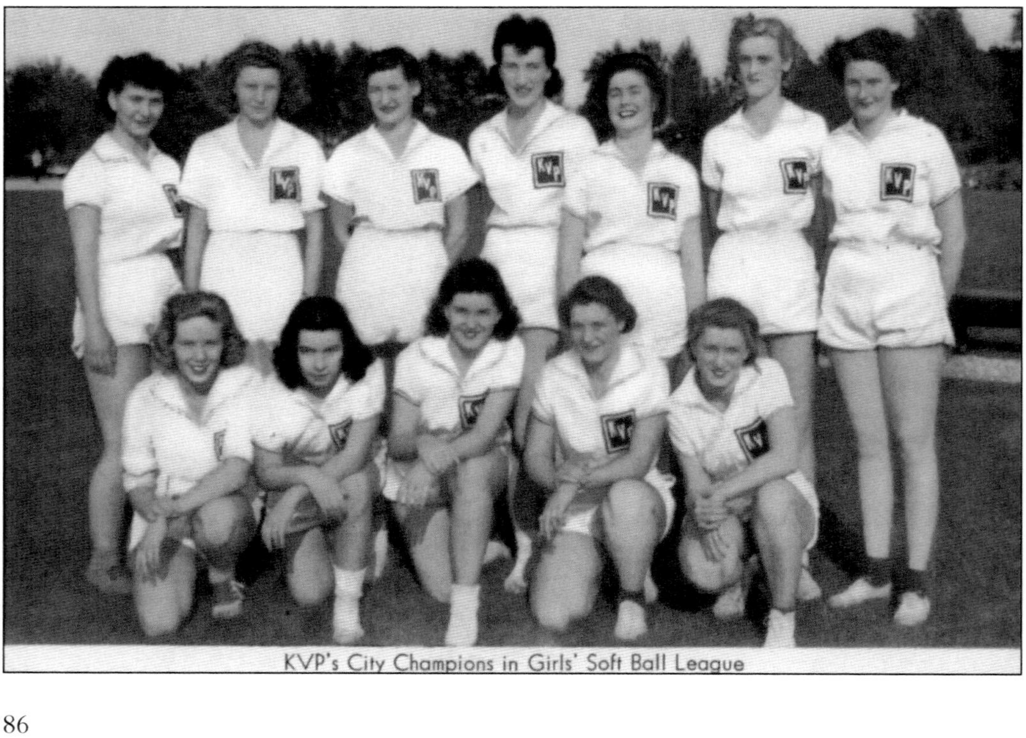

KVP's City Champions in Girls' Soft Ball League

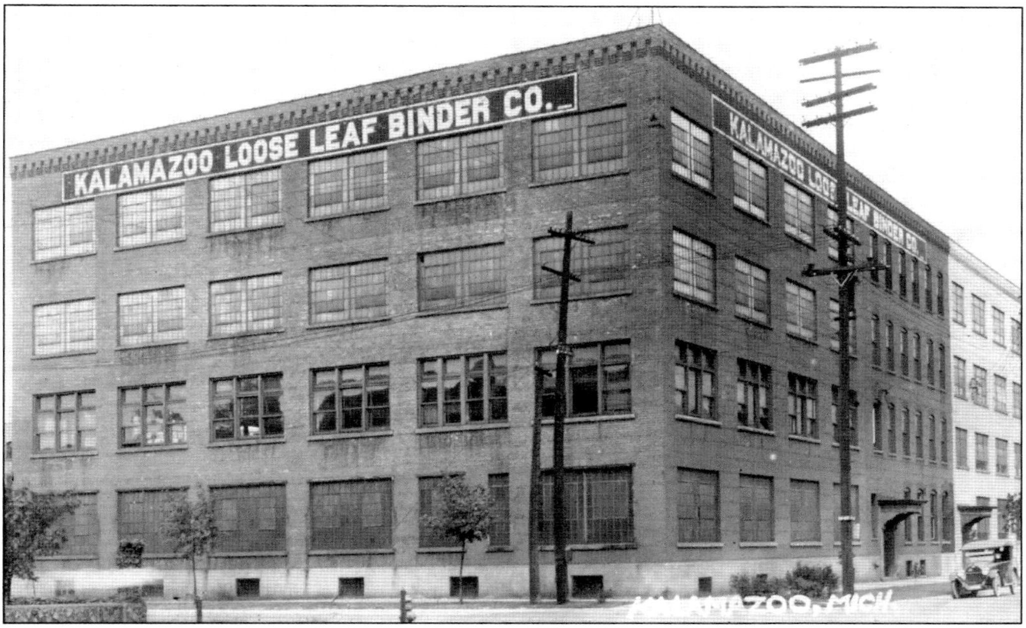


The Kalamazoo Loose Leaf Binder Company is an example of one of the many spin-off businesses generated by the presence of paper mills. It produced paper-based office products such as binders, ledgers, catalog covers, and ruled sheets. This building opened in 1906 and was steadily expanded until it filled the block. It has housed several different businesses over the years, including the Saniwax Company, which produced waxed food wrappers. It is known today as the Park Trades Center.

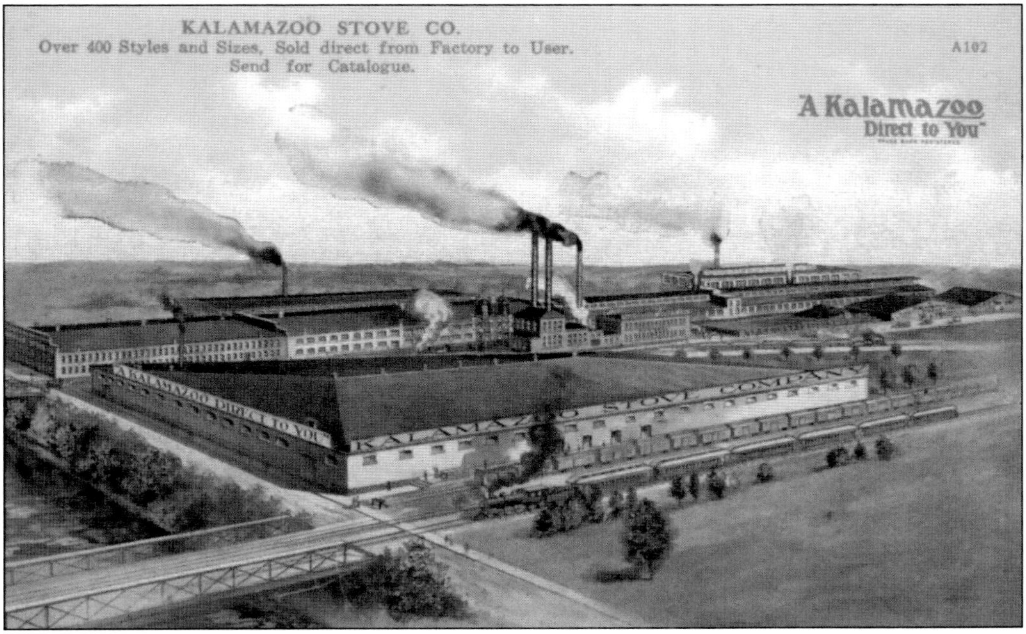


Kalamazoo made more than paper. In 1902, the Kalamazoo Stove Company opened. It experienced great success by selling its product direct to the consumer via mail order. The firm's slogan, "A Kalamazoo Direct To You," is visible on this postcard of the factory. At its peak, it produced over 100,000 stoves a year. It declined after World War II and folded in 1952.

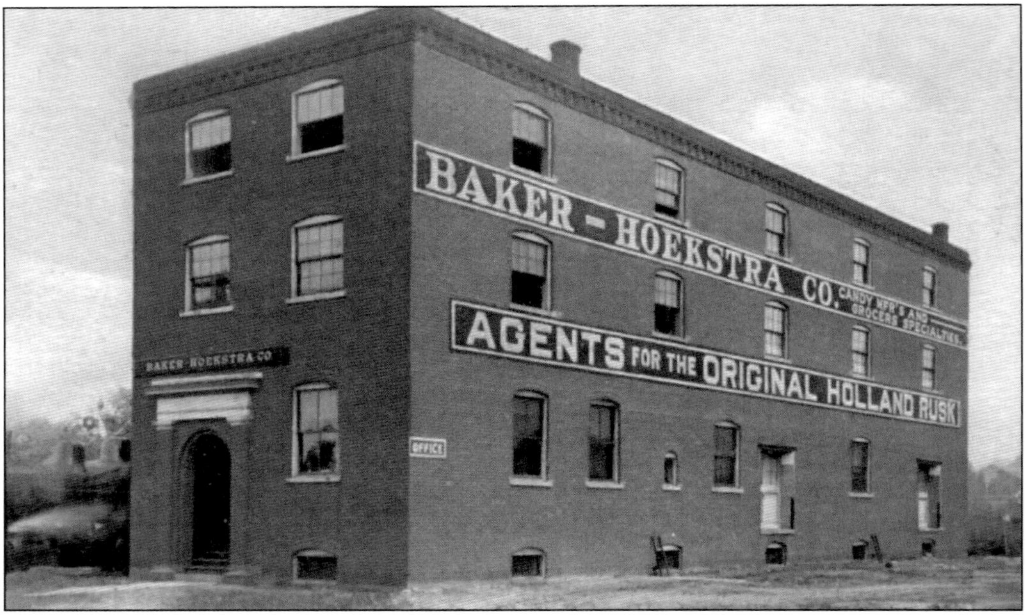


Kalamazoo has been home to a number of candy manufacturers over the years. Shown here is the Baker-Hoekstra Company. It was later bought out by another candy firm, the Hanselman Candy Company, which continued to operate here until the mid-1920s. Although the smells of candy being manufactured are long gone, the building has found new life as a popular bar and performance space, the Olde Dog Tavern.

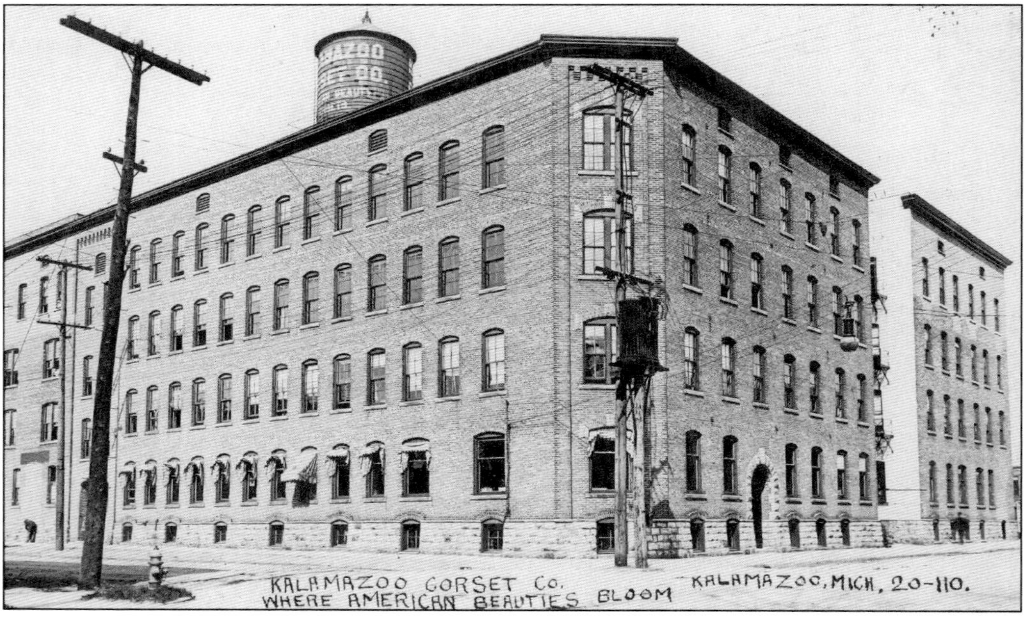


In the late 19th and early 20th centuries, shape-forming corsets were a must in women's fashion. The Kalamazoo Corset Company flourished upon moving to the city in 1891. The firm employed a largely female workforce that famously went on strike in 1912, demanding better working conditions. In later years, the firm was known as the Grace Corset Company. It went into a long decline after corsets went out of style in the 1920s. The firm managed to survive until 1957, when it closed.

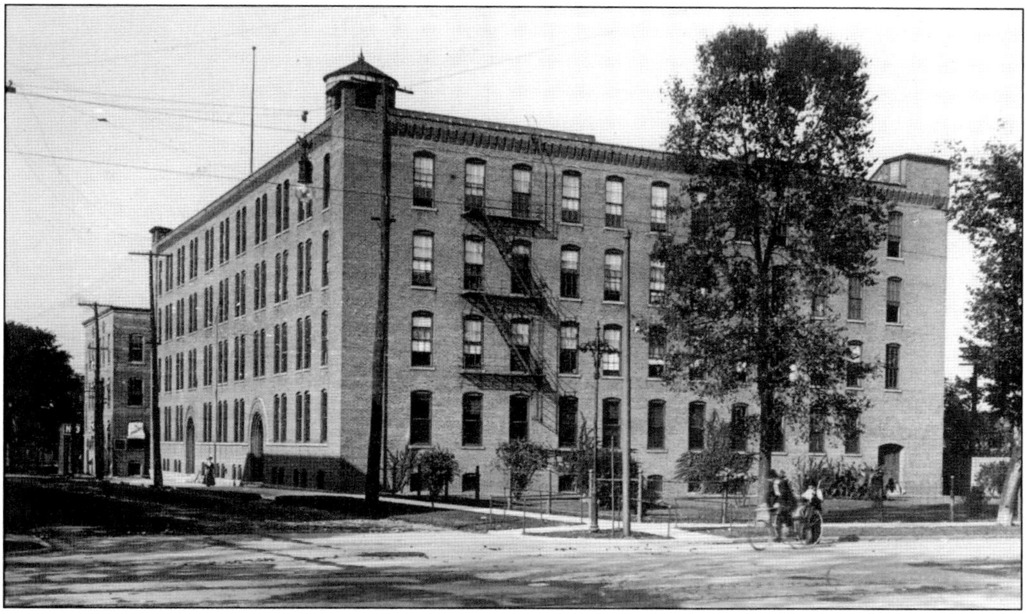

The Henderson-Ames Company manufactured uniforms and regalia used by bands, military groups, and fraternal societies. The firm, established in Kalamazoo by Frank Henderson in 1860, became known as Henderson-Ames in 1893. It built this massive factory at Main and Park Streets in 1900 and would call it home until the firm ceased local operations in 1940. The factory site is now a parking lot. (Courtesy of the Kalamazoo Public Library's Local History Room.)

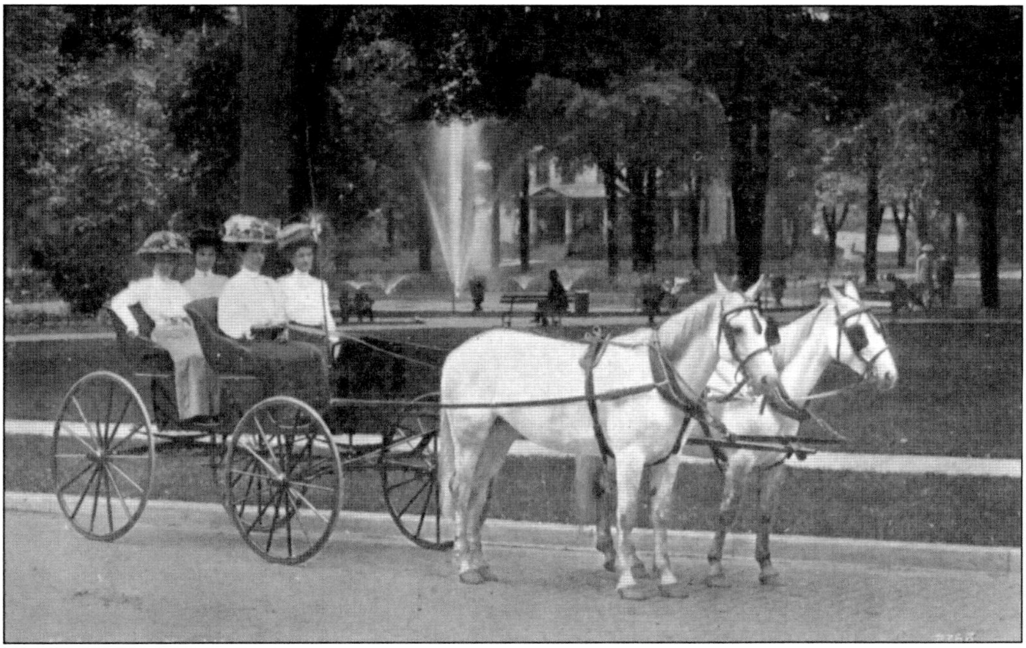

By 1887, there were 18 firms producing buggies, carriages, and sleighs, and the Kalamazoo-produced vehicles could be found nationwide. One was Linford C. Lull's Lull Carriage Company. Although incorporated in 1902, the firm had its roots in earlier business ventures dating to 1883. As with most horse-drawn-vehicle businesses, Lull did well until the popularity of automobiles made its product obsolete. The business was sold to the Dort Motor Car Company in 1920.

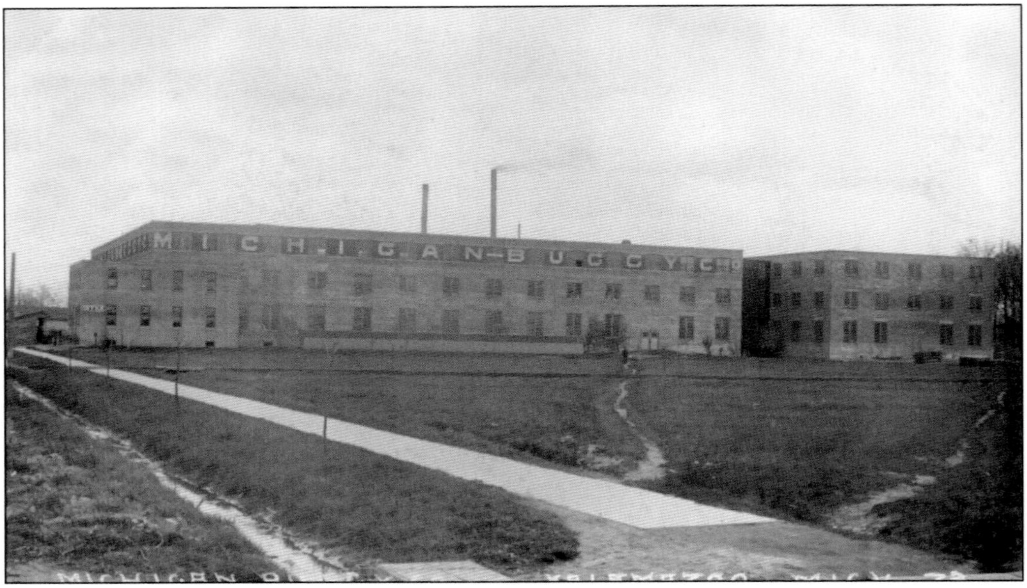


The Michigan Buggy Company was another of Kalamazoo's successful horse-drawn-vehicle manufacturers. However, the firm led a stormy life. It was founded in 1883 as a family business by father and son George and Frank Lay, as well as Moses Henry Lane, who was related to the Lays through marriage. It quickly rose to the top of the industry. The impressive stone castle that Lane built for himself at the corner of Main and West Streets (below) demonstrates the firm's success. Yet, the business was nearly ruined when the factory burned to the ground in 1896. Michigan Buggy managed to rebuild, only to see its factory burn to the ground a second time, in 1902. A third factory (above) was built of fireproof, reinforced concrete on the city's east side. In 1909, the company entered the automobile business with the "Mighty Michigan 40," a 40-horsepower car that was unwisely sold for less than it cost to produce. The venture ruined the business, which collapsed amid bankruptcy and scandal in 1913.

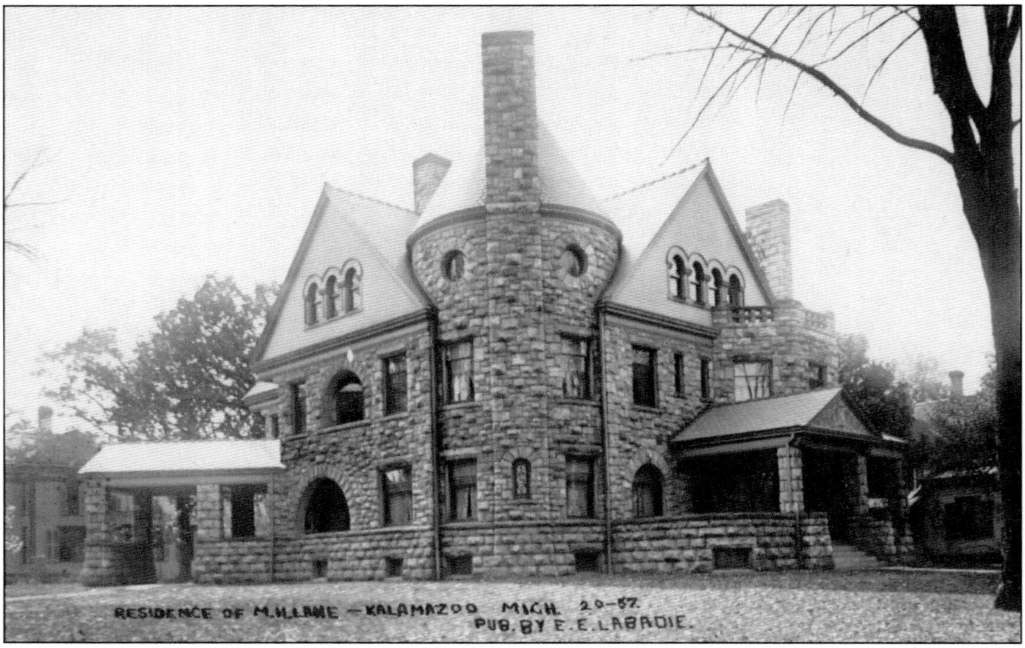

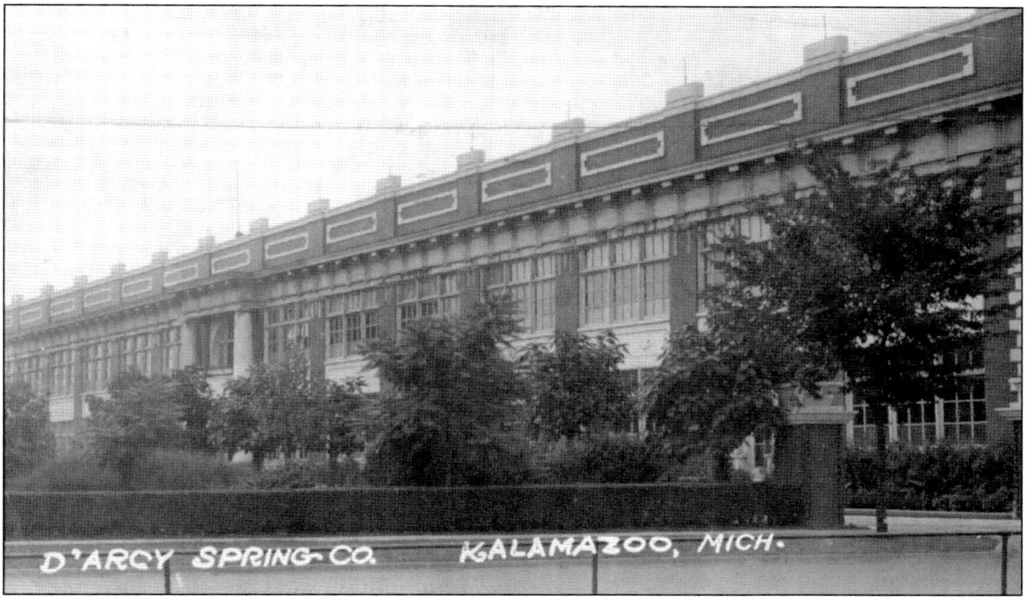


The D'Arcy Spring Company, located on the northwest corner of Paterson and Pitcher Streets on the city's north side, produced parts for various automobile manufacturers, including local firm Roamer. Business boomed during the 1920s, and Frank D'Arcy had this handsome factory built. However, the firm's tenure in the structure would be short-lived. The company moved after 1931; in 1936, the Sutherland Paper Company occupied this building. It was demolished in 1996.

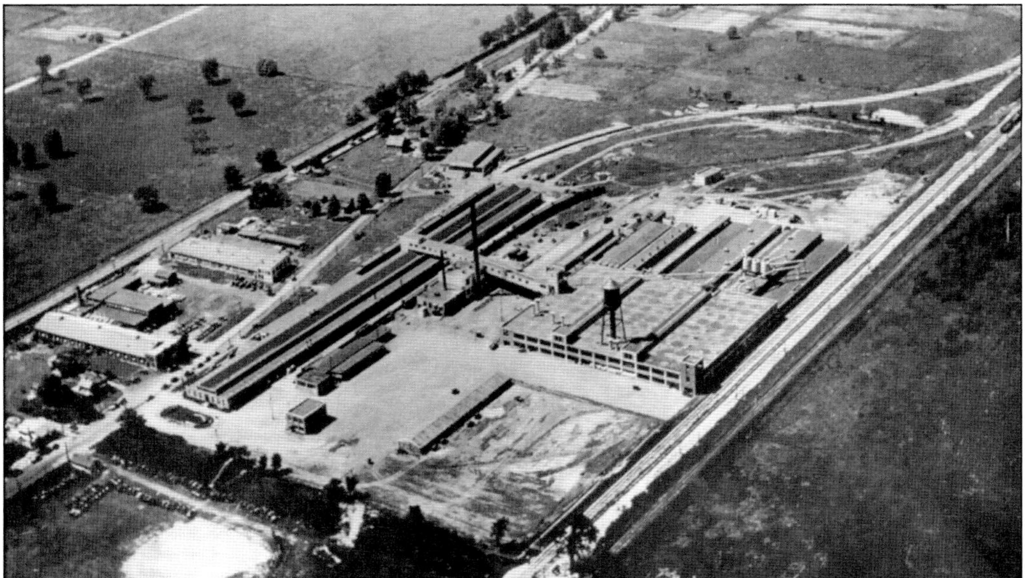

Several automobile manufacturers were established in Kalamazoo during the first years of the 20th century. However, only one survived the Great Depression. That firm, the Checker Motors Corporation, made Kalamazoo proud. Morris Markin moved his young company from Chicago to Kalamazoo in 1923. The taxicabs he built here quickly earned a reputation for reliability and endurance. In 1956, this plant on Pitcher Street began production of the firm's most iconic design, and the Checker would remain largely unchanged until taxi production ended in 1982. Checker Motors continued to produce automobile parts until it closed in 2009.

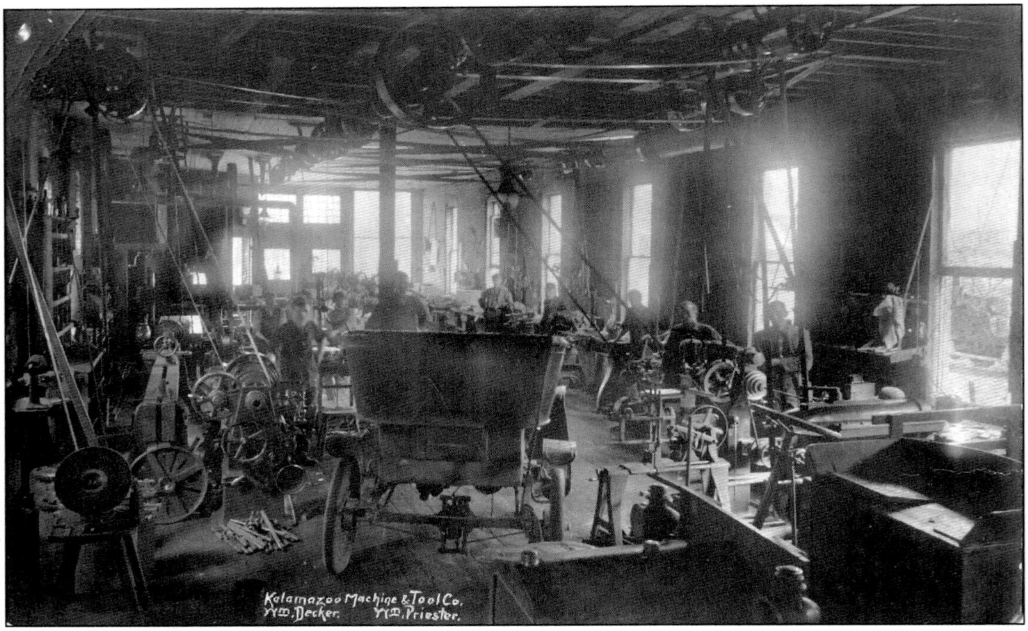


This photograph shows the cluttered interior of the Kalamazoo Machine & Tool Company. The machine shop opened shortly after the turn of the 20th century and operated through the 1930s, first at a location on North Rose Street, and later a block over on Church Street. The firm offered Kalamazoo's early motorists one of the few options then available for automobile repair. (From the Collection of the Kalamazoo Valley Museum.)

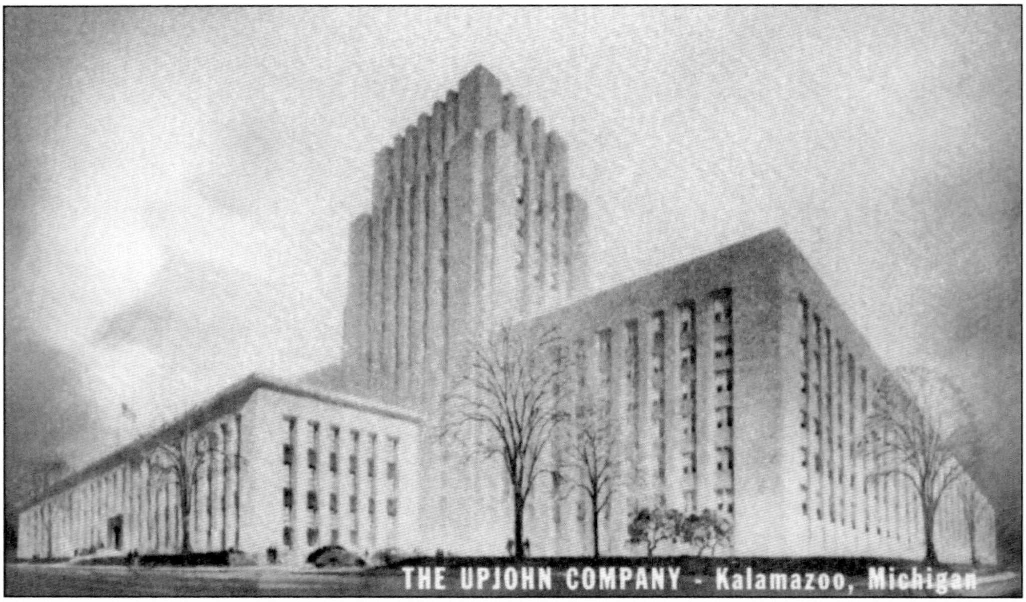


William E. Upjohn developed the "friable pill" in 1885; before long, his Upjohn Company was on its way to becoming not only one of Kalamazoo's most important businesses, but one of the most important pharmaceutical firms in the nation. This streamlined rendering shows the company's new headquarters and plant, built in 1935. Upjohn has since been absorbed into pharmaceutical giant Pfizer. The skyscraper fell in 2005, but the headquarters remains a downtown landmark.

# Seven

# HEALTH

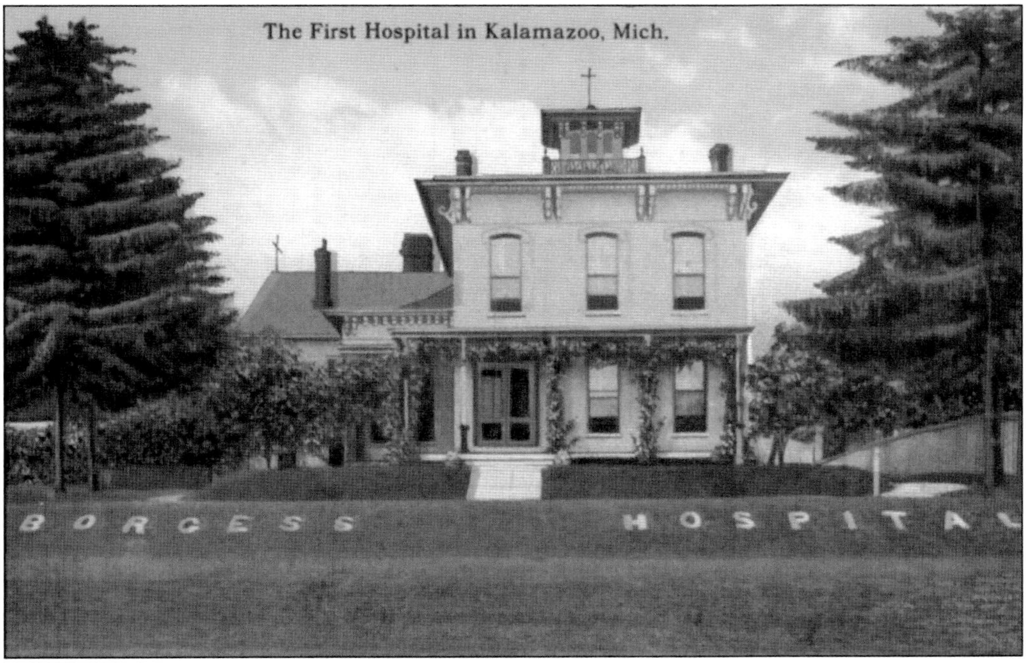


In 1889, eleven nuns from the Sisters of St. Joseph arrived in Kalamazoo to open Borgess Hospital in this 1853 home on Portage Street. The old home, along with an addition built onto its rear, provided a 20-bed facility that was Kalamazoo's first hospital. It was a relatively modest affair by today's standards, but it served as a foundation upon which 20th-century medicine would grow in the city. (Courtesy of the Kalamazoo Public Library's Local History Room.)

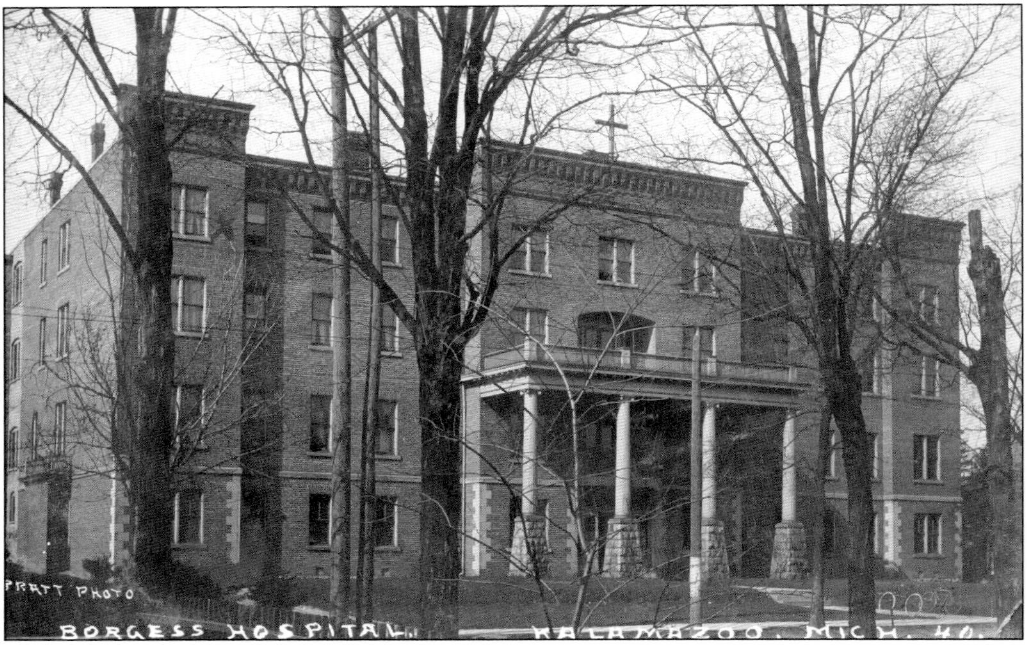


Borgess continually expanded in order to keep up with the needs of a growing city. By the early 20th century, new additions completely obscured the original house and provided space for 100 beds. This photo postcard shows the hospital on Portage Street at its greatest size. In 1917, a substantial new building was erected on Gull Road. The Portage Street buildings continued to be used until 1929, when all of the hospital's operations were concentrated on the Gull Road site.

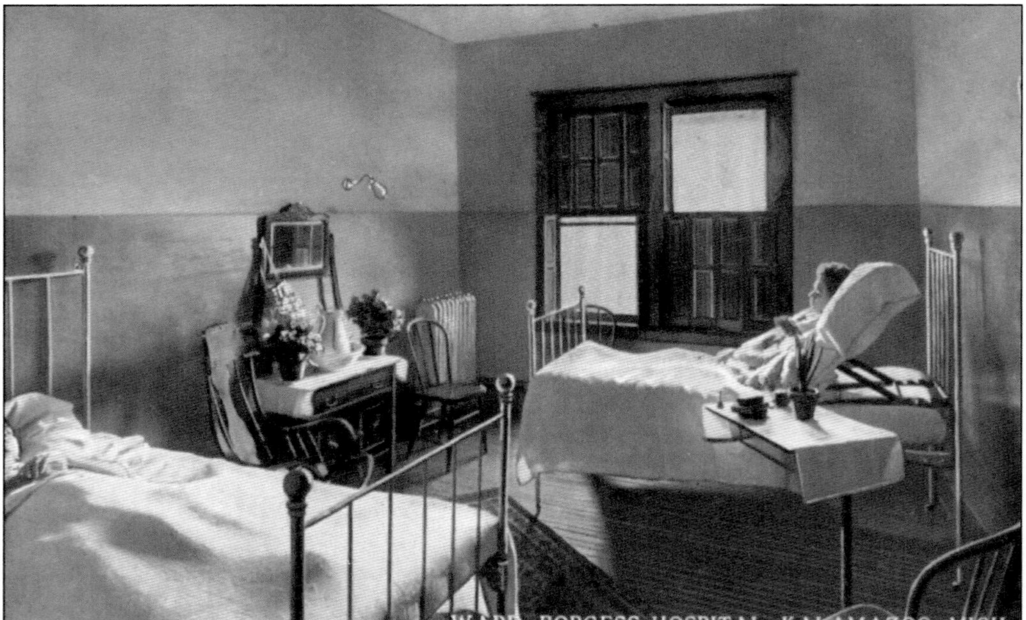


This postcard shows the type of accommodations one could expect at Borgess's Portage Road hospital. Most rooms were shared, but they were provided with plenty of light and sanitary conditions. (Courtesy of the Kalamazoo Public Library's Local History Room.)

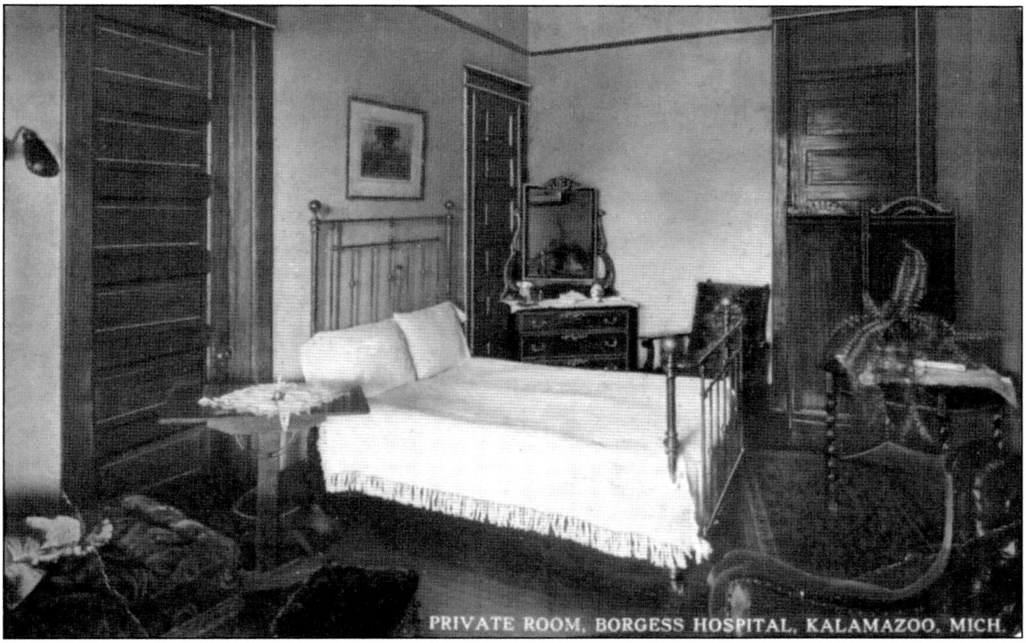


In contrast to the previous image, this postcard shows a less-than-typical private hospital accommodation. The room resembles that of a private home more than a hospital.

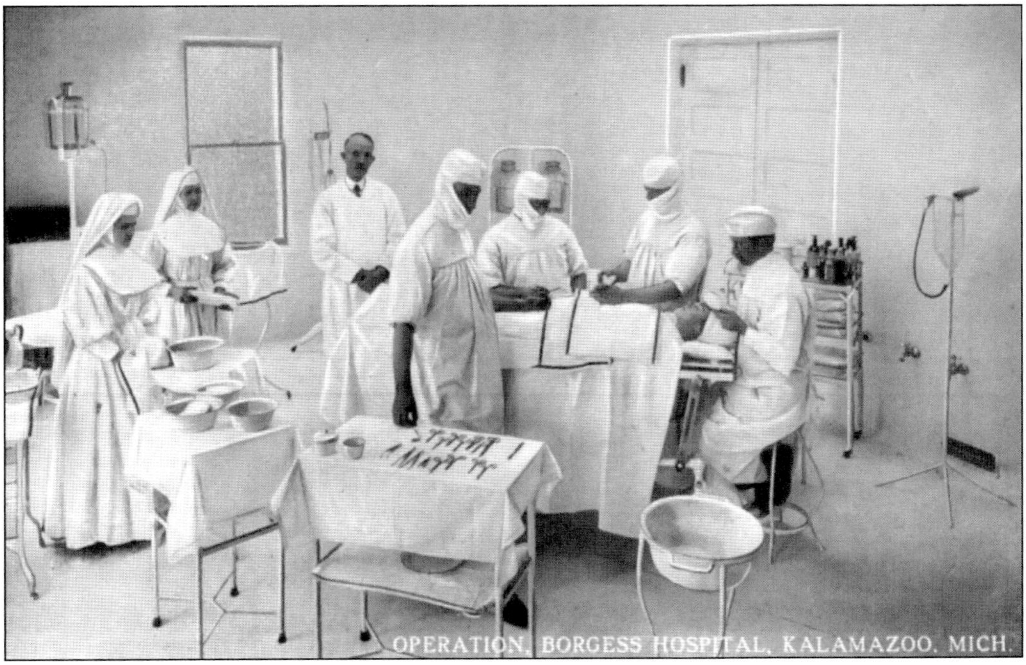


This postcard shows an operating room with a procedure in progress. The operation was likely staged for the benefit of the photographer. The white walls help give a sense of cleanliness. The two nuns on the left are a reminder of the hospital's religious connection. (Courtesy of the Kalamazoo Public Library's Local History Room.)

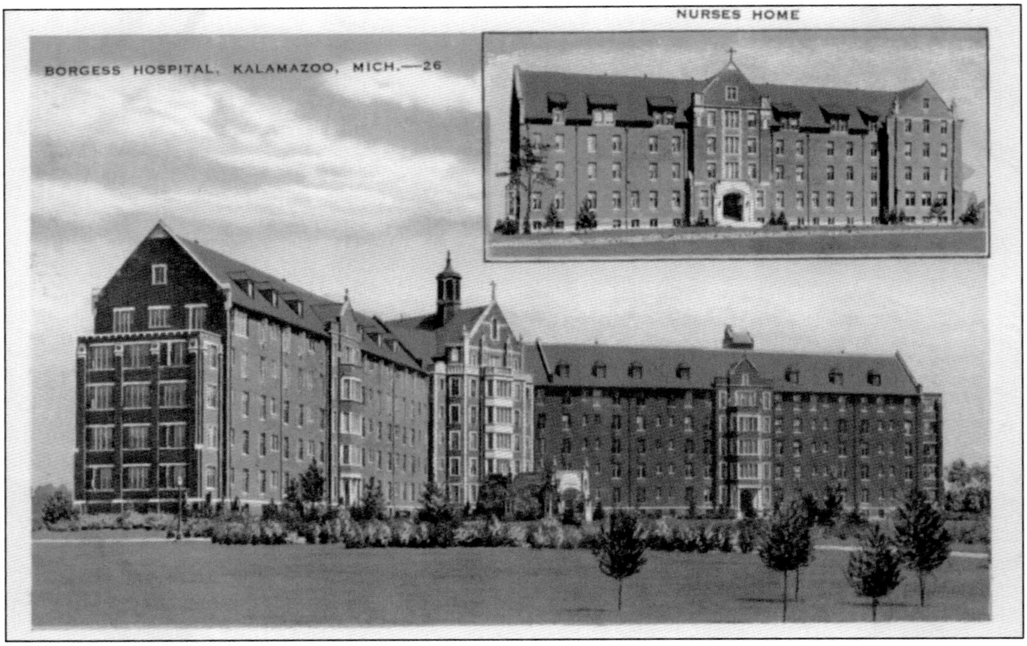


In 1927, Borgess completely revamped and expanded its hospital on Gull Road. The result was this impressive Gothic facility with an adjacent dormitory for nurses. Once this complex was completed, the hospital's original buildings on Portage Street were sold. Borgess continues to operate out of this hospital, although it has been greatly expanded and the nurses' home razed.

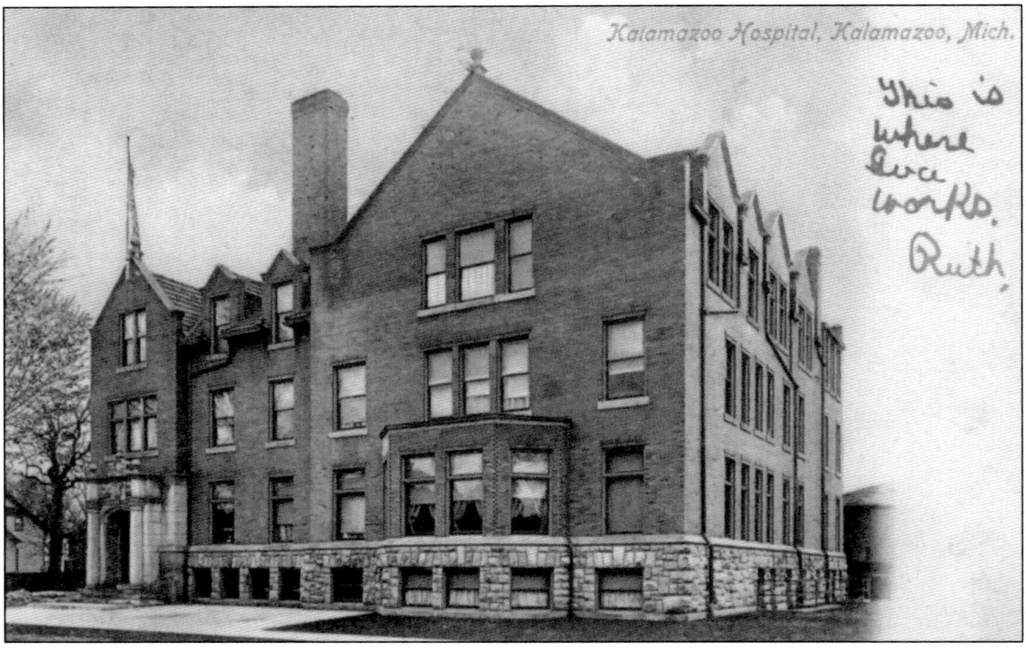


Kalamazoo's other major hospital, Bronson, had its beginnings in 1900. Known as Kalamazoo Hospital at the time, it completed this fine building on John Street in 1905. The hospital changed its name two years later to Bronson, in honor of Kalamazoo's founder, Titus Bronson. Like Borgess, Bronson has continued to grow. Today, it occupies a vast complex on the southeast side of downtown. Sadly, this building was demolished in 2001.

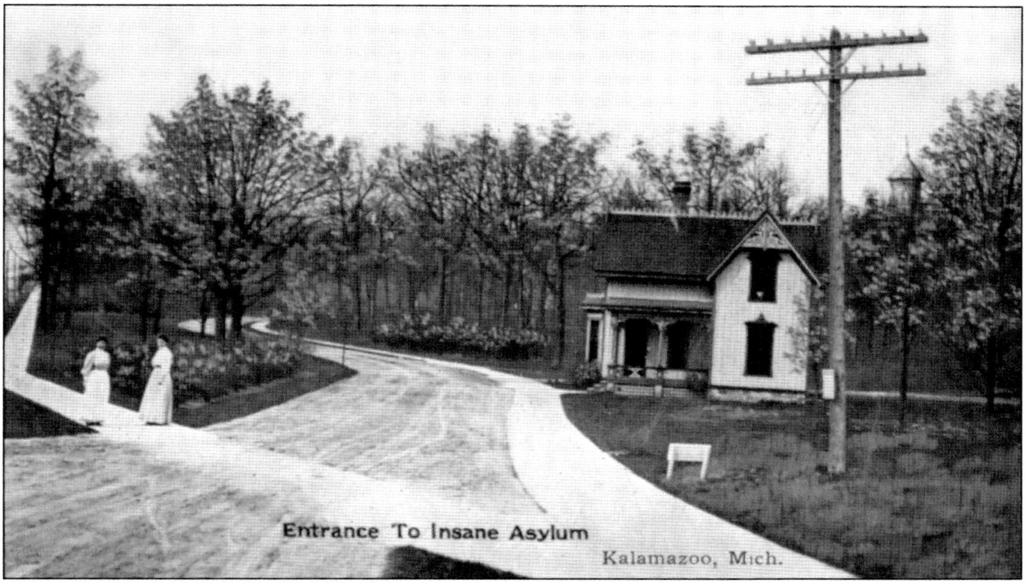


Kalamazoo's first health facility opened decades before either Borgess or Bronson. The Kalamazoo Psychiatric Hospital opened in 1859 after a fierce competition among local communities to secure the new mental-health complex from the state. It was located on Asylum Drive, now named Oakland Drive. This is the complex's gatehouse at the hospital entrance. This home remains a landmark and is one of only two of the hospital's 19th-century structures to survive.

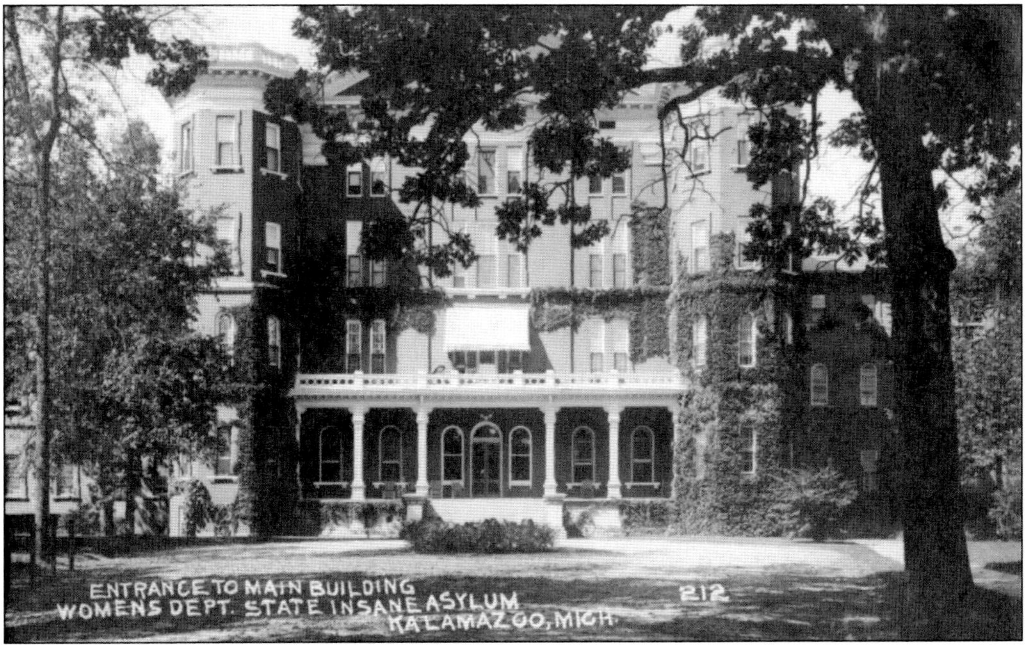


The varied buildings on the hospital's vast grounds reflected changing attitudes toward the proper treatment of mental health. The first structures were known as Kirkbrides, after architect Thomas Story Kirkbride, who advocated their unique design as beneficial to curing the insane. The grand structures included airy private rooms arranged along corridors. The scale of the building was reduced by having the long halls broken up into snake-like wings. This 1916 photograph shows the entrance of the original 1859 Kirkbride, which housed women.

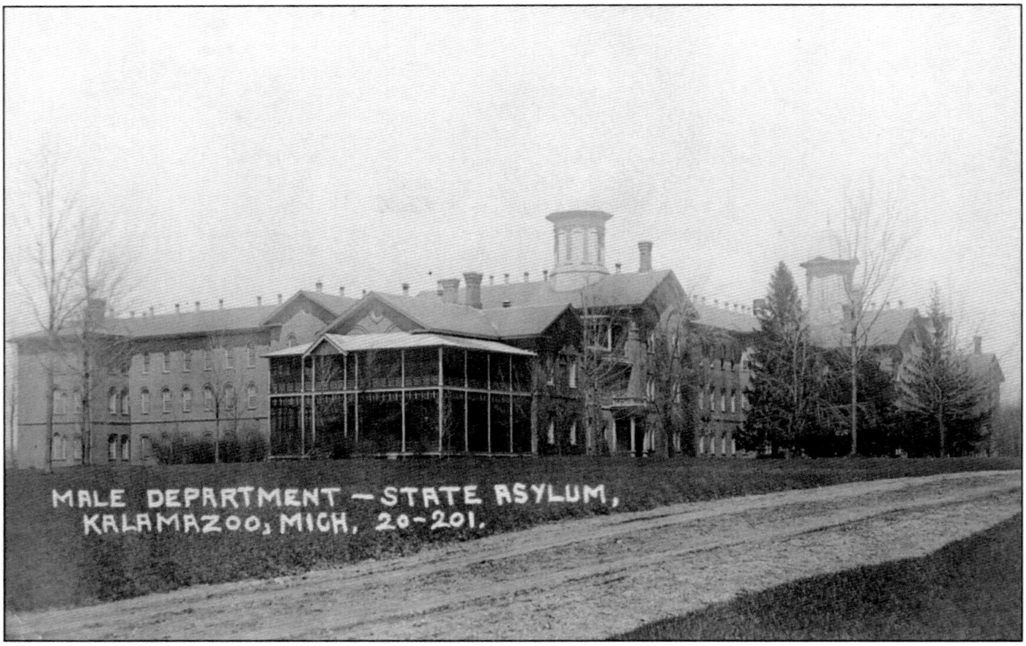


This second Kirkbride was built in 1871 to house men. The structure's vast size is apparent, as are the multiple wings. The screened-in porches at the building's end were provided to allow patients access to fresh air. By the 1960s, treatment of mental health began to shift from hospitalization to medicine and home care. As a result, the hospital began to reduce its facilities. The two Kirkbrides were demolished in 1969 and 1976.

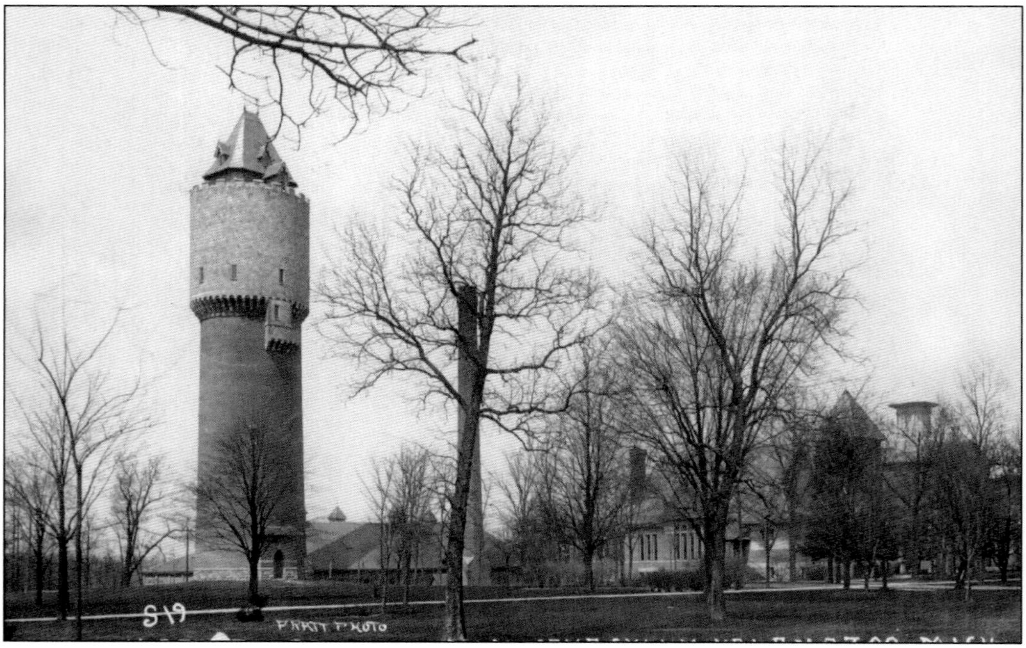

This soaring water tower was built in 1895 in the Gothic style. It was located halfway between the male and female Kirkbrides, in a fairly open area. The hospital's chapel is also partially visible in this postcard. Escaping demolition in the 1970s, the water tower remains a landmark today and can be seen from a great distance throughout the city.

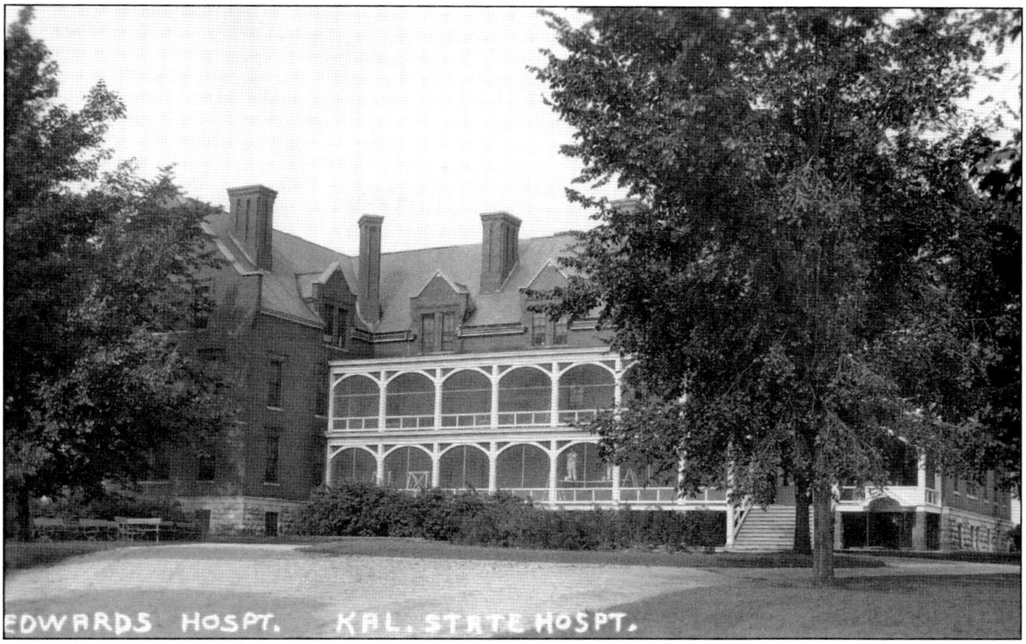


In the late 19th and early 20th centuries, the architecture of mental health facilities shifted, from enormous Kirkbrides to smaller, detached "cottages." These buildings, such as Edwards Hospital (above) and Fletcher Hospital (below), were intended to alleviate overcrowding in the older structures and to provide patients with smaller communities. Note the airy enclosed porches and less-imposing design. Fletcher opened in 1897 and Edwards in 1905.

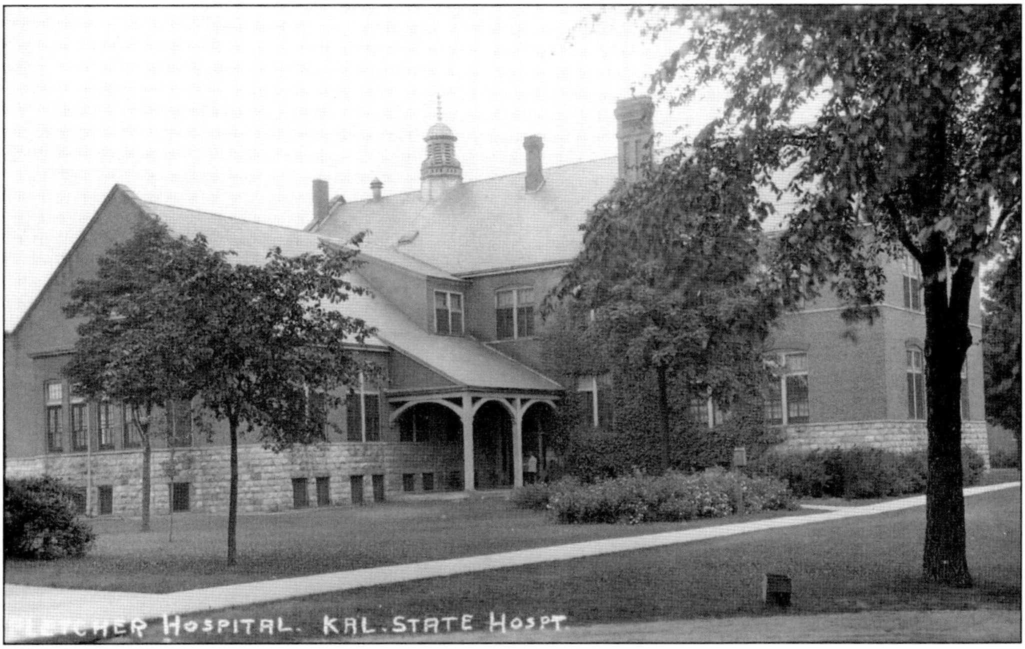

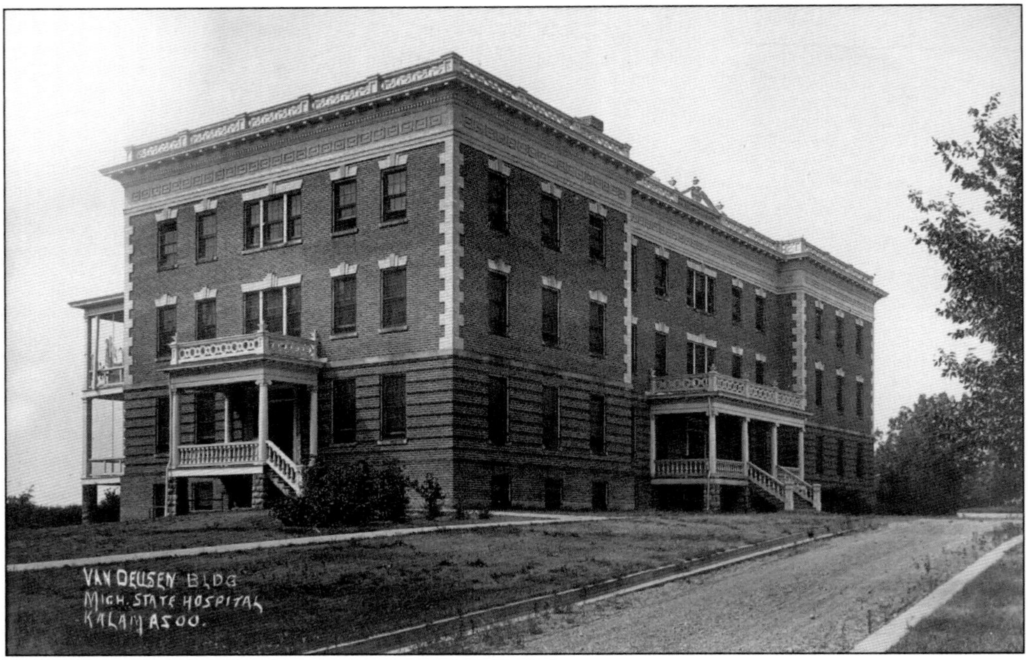


The boxy Van Deusen Hospital opened in 1908. It was built as a receiving hospital for new female patients. The Van Deusen, Edwards, and Fletcher buildings were all demolished in 1988. The property on which they stood has been transferred to Western Michigan University.

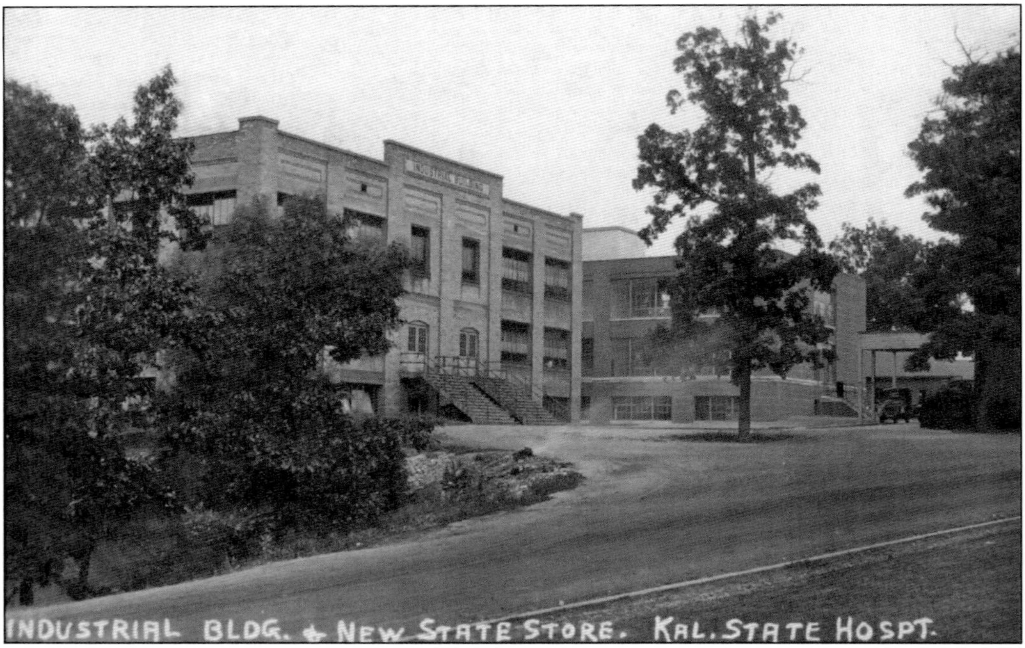


These simple industrial buildings were located behind the main hospital structures. They provided shop space for the hospital's physical needs as well as work opportunities for patients. They survived until 2005, when they were demolished by Western Michigan University.

## *Eight*

# EDUCATION

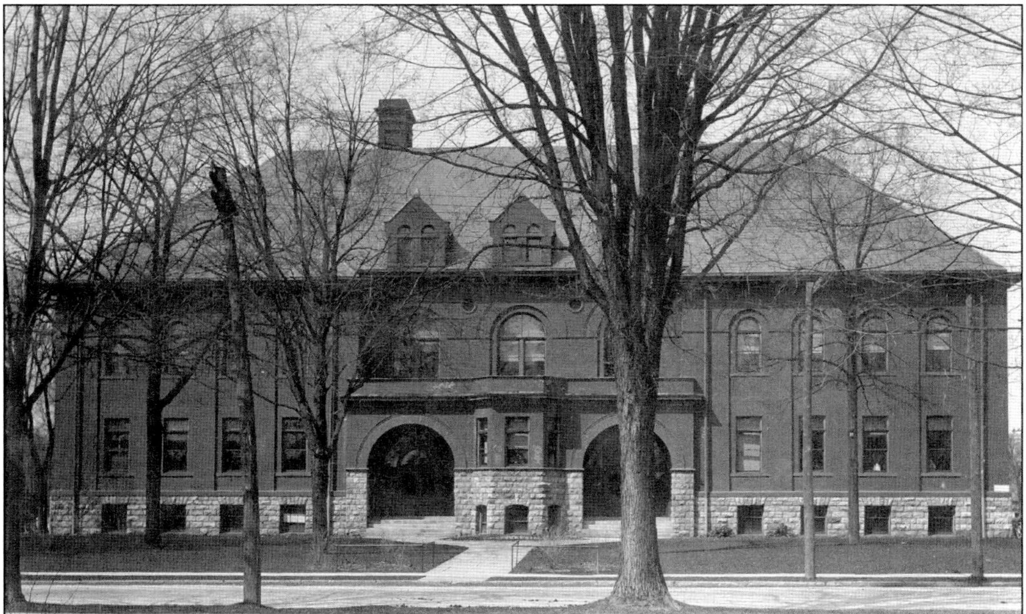


Education has been as important to Kalamazoo as any industry. The public school system has represented the city's commitment to education and has consistently provided the children of Kalamazoo with up-to-date facilities. This postcard shows the city's central high school, which was built in 1898 and was already the third building used for the purpose. The most significant event in this building's history was its hosting of the first classes of the new Western State Normal School in 1903, known today as Western Michigan University. Western's own building would not be completed until the following year.

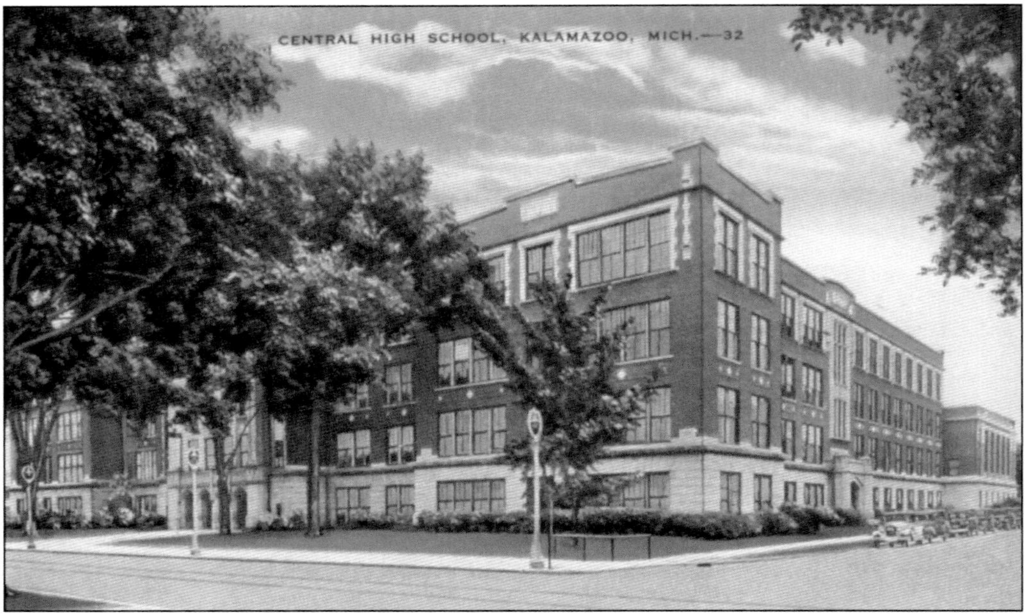


The high school was still fairly new when, in 1912, work began on its successor. The new Central High was built in stages, so that the old building could continue to be used while the new one went up. The new school (pictured) was completed in 1923. The familiar South Westnedge Avenue landmark remained in use until 1972. Although it is no longer a regular high school, it continues to serve the education needs of the community with adult and summer programs. (Courtesy of the Kalamazoo Public Library's Local History Room.)

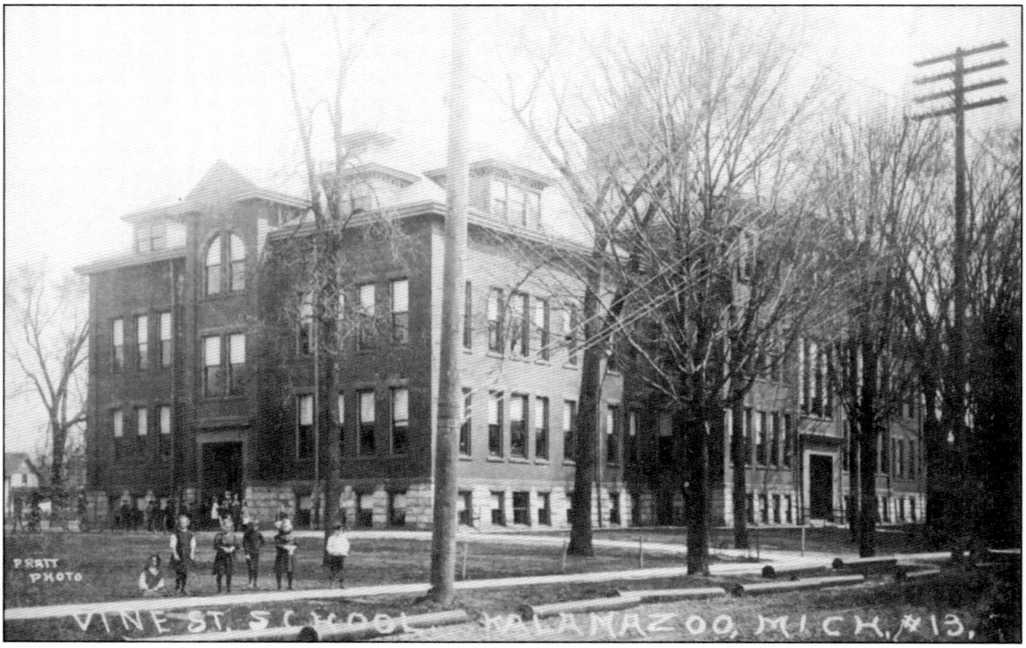


The massive Vine Street School (pictured) was located on the same block as Central High School. The building was erected in 1904 to replace an earlier school that had burned down. An addition was built onto this school in 1924. That addition remains in use as El Sol Elementary, but this building was demolished in 1963.

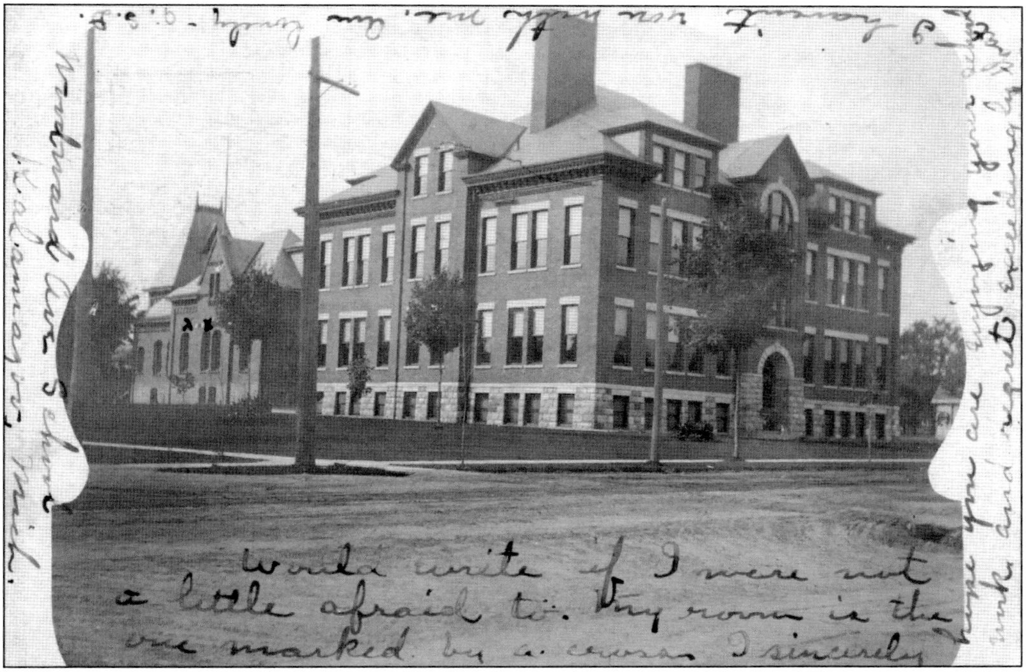


The Woodward Avenue School has served the city's northwest side since 1880. Its development reflects the rapid growth of the city. Careful examination of this postcard shows the original 1880 building on the left and a 1903 addition on the right. The 1903 building lasted until 1962, when the fire marshal declared it a hazard and ordered it demolished.

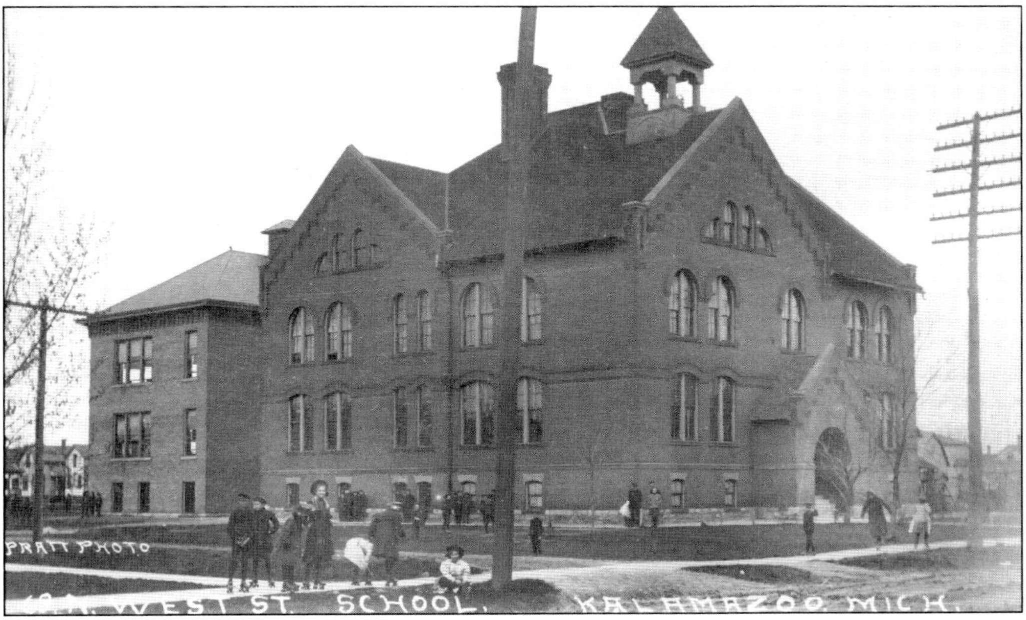


The North West Street School opened on the city's north side in 1888. The graceful 19th-century building is seen here, as is a boxy 1907 addition built at the rear. A second addition in 1926 would obscure the original design. When West Street was renamed Westnedge Avenue in 1919, the school followed suit. Like Woodward, it was declared a fire hazard in 1962; it was demolished in 1965. It was the oldest active building in the public school system at the time of its closure.

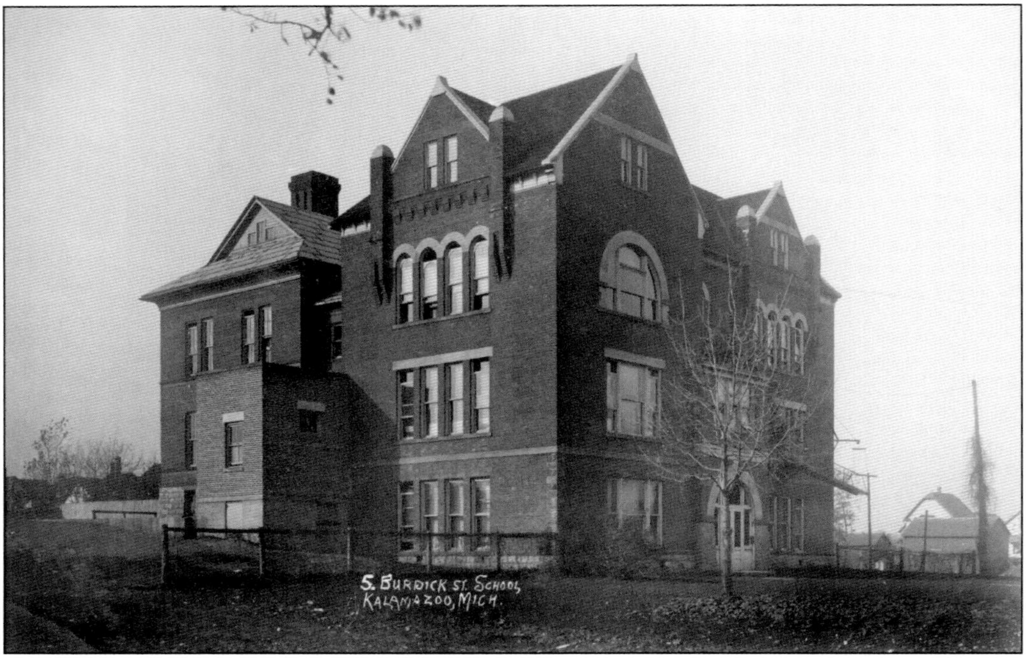


The Burdick Street School served the south side at the corner of Burdick and Emerson Streets. The building pictured here was erected in 1886. A new Burdick Street School opened in 1914, farther south at Cork Street. The old building became part of the new Mckinley School. The old school was torn down in 1940. The rest of Mckinley fell in 1988 to make way for the Salvation Army headquarters.

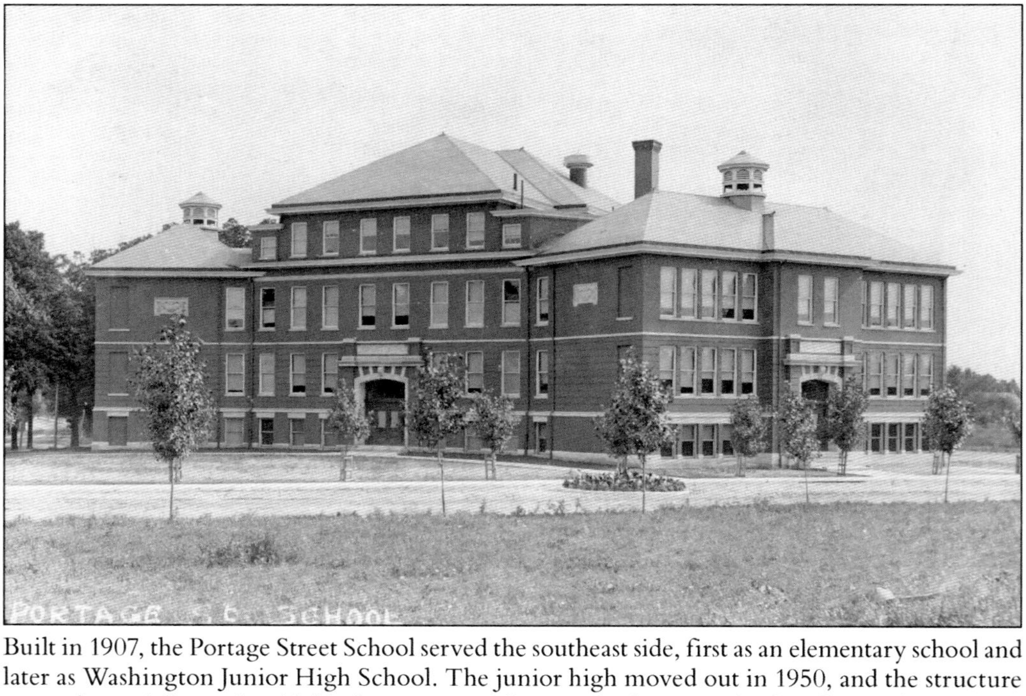


Built in 1907, the Portage Street School served the southeast side, first as an elementary school and later as Washington Junior High School. The junior high moved out in 1950, and the structure was only partially used, with kindergarten and first-grade classes on the first floor. The building was torn down in 1963 on orders of the fire marshal.

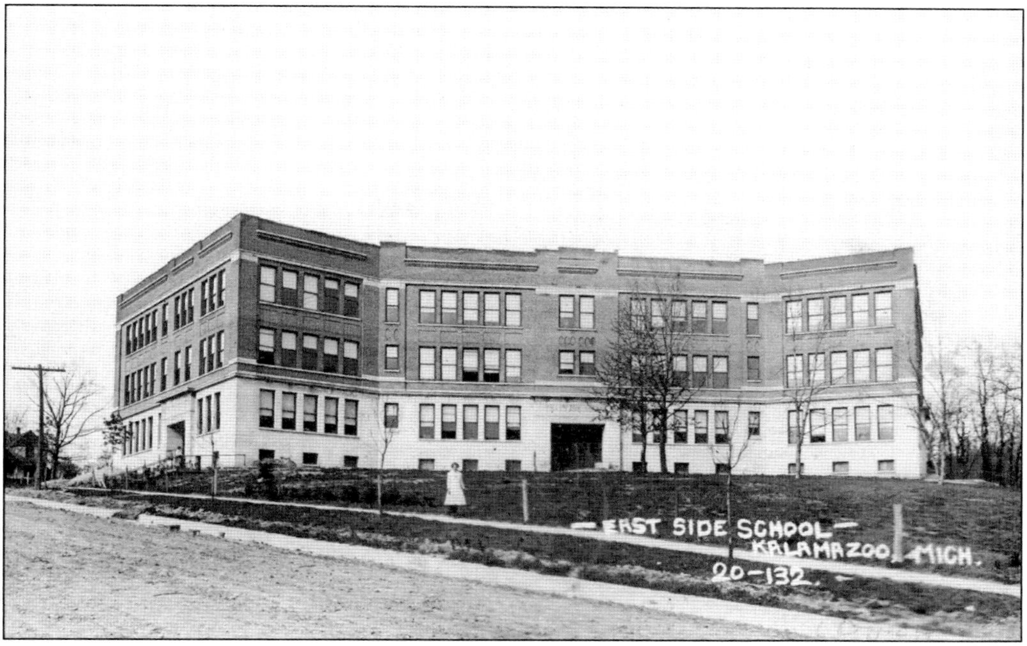


The East Side School served the community from 1909 until 1975. It was renamed Roosevelt Elementary in 1926, an example of a trend in the city to name schools for past presidents. The building was demolished in 1988.

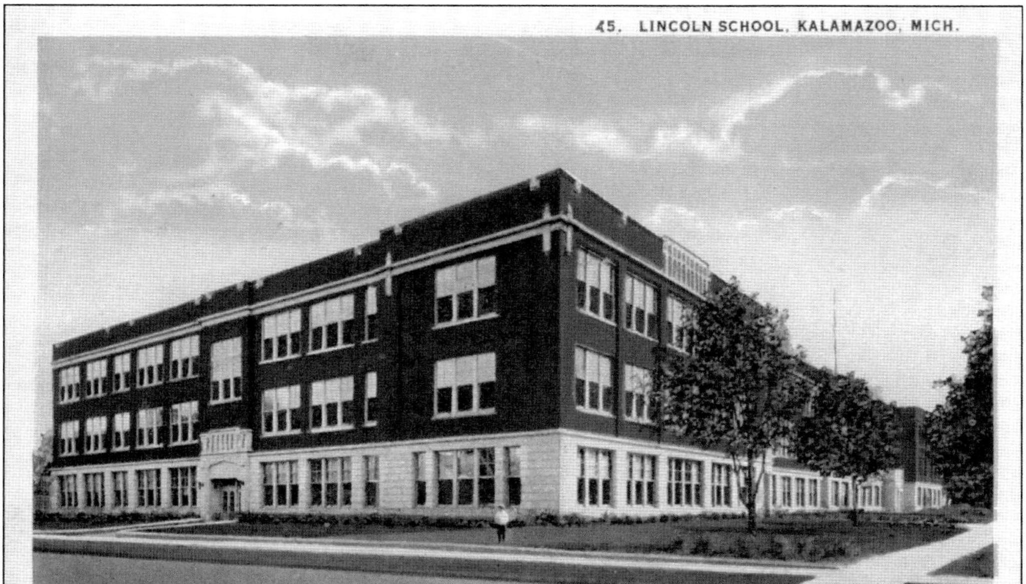


Lincoln School was built as a high school in 1922, but it never served that purpose. Instead, it has shifted over the years, being both a middle school and an elementary school. Its demographics have also shifted. When first built, it anchored a largely Dutch neighborhood. But by the 1970s, it was known as Kalamazoo's "black school." Lincoln remains a north-side institution today.

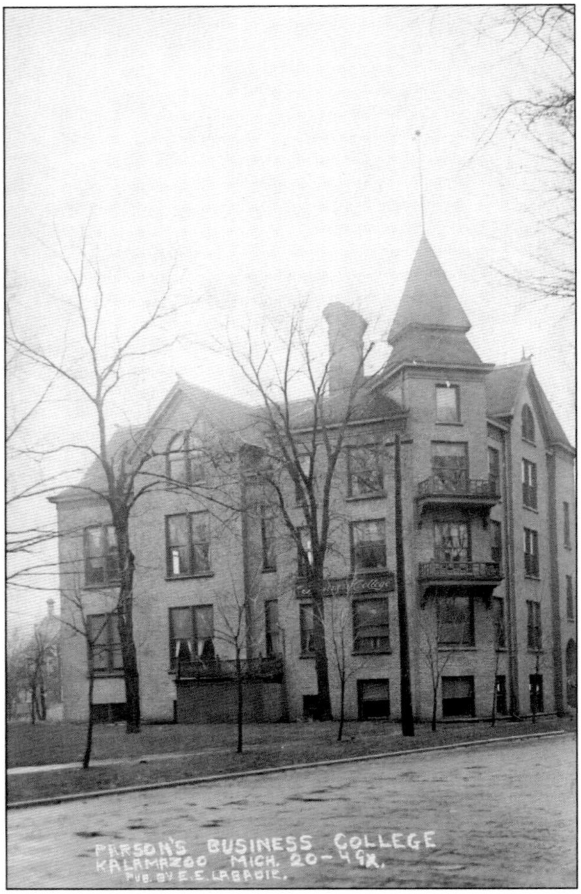


Parson's Business College opened in this building on West Street in 1901. The school provided professional training to serve the needs of a growing white-collar workforce. The curriculum included classes in business administration, accounting, advertising, and salesmanship.

This interior view shows the large lower-level classroom of Parson's Business College. If nothing else, the photograph speaks of the popularity of the education the school provided. The Veterans Administration occupied the former Parson's building after World War II. It was demolished in the 1950s; the site is currently occupied by St. Augustine Parish.

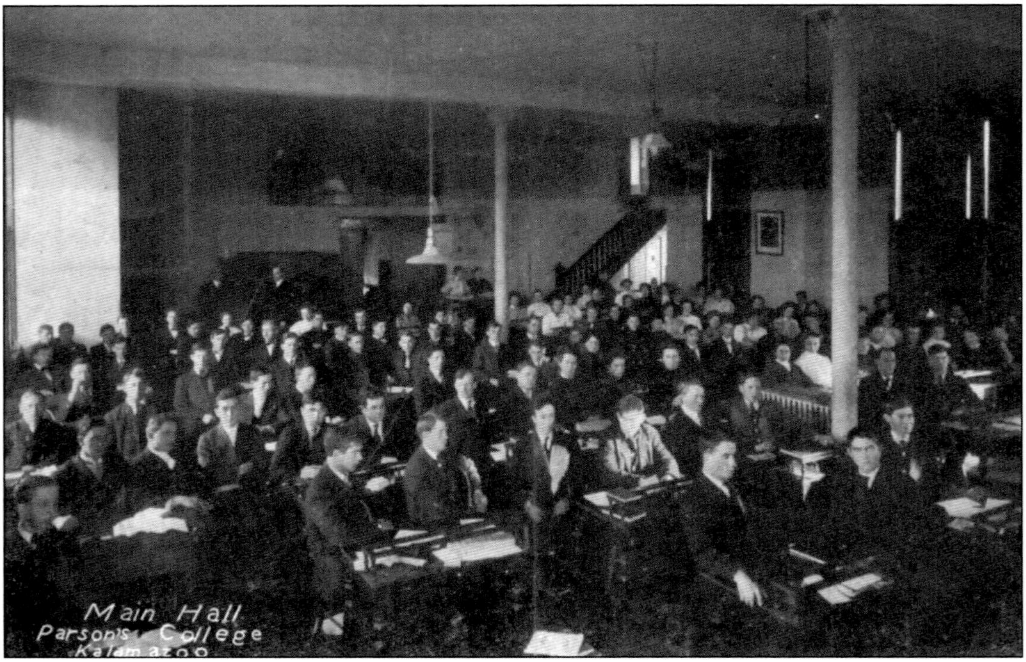

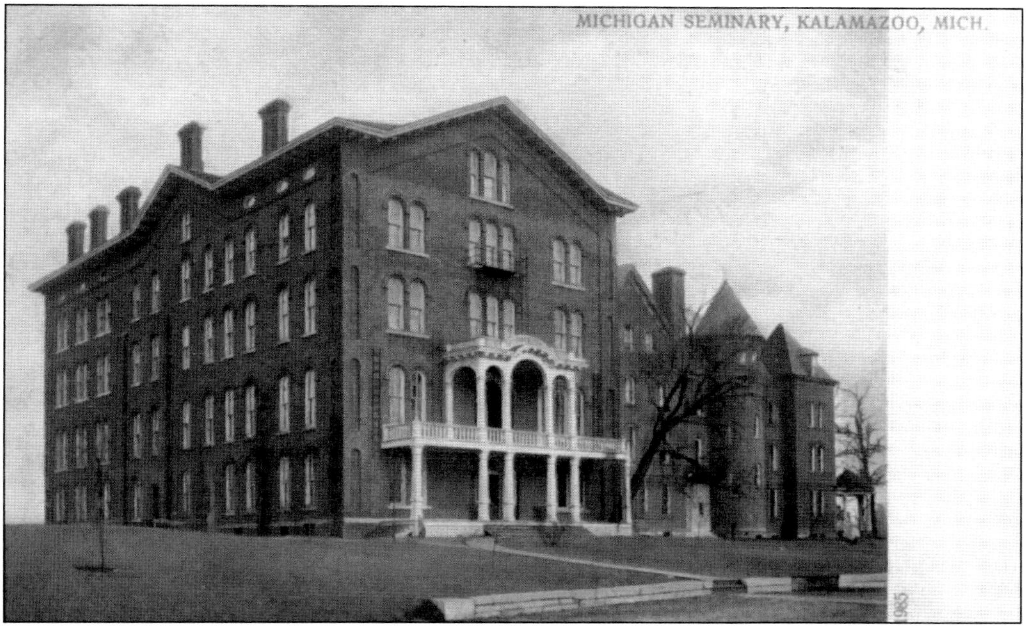


The Michigan Female Seminary opened in 1856 and occupied this handsome building overlooking Gull Road. The school provided a strong religious-based education that was the equivalent of two years of college. It prospered for over 40 years, closing in 1907. The buildings were razed in 1935 to reduce the property's taxable value.

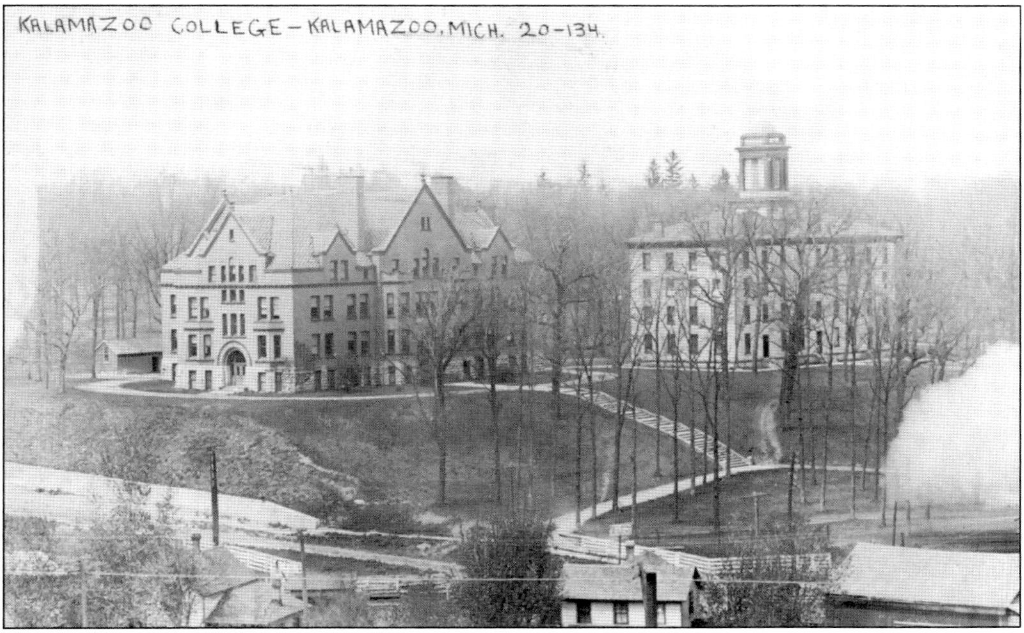


Kalamazoo's first institution of higher learning, Kalamazoo College, opened in 1833. Development of the school's present campus began in 1845. Shortly thereafter, the large building on the right was erected. The building served as the men's dormitory and was later known as Williams Hall. The building on the left is Bowen Hall. Completed in 1902, it contained classrooms and administrative space. Both of these buildings have given way to the school's current architecture. Williams fell in 1936, and Bowen followed in 1969.

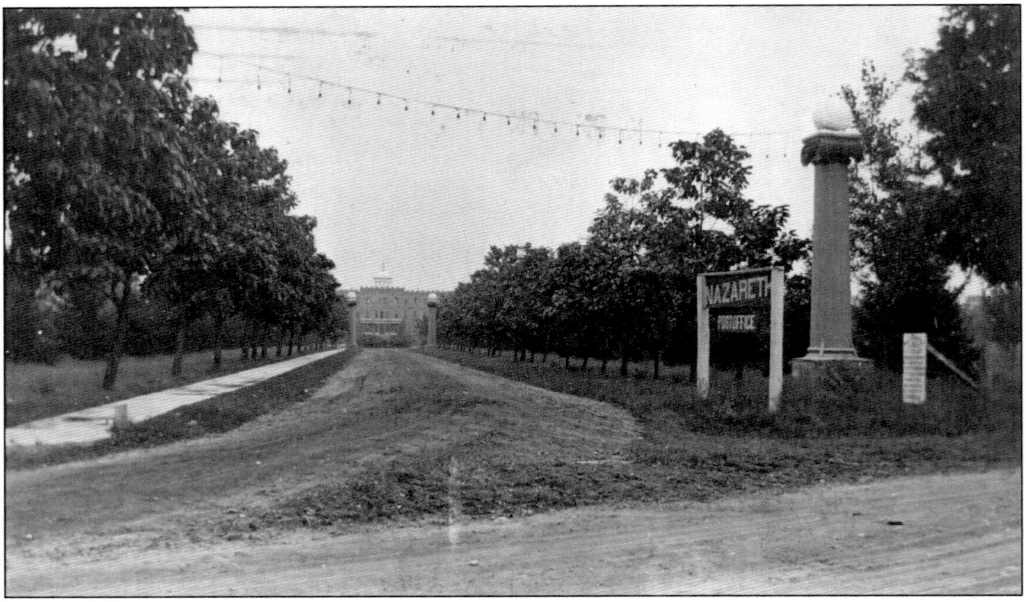


The Sisters of St. Joseph came to Kalamazoo in 1889 to help establish and run the new Borgess Hospital. In 1897, they built a home for themselves called Nazareth east of town on Gull Road. The entrance to that campus is seen here, with the main convent visible at the end of a long drive.

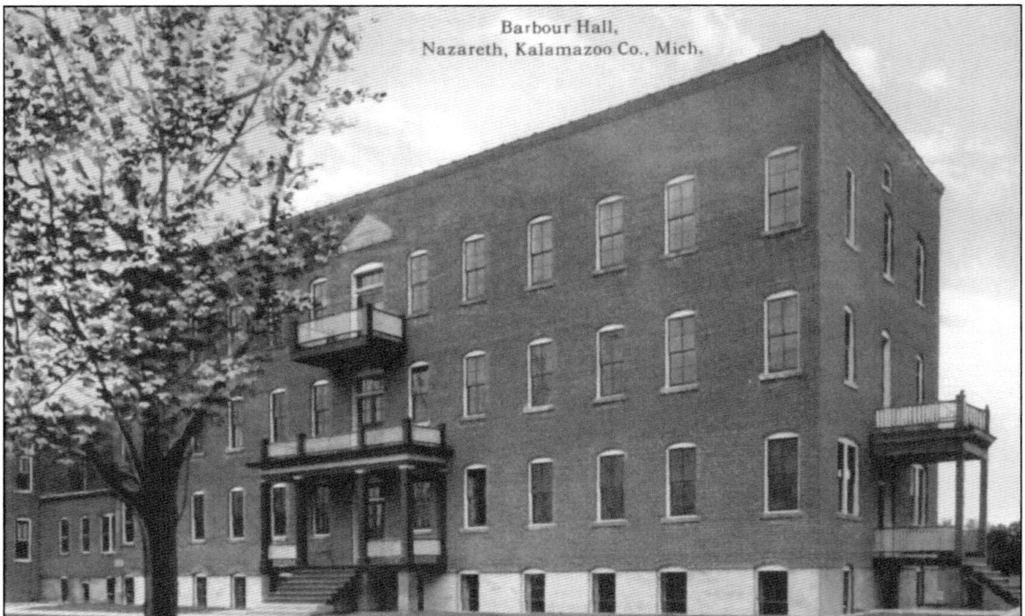


In addition to providing a home for themselves, the sisters opened a school for girls, Nazareth Academy. The school proved popular, and a boys' school followed in 1902. This postcard shows Nazareth Academy's main building, Barbour Hall.

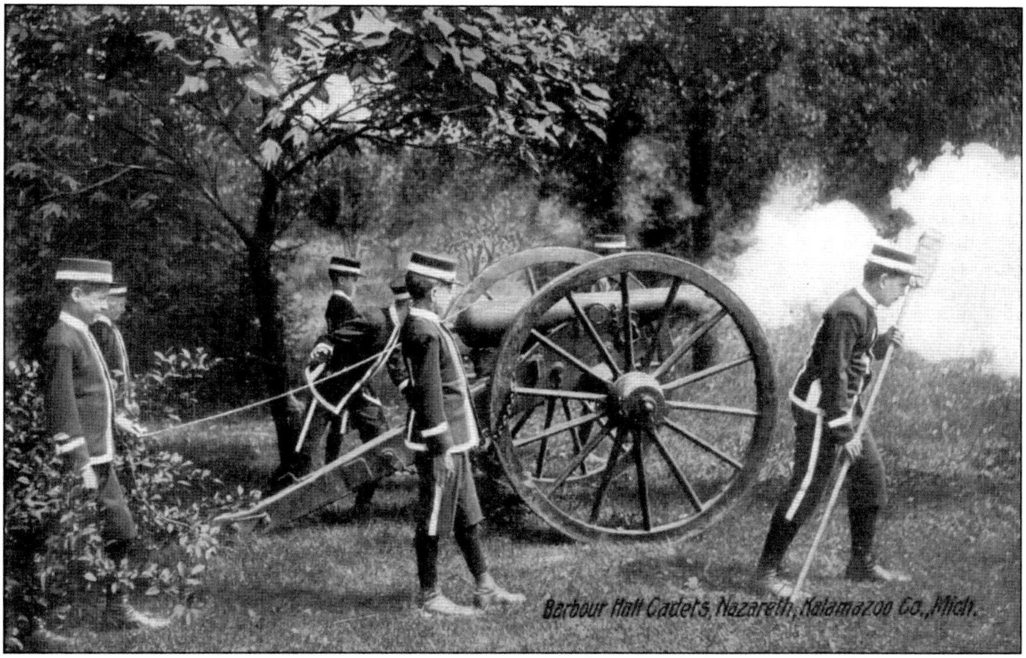


The boys' academy at Nazareth included military-style training, such as drills, bands, and, in this case, artillery. Nazareth Academy was closed in 1979 after years of declining enrollment. Barbour Hall came down the following year.

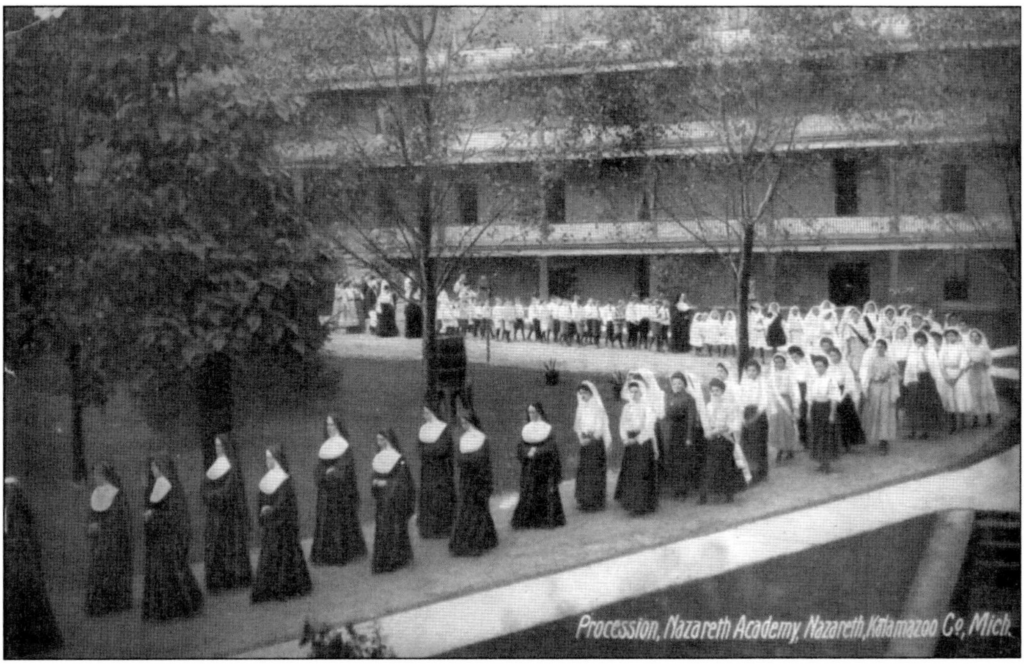


Nazareth's religious connections are readily apparent in this postcard, showing the Sisters of St. Joseph leading a procession of students through the campus grounds. The sisters did not limit their educational mission to girls and boys. They opened Nazareth College as a nursing school in 1924. Like the academy before it, Nazareth College opened first for women. Men were not admitted until 1971.

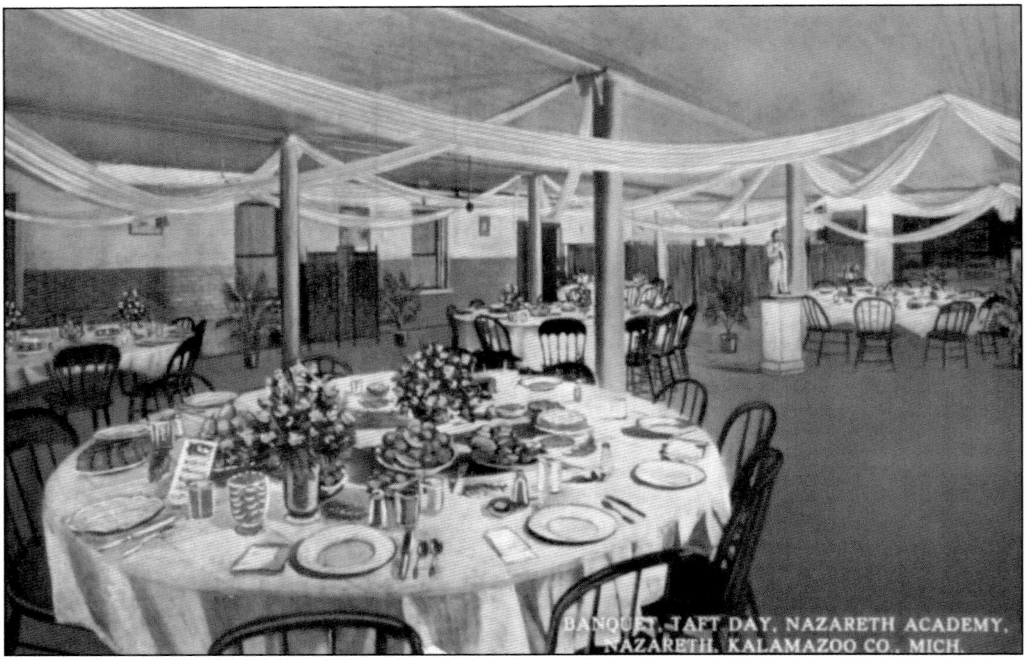


The basement chapel of Nazareth's main building is decked out for Pres. William Howard Taft's visit in 1911. Taft took a whirlwind tour of the city that included, along with the stop at Nazareth, laying the cornerstone of the new YMCA and dedicating the new Burdick Hotel. Nazareth College closed in 1991. The Sisters of St. Joseph remain on the site.

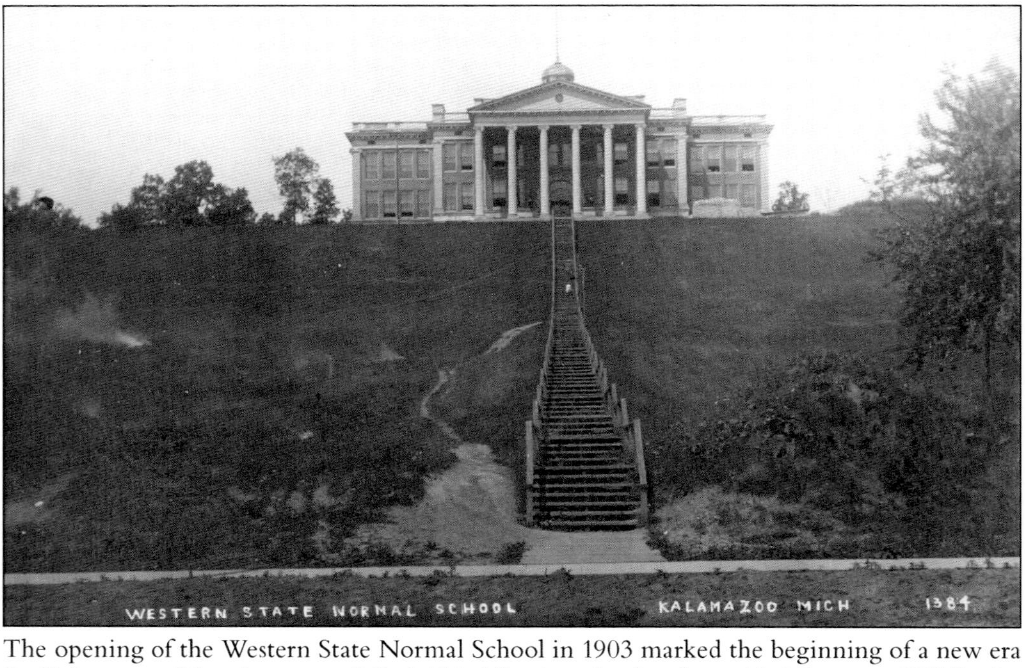


The opening of the Western State Normal School in 1903 marked the beginning of a new era for Kalamazoo. The city successfully lobbied for the school and provided Prospect Hill for the campus. Although no one knew it at the time, the small teachers college would eventually grow to become one of the main public universities in the state. This view shows the newly completed first section of East Hall, built in 1904.

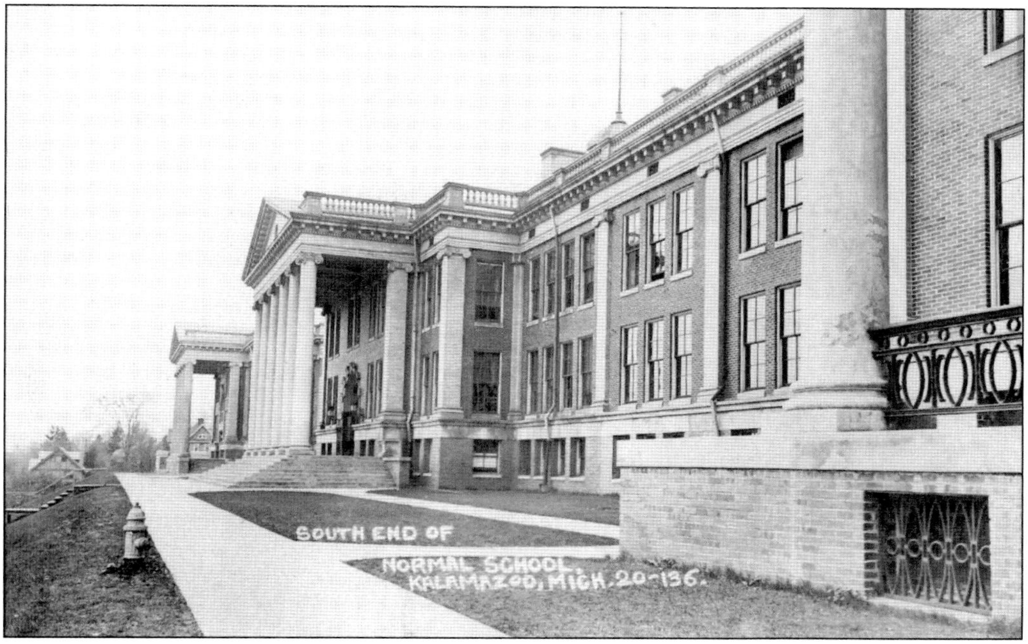


The core of East Hall was completed in 1904, but it was soon expanded with additional wings to meet the growing school's demands. This photograph shows the completed East Hall, with a gymnasium wing (foreground) and a training-school wing (background), built in 1908 and 1910, respectively. The three identical porticos were a landmark for decades. Sadly, most of East Hall was leveled in 2014.

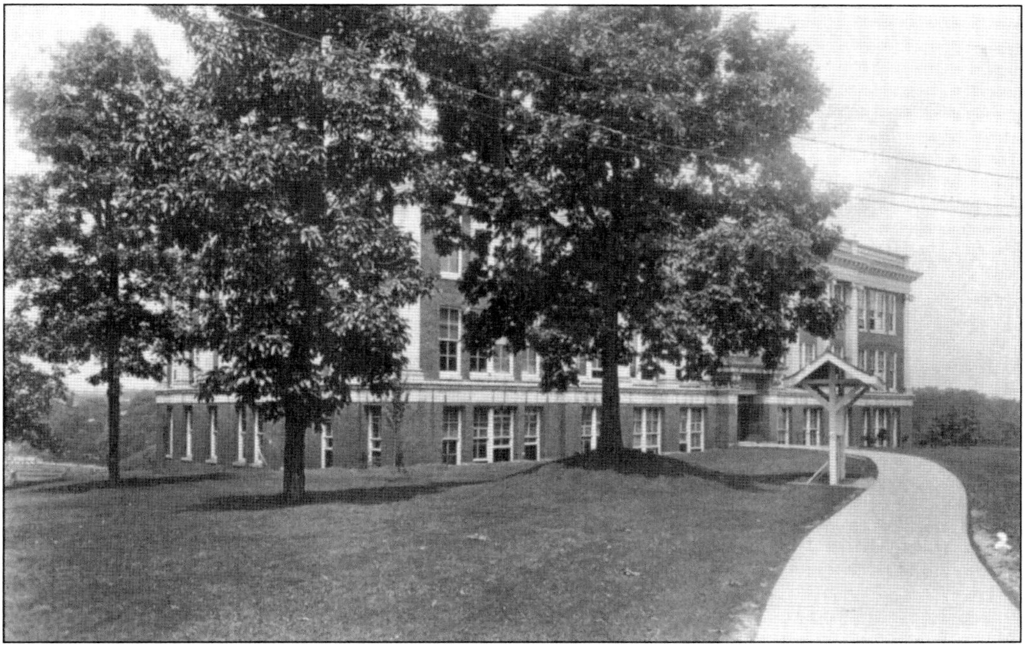

West Hall, the college's science building, was added to the opposite side of Prospect Hill in 1913. The building, featuring architecture compatible with the earlier East Hall, contained classrooms and lecture halls. It was demolished in 2013 as part of a controversial redevelopment of Western's East Campus.

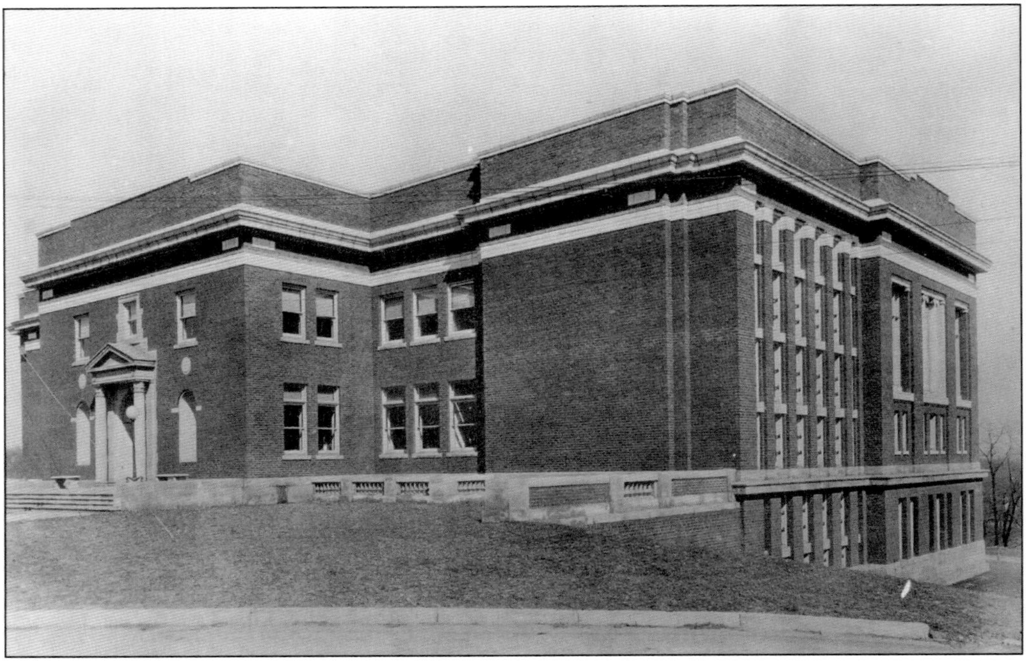

In 1924, East and West Halls were joined by this new library. It was the college's showplace, with a two-story reading room that offered stunning views of the city. When the library moved to a new building on the school's West Campus in 1957, the old library continued to serve as classroom space and as book storage. Known as North Hall in its later years, it was demolished in 2014.

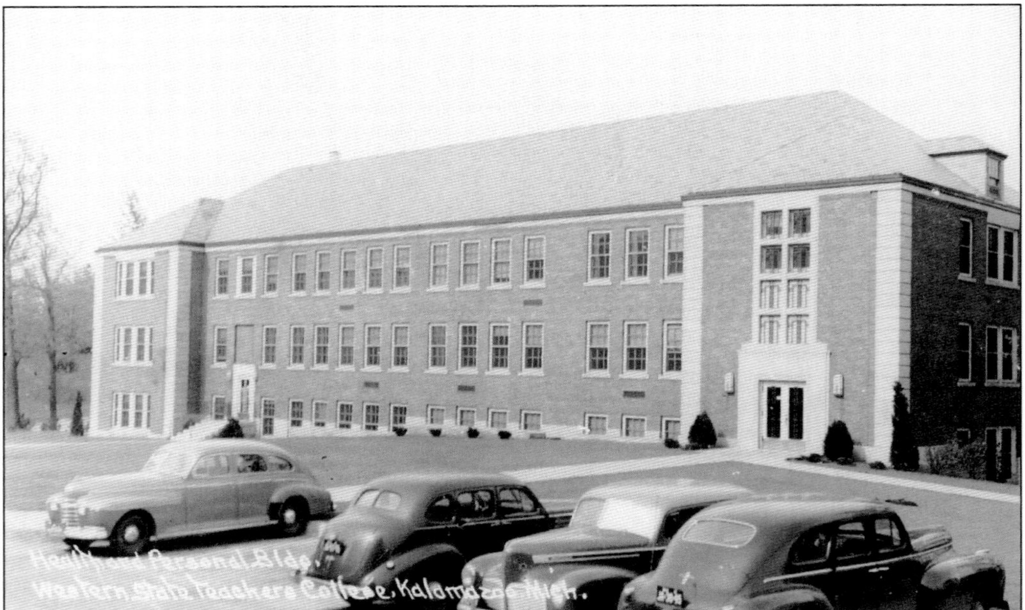


Built in 1939, the Health and Personnel Building was the final structure erected atop Prospect Hill. It contained a small medical center as well as advising offices and the graduate school. In later years, it housed the speech pathology department. It was vacated after 2003 and demolished in 2013.

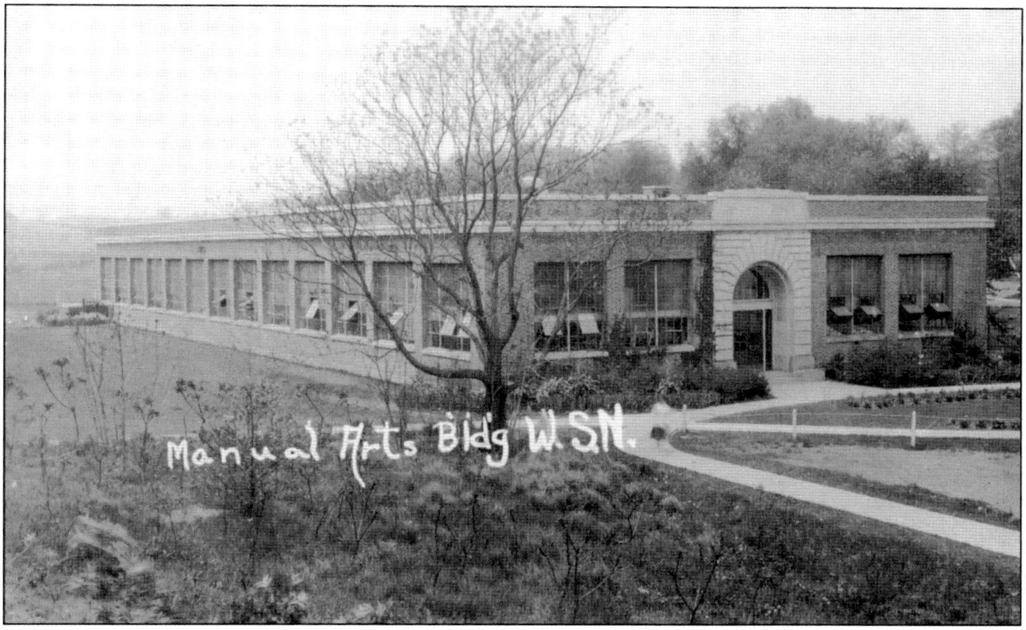


In the 1920s, Western found it necessary to build beyond the crowded confines of Prospect Hill. The Manual Arts Building, completed in 1922, was one example. This building still exists between Oakland and Stadium Drives.

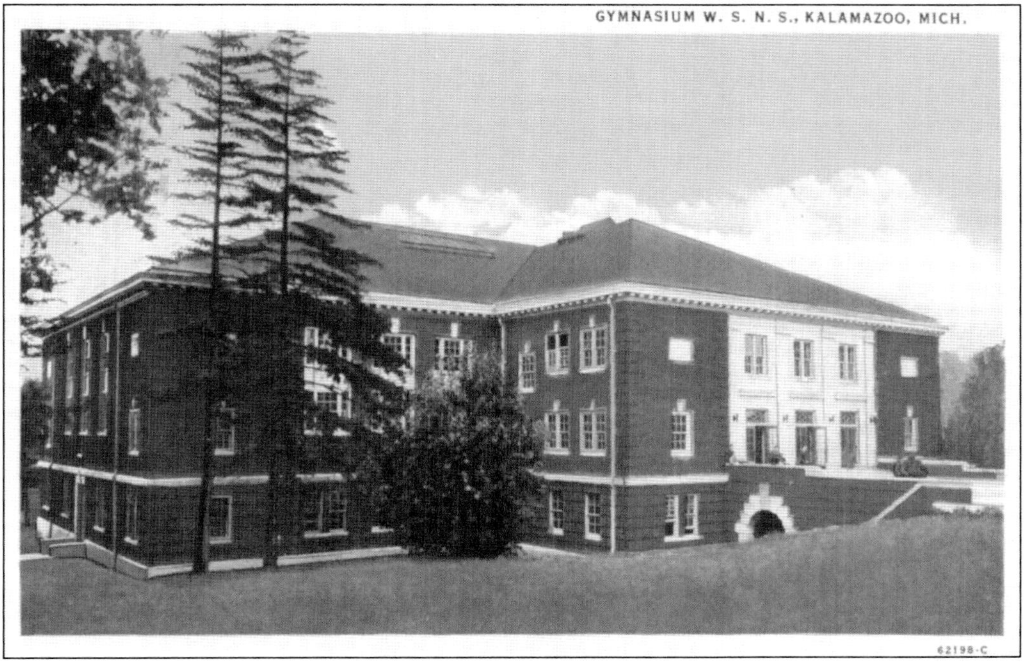


By 1925, the gymnasium in East Hall was no longer sufficient. This new gym was built opposite Prospect Hill, on Oakland Drive. The facility housed the college's athletic programs as well as basketball games. It was demolished in 2003 for the new Seelye Center. The main facade was retained and included in the new design.

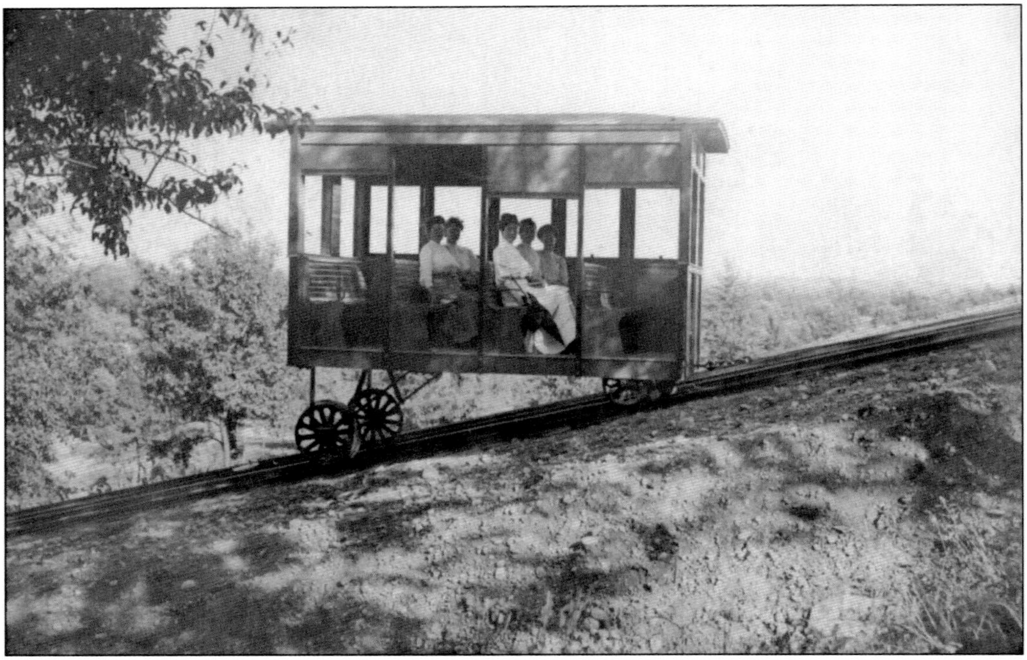

Because the main campus was located on a hilltop and the majority of students lived in the Vine neighborhood below, a special railroad was constructed to ease the daily commute. These cable cars operated from 1910 to 1948. The weight of one car would help pull the other up the hill. Although no trace of the railroad survives, a replica car was built by a group of engineering students in 2003.

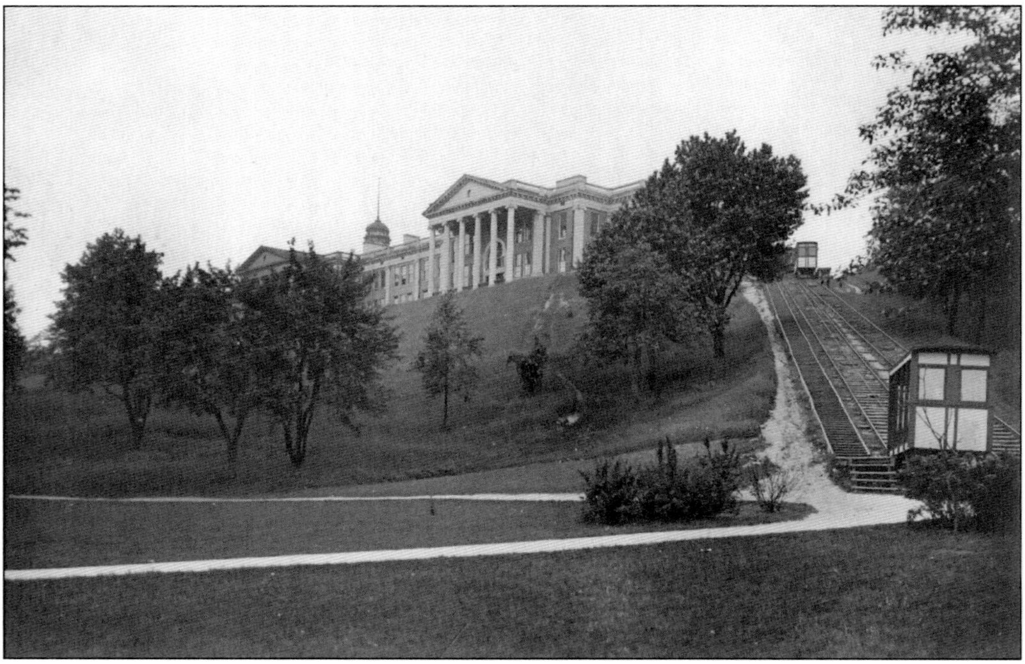

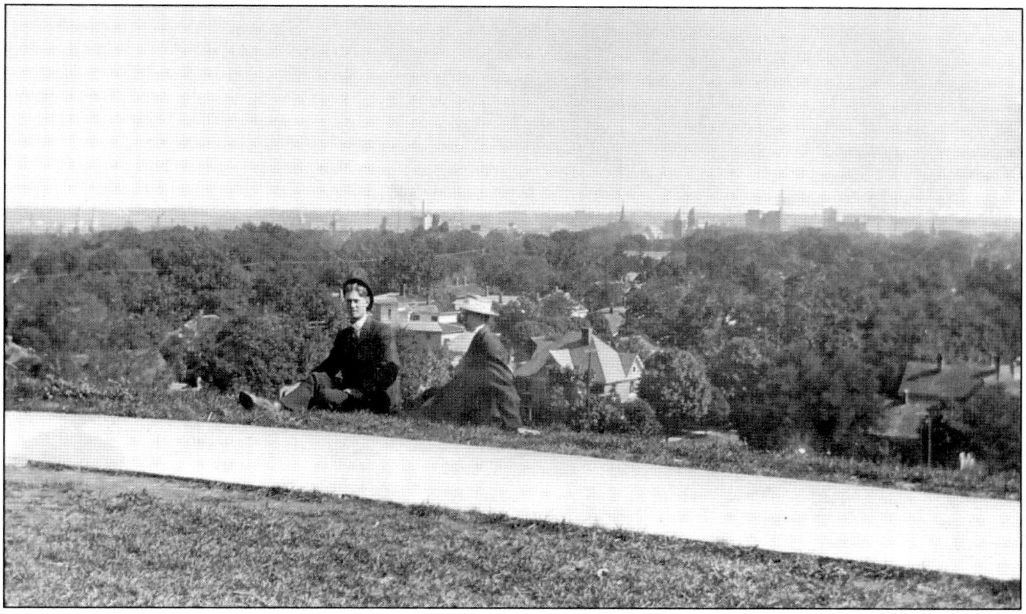

The placement of Western's original campus atop Prospect Hill gave it a highly visible presence throughout the city and provided stunning views of the Kalamazoo Valley. Here, a group of students relax in front of East Hall. The Vine neighborhood is immediately below them. Visible in the distance are the steeples of Kalamazoo's downtown churches, as well as new skyscrapers. Based on the buildings, the photograph dates from 1911.

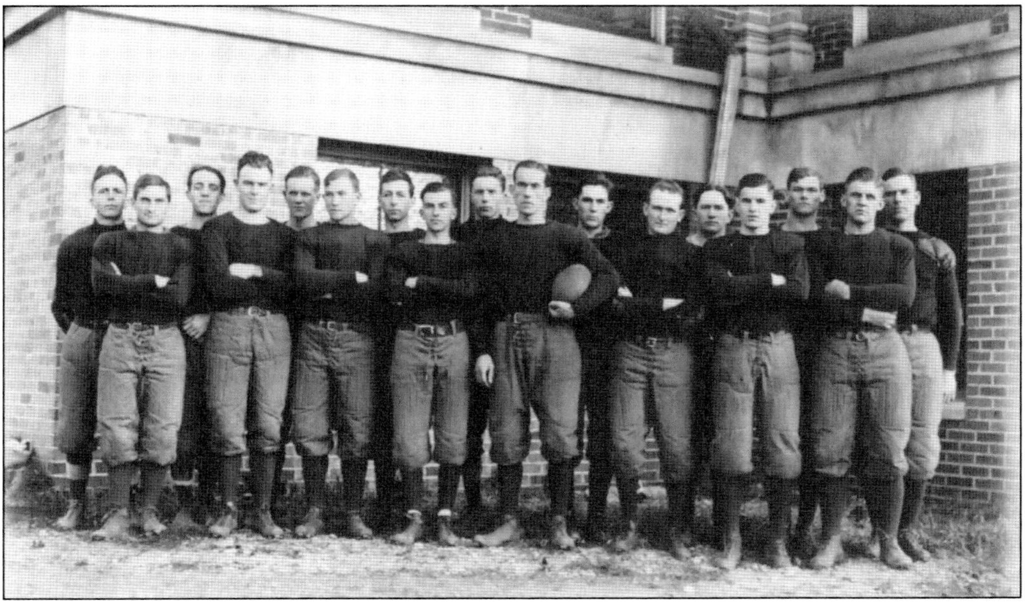

Athletics have long been an important part of the educational experience. This is especially true of the 20th century, when sports were viewed as a good way to promote health and school spirit. Here, an early Western football team poses in front of East Hall.

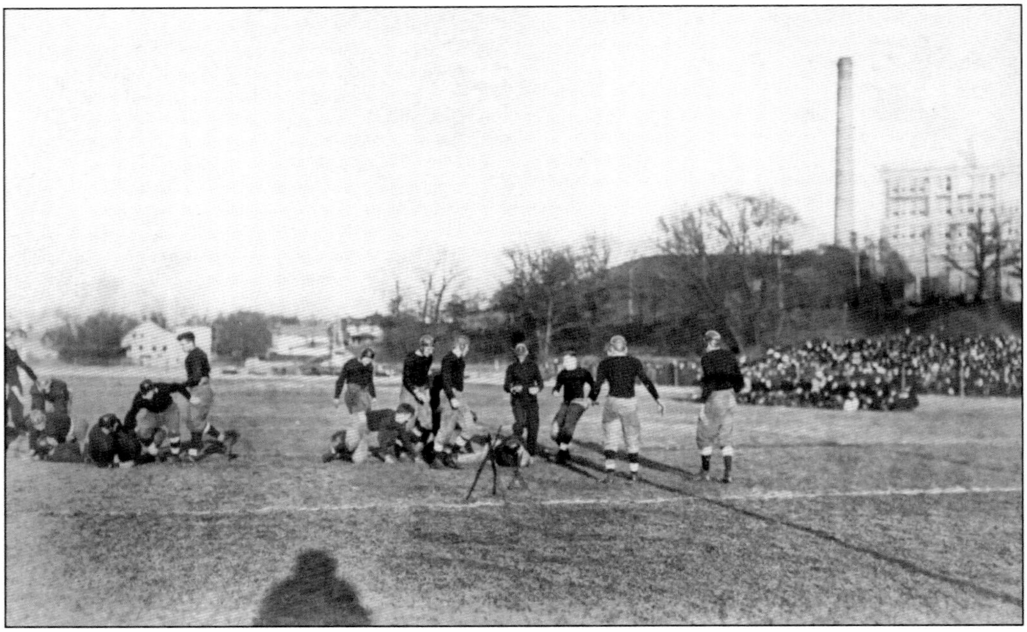

Western played its various sporting matches on a field located along Stadium Drive, below Prospect Hill. Here, an early football game is in progress. Note the photographer's shadow. The hilltop campus and West Hall are visible in the background.

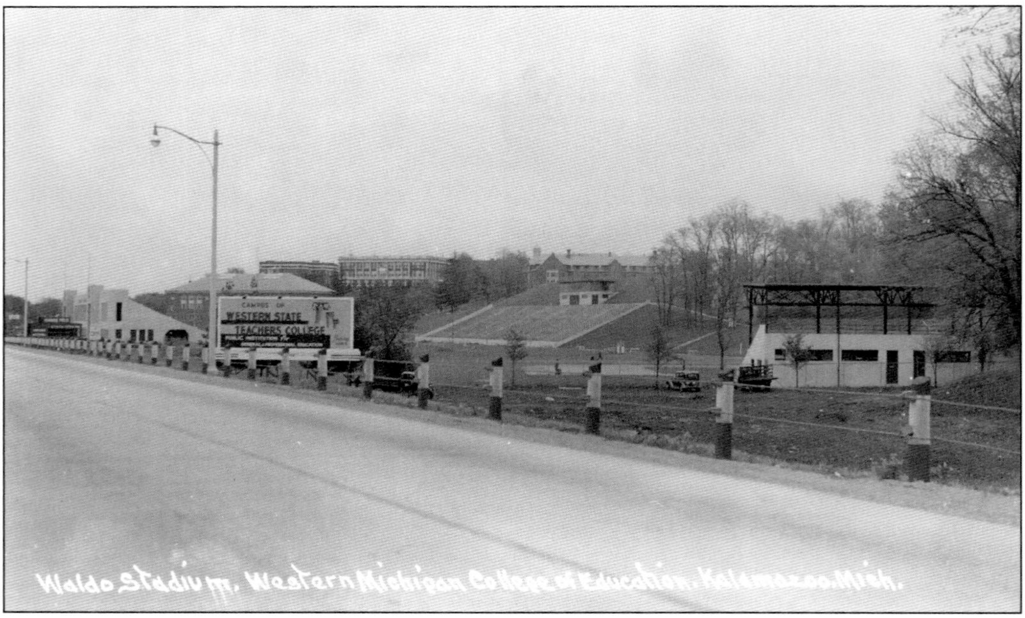


In 1939, the sporting grounds were dramatically improved with the construction of proper stadiums. This view shows both Waldo Stadium, the football field, and Hyames Field, the baseball stadium. Hyames Field is especially notable as the site of the 1947 and 1948 College World Series. The 1947 contest included a first baseman from Yale named George H.W. Bush, future president of the United States. Both fields still exist, although heavily altered.

*Nine*

# Events

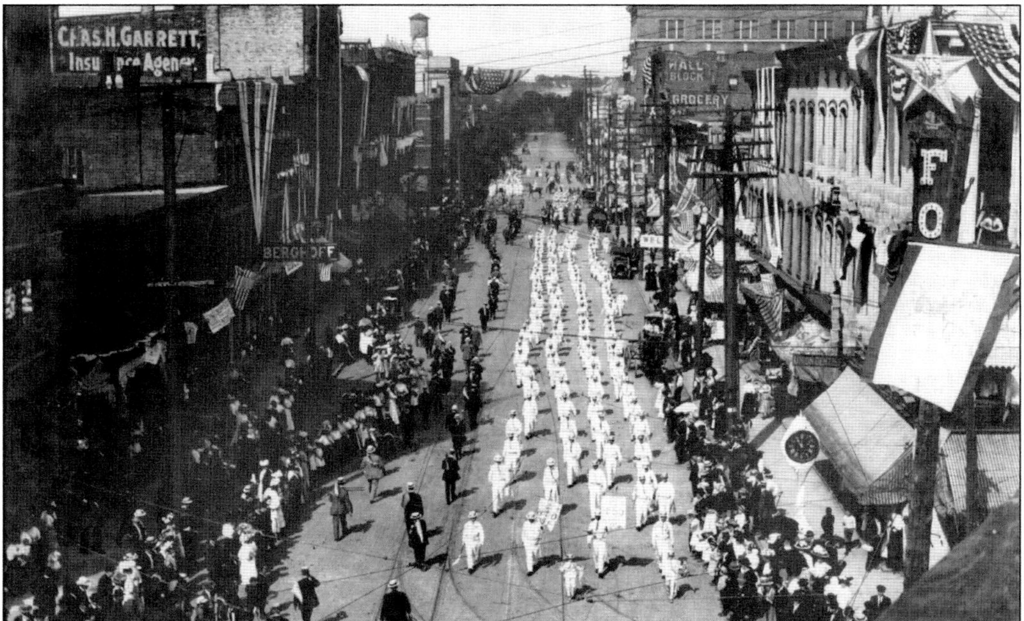


Parades and other civic celebrations were a popular subject for postcard publishers. Seen here is a 1908 Elks parade on East Main Street. The parade was the grand finale to a statewide Elks convention held in Kalamazoo that year.

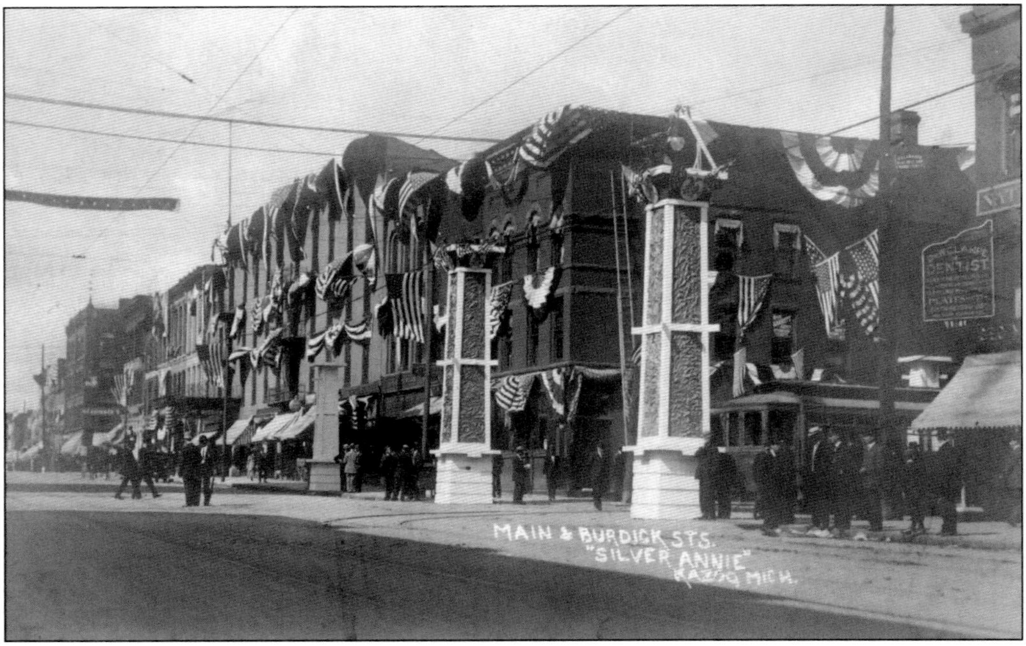


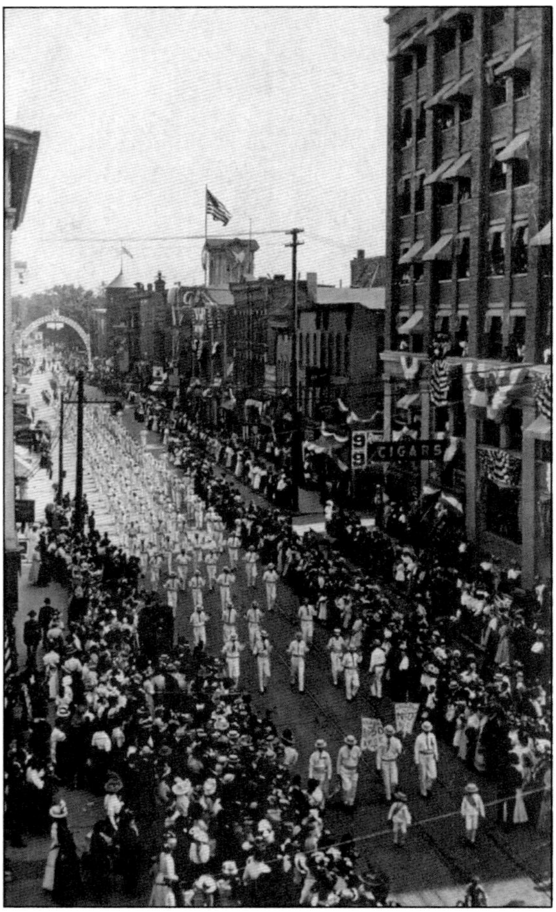

Perhaps the biggest bash downtown Kalamazoo ever saw occurred in October 1909. In that year, the community celebrated its 25th anniversary as a city. Buildings throughout the city were decked out in patriotic bunting. This view shows the block on Main Street, including the Burdick Hotel, which would burn to the ground two months later.

The "Silver Annie" celebrations included several parades held by local fraternal organizations as well as the GAR. Here, one of these parades makes its way north on Burdick Street. The eight-story Kalamazoo National Bank Building is decked out with flags.

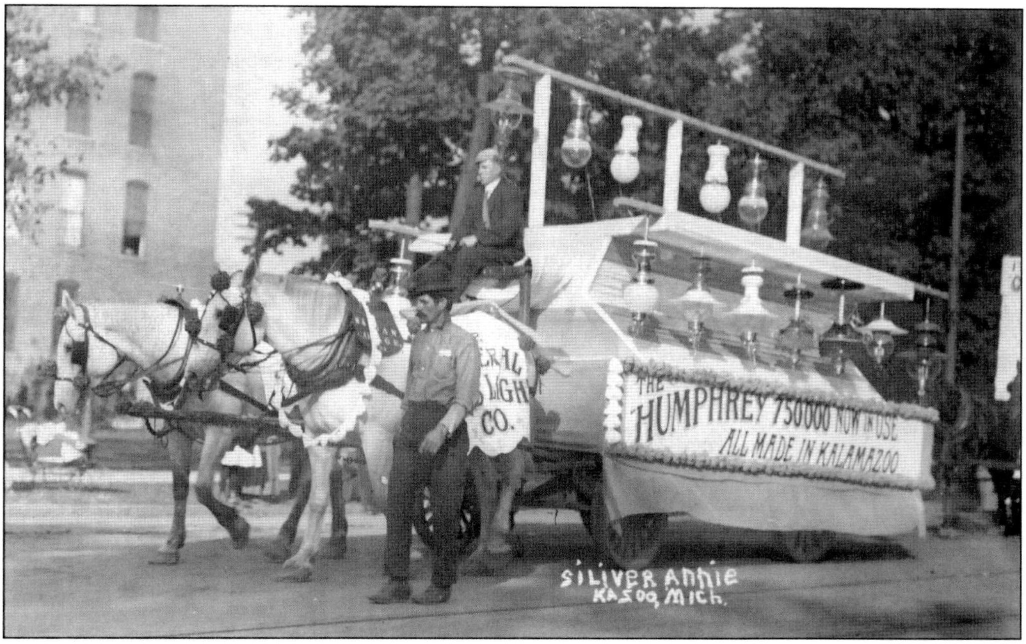


Local business got in on the festivities, and many created elaborate floats to promote their products. This float, built by the Humphrey Gas Lamp Company, boasts that over 750,000 of its products have been produced locally. Note the gas lamps hanging on display. (Courtesy of the Kalamazoo Public Library's Local History Room.)

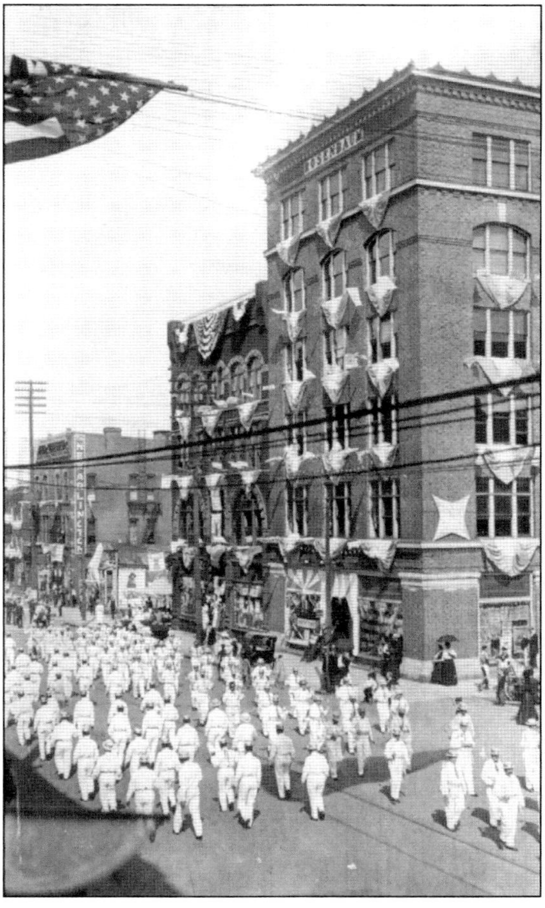

This parade scene shows the "Silver Annie" festivities on East Main Street. The Rosenbaum Building and the Arlington Hotel can be seen in the background. All of these buildings survive. (Courtesy of the Kalamazoo Public Library's Local History Room.)

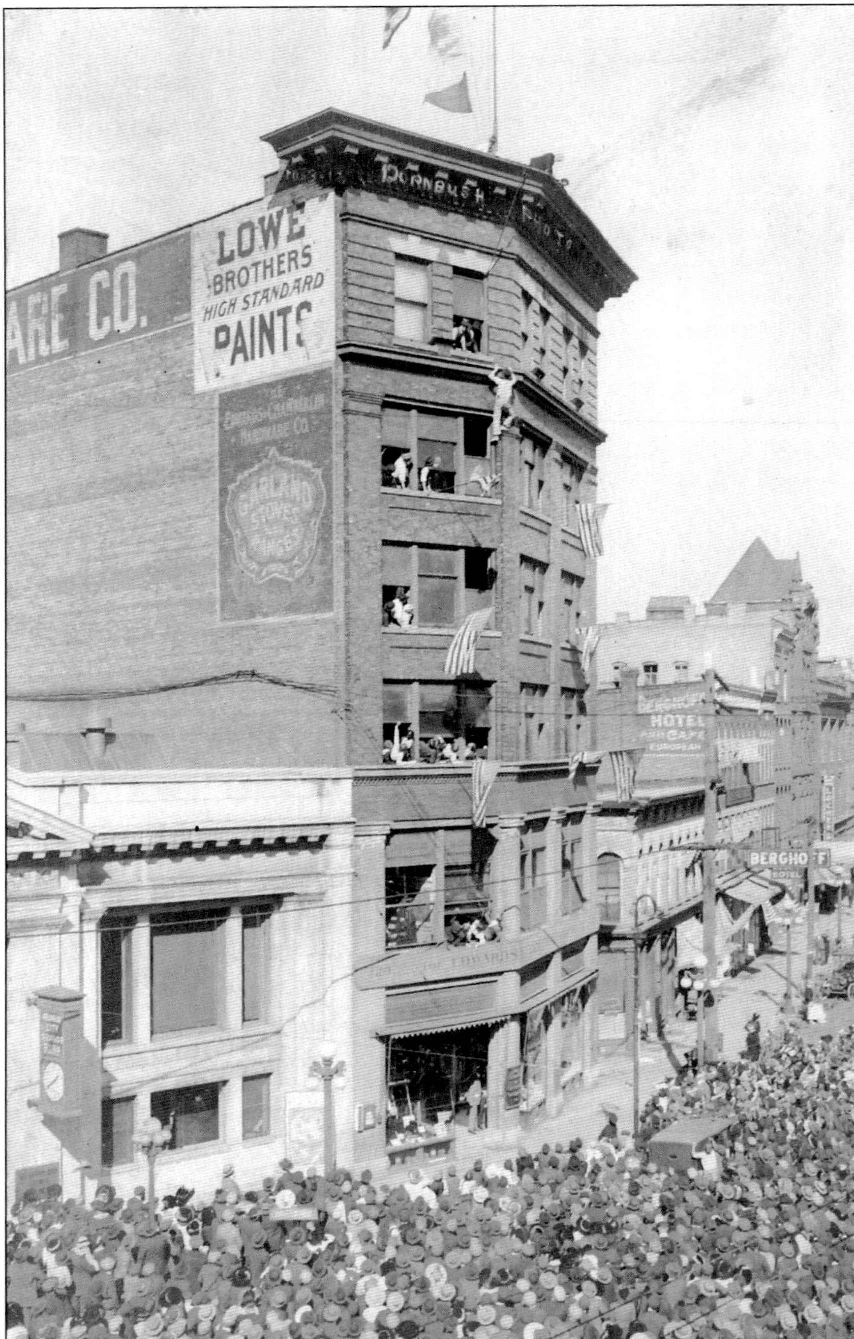


One of the most unusual events to be held downtown occurred during the Kalamazoo County Fair in 1916. The *Kalamazoo Gazette* hired a stunt performer named Jack Williams to climb local landmarks. Williams, nicknamed "The Human Fly," proudly boasted to the paper that anyone who came to see him fall to his death would be disappointed. Here, he climbs up the facade of the Edwards and Chamberlin Hardware Store. He would climb the Hanselman Building later that evening. True to his word, he did not fall. (From the Collection of the Kalamazoo Valley Museum.)

Fires were another popular postcard subject. Kalamazoo's most well-documented fire was the blaze that leveled the Burdick Hotel on the night of December 8–9, 1909. The fire broke out in the Star Bargain House and soon spread to the neighboring hotel. Most postcards show the aftermath, but this remarkable view shows the blaze in progress. The massive hotel and most of the city block were reduced to ruins. Remarkably, no one was killed.

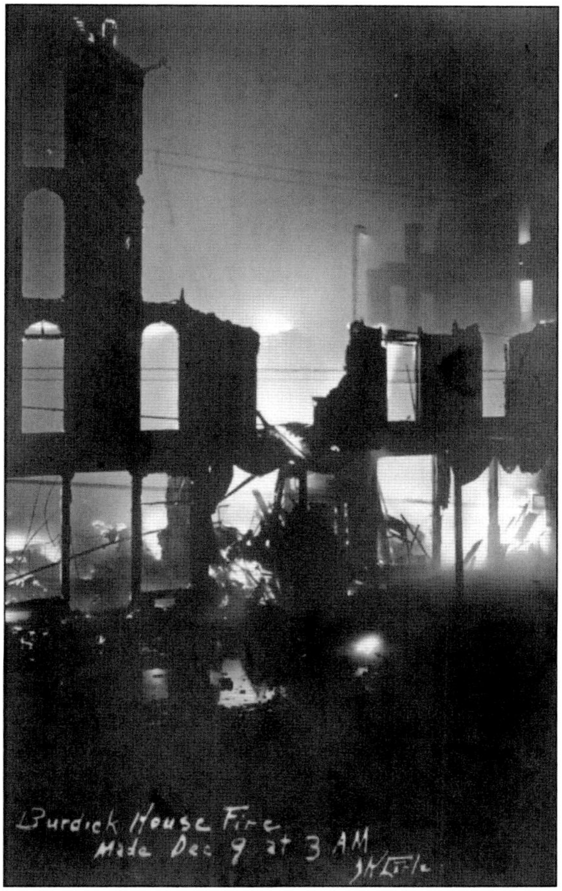


The Burdick blaze quickly overwhelmed Kalamazoo's fire department. The departments from Battle Creek and Grand Rapids made the long journey to provide assistance. Water from the state hospital's water tower had to be used via a long chain of hoses. This postcard shows one of Grand Rapid's fire engines at the scene.

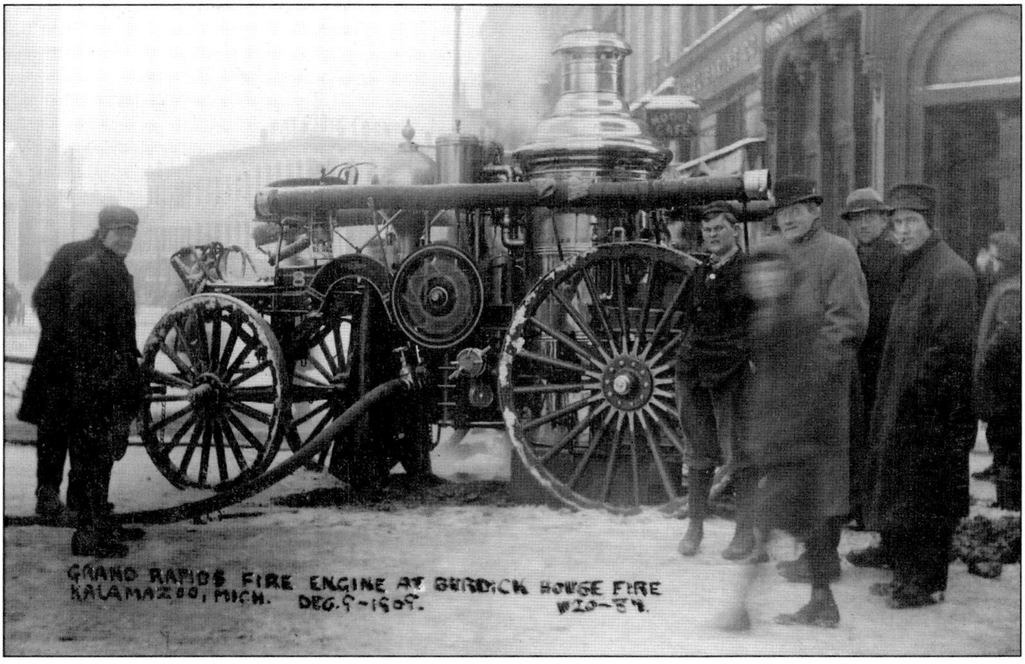

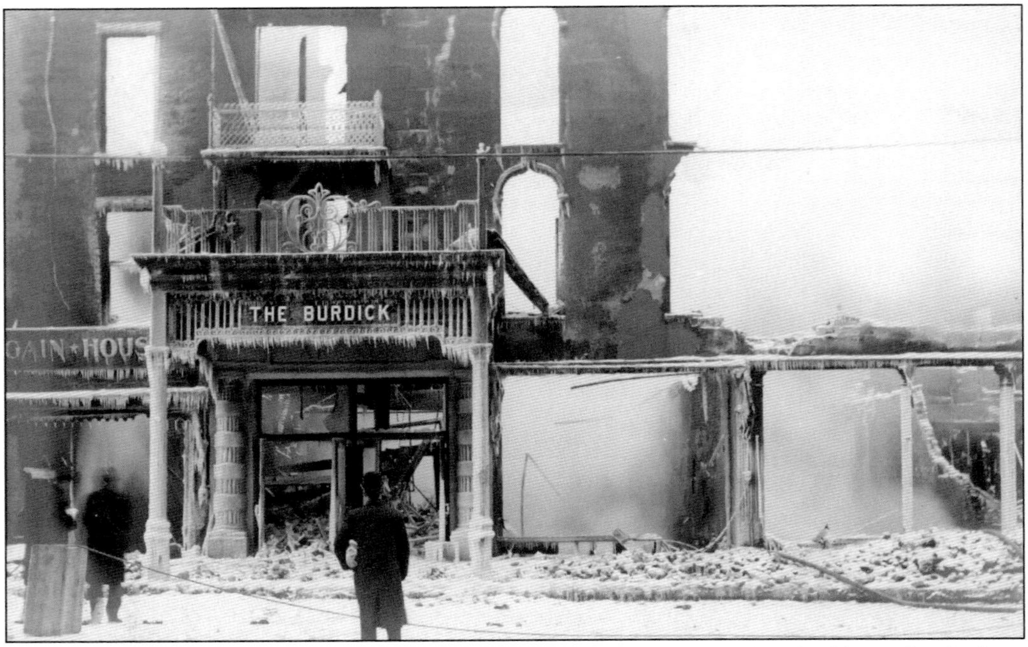


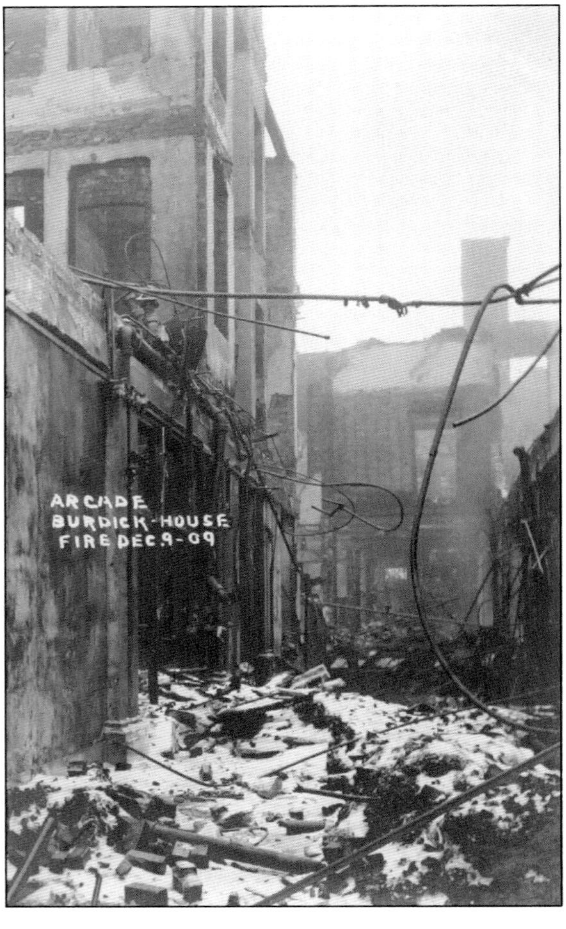


In the hours after the blaze, shocked city residents were drawn to the smoldering and ice-encrusted ruins. Only the front entrance and unstable wall fragments remained of Kalamazoo's best hotel. Walls continued to collapse throughout the morning; the rest were quickly pulled down for safety reasons.

Before the fire, the Burdick's retail arcade that ran between Main and Water Streets had been the hotel's most distinguishing feature. This photograph shows that space in ruins, a sharp contrast to the image on page 40. Nothing remained of the onyx marble paneling or the fine shops. Even as the smoke continued to rise over Kalamazoo, the hotel's owners set up an office across the street to begin making plans to rebuild the hotel even bigger than before.

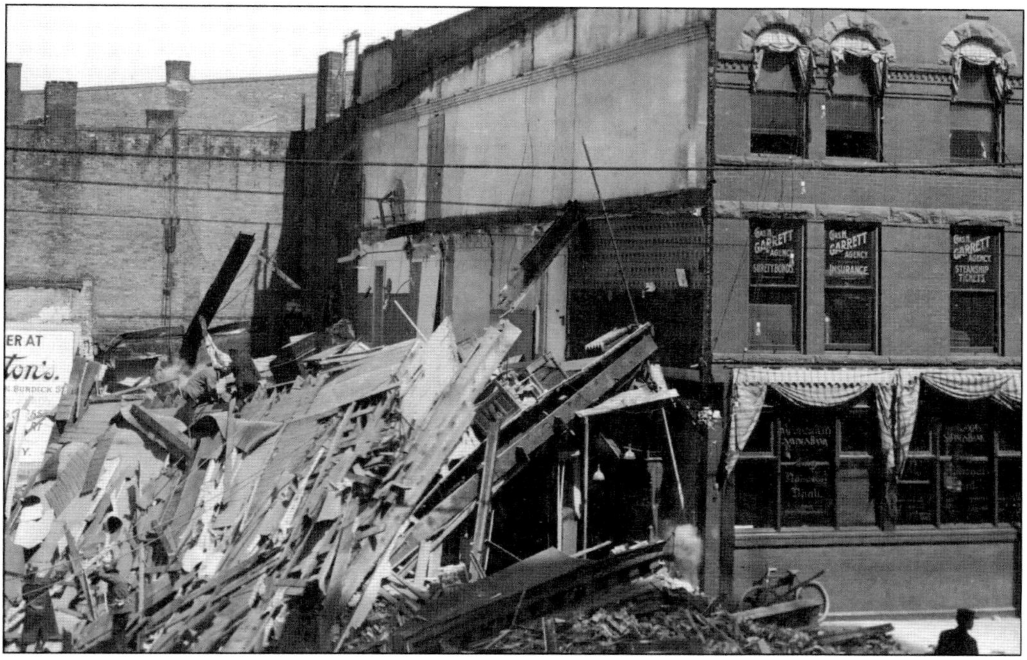


The fire claimed more than just the Burdick. On March 21, 1910, the undamaged E.M. Kennedy Drug Store suddenly collapsed into the void left by the demolished ruins. Despite the fact that the store was fully occupied at the time, everyone was pulled from the rubble alive. It was determined that the neighboring demolition had compromised the drugstore's foundations.

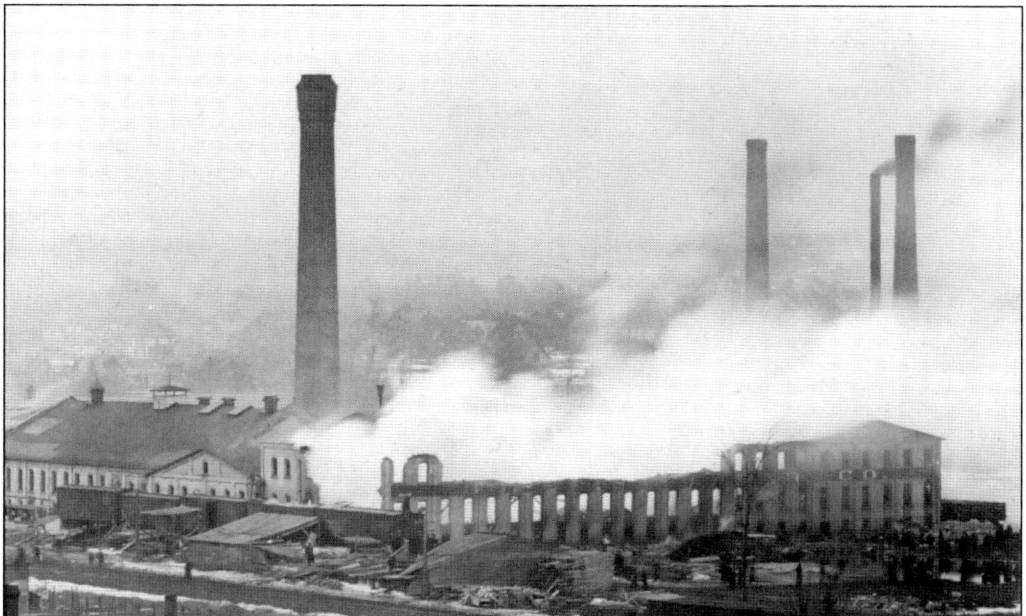

This postcard shows the results of a devastating 1910 fire at the Superior Paper Company on Alcott Street. Despite using a slow-burning "fireproof" construction, the mill was nearly totally reduced to ruin. It would be rebuilt, and the firm eventually merged with the neighboring Bryant Paper Company.

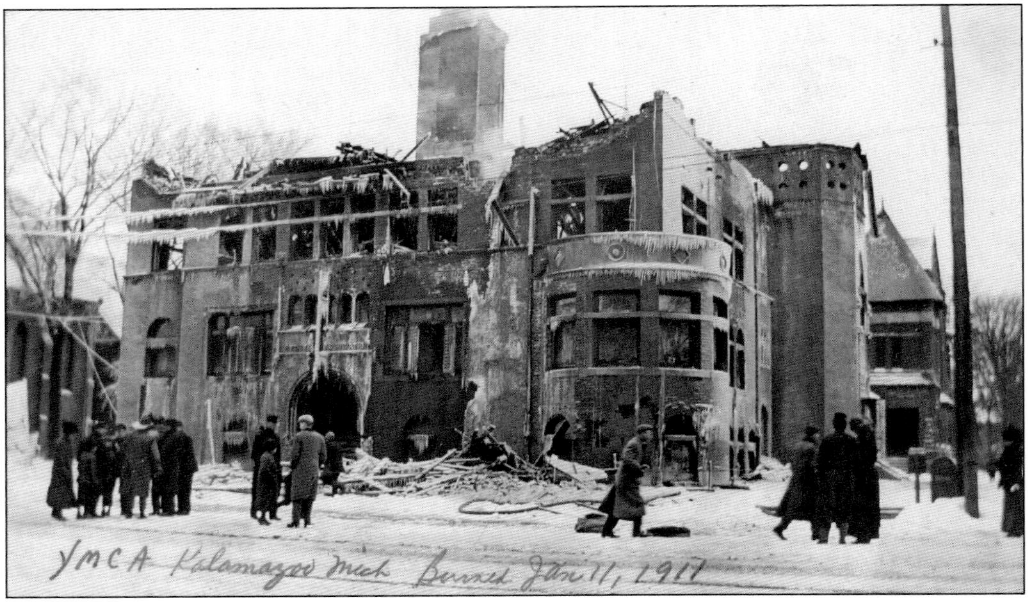


The January 1911 fire that claimed Kalamazoo's YMCA was as picturesque as the Burdick fire. The brick castle was quickly reduced to an unrecognizable mass of brick and ice. The rubble was cleared away by September so that President Taft could lay the cornerstone for the new building during his visit to the city.

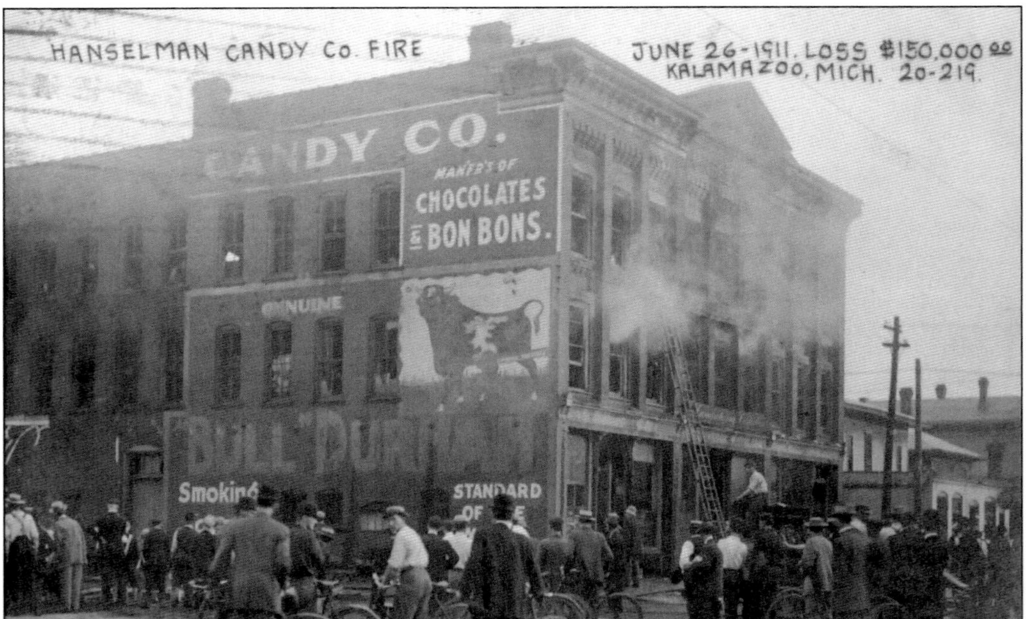


Another big 1911 fire claimed the Hanselman Candy Company on East Main Street. Not only did the business recover from this setback; the blaze did nothing to slow down George Hanselman's plans to build the city's tallest skyscraper. That building was completed the following year. The candy company remained in business until 1925.

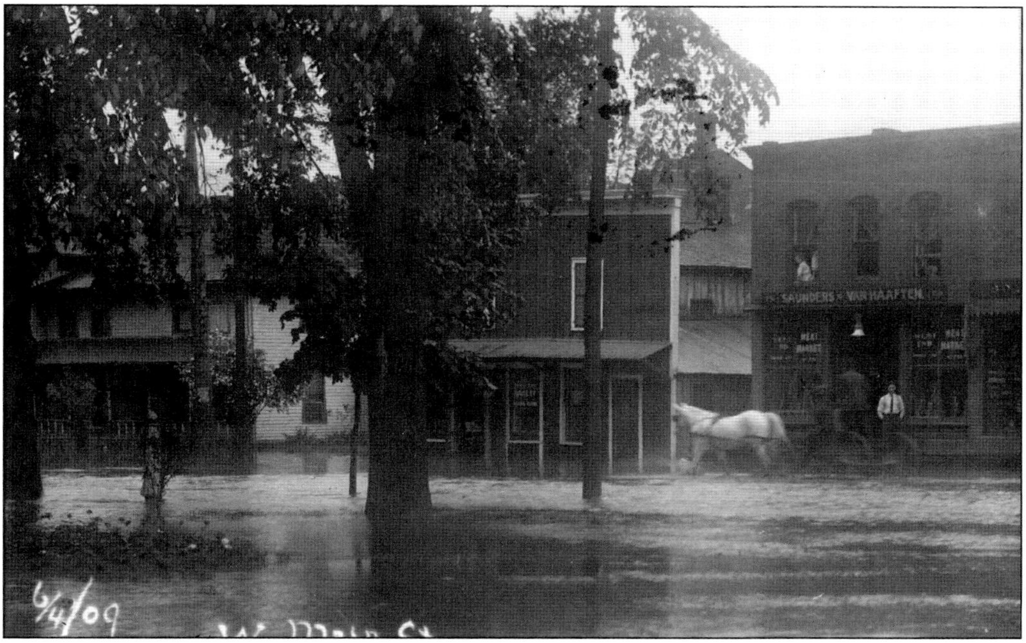


Floods were another common disaster. This postcard shows the aftermath of Arcadia Creek overflowing after a rainstorm on June 4, 1909. The west side of the city was largely submerged, and both streetcar traffic and the railroads experienced significant delays. However, the water seems to have little effect on this horse-drawn wagon as it makes its way down West Main Street. Fortunately, sewage and drainage improvements have made floods less frequent. (Courtesy of the Kalamazoo Public Library's Local History Room.)

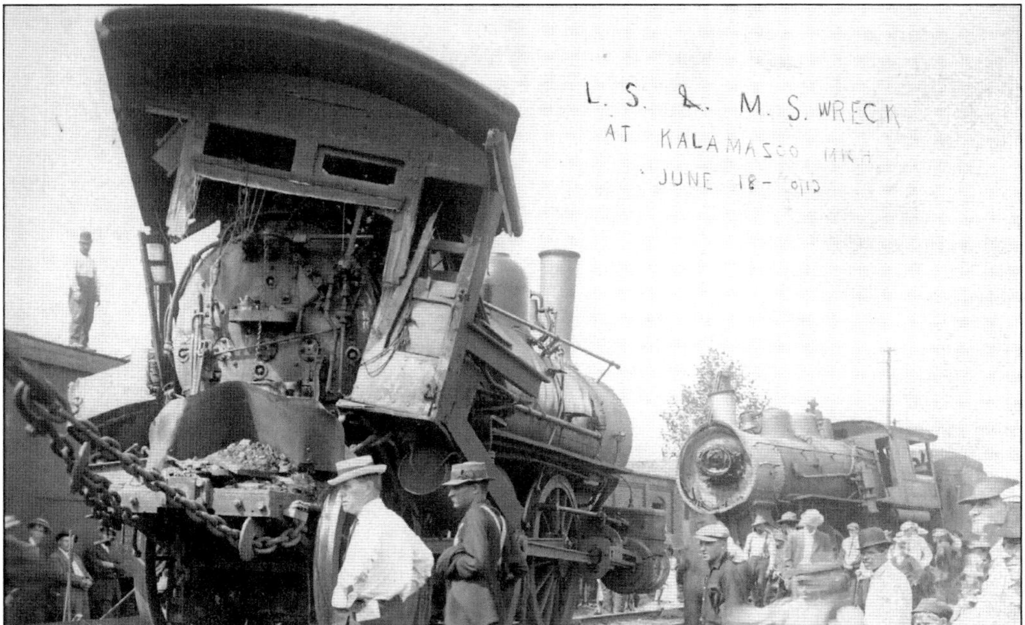


Railroads brought their own dangers. Derailments were the most frequent misfortune. This 1912 photo postcard shows an even greater disaster, a head-on collision. The massive steam locomotives have been reduced to scrap iron. (From the Collection of the Kalamazoo Valley Museum.)

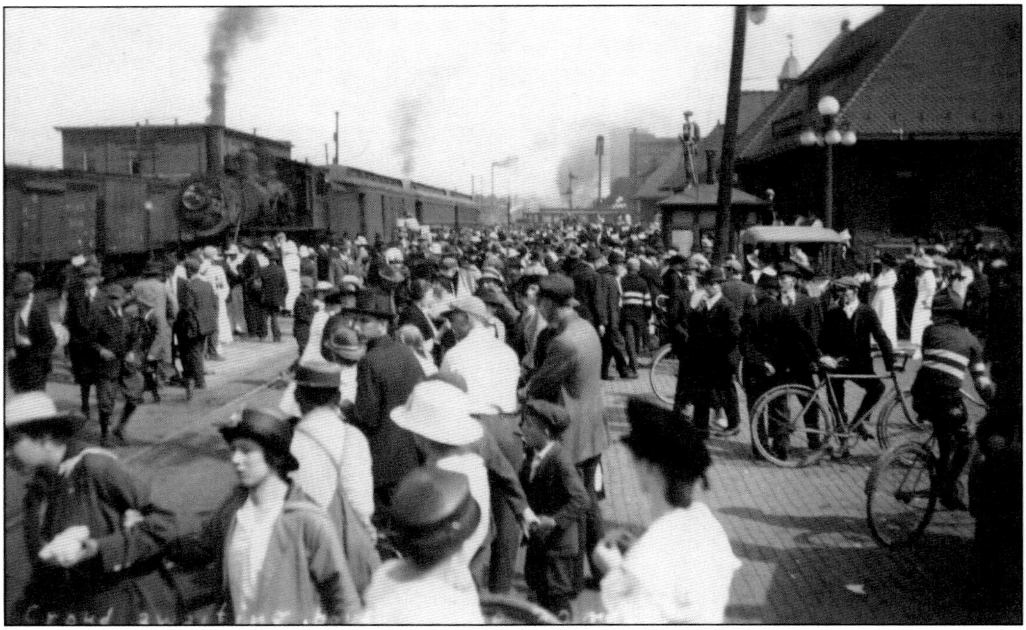

Not all events were celebrations or disasters. These photo postcards show the scene at the Michigan Central Station as local doughboys prepare to leave on the first leg of their journey to the distant battlefields of World War I. Less than two years later, the same platforms would see a more joyous event, the soldiers coming home. (Both, courtesy of the Kalamazoo Public Library's Local History Room.)

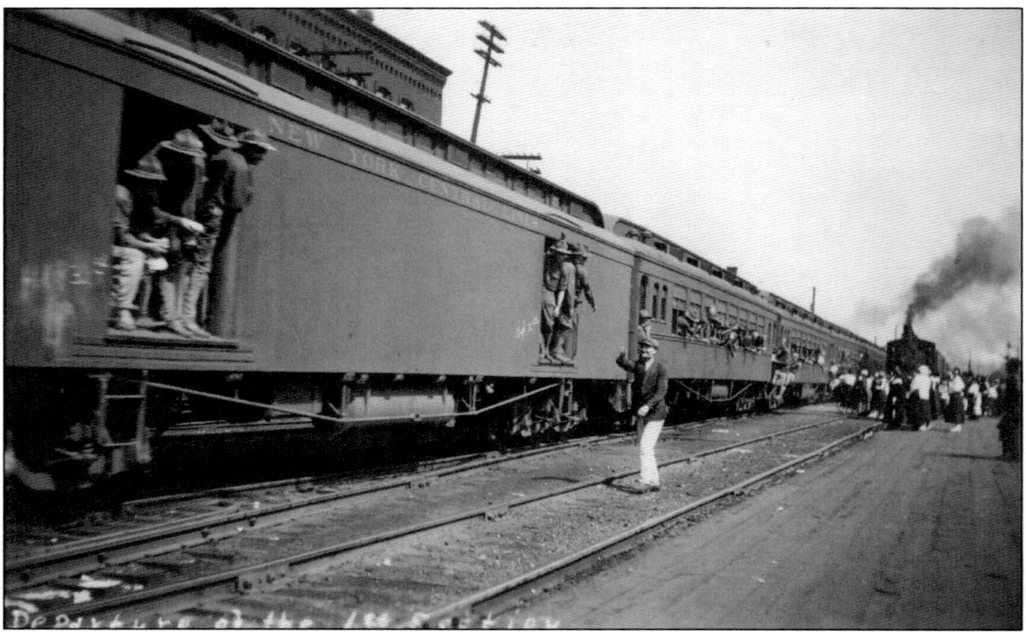

# Bibliography


Decker, William A. *Asylum for the Insane: A History of the Kalamazoo State Hospital.* Traverse City, MI: Arbutus Press, 2008.

Dunbar, Willis. *Kalamazoo and How it Grew.* Kalamazoo: Western Michigan University, 1959.

Henehan, Brendan. *Walking through Time.* Kalamazoo: Kalamazoo Historical Commission, 1981.

Houghton, Lynn, and Pamela Hall O'Connor. *Kalamazoo Lost and Found.* Kalamazoo: Kalamazoo Historic Preservation Commission, 2001.

Massie, Larry, and Peter Schmitt. *Kalamazoo: The Place behind the Products.* Sun Valley, CA: American Historical Press, 1998.

Mayer, Elizabeth. *Yes, There Were Germans in Kalamazoo.* Kalamazoo: The Kalamazoo County Historical Society, 1979.

Schmitt, Peter. *Kalamazoo: Nineteenth-Century Homes in a Midwestern Village.* Kalamazoo: Kalamazoo Historical Commission, 1976.